U0920362

感动世界的文字：

每天读点世界名著

英汉双语版

周芬 罗莉 编著

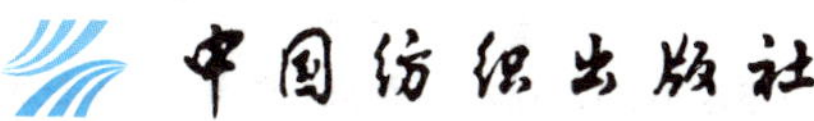

图书在版编目（CIP）数据

感动世界的文字：每天读点世界名著：英汉双语版 / 周芬，罗莉编著. —北京：中国纺织出版社，2016.5（2023.1 重印）

ISBN 978-7-5180-2300-4

Ⅰ.①感… Ⅱ.①周… ②罗… Ⅲ.①英语—汉语—对照读物 Ⅳ.①H319.4

中国版本图书馆CIP数据核字（2016）第018576号

策划编辑：张向红　　责任编辑：张向红
责任设计：林昕瑶　　责任印制：储志伟

中国纺织出版社出版发行
地　　址：北京市朝阳区百子湾东里A407号楼　邮政编码：100124
销售电话：010—67004422　传真：010—87155801
http: //www. c-textilep. com
E-mail: faxing@c-textilep. com
中国纺织出版社天猫旗舰店
官方微博 http: //weibo. com/2119887771
北京兰星球彩色印刷有限公司印刷　各地新华书店经销
2016年5月第1版　2023 年 1 月第 3 次印刷
开　　本：880 × 1230　1 / 32　印张：16
字　　数：450千字　定价：68.00元

Preface
前言

这是一本汇集了百部世界文学名著的书籍。该书中各部世界名著的中文导读和作者简介，有利于读者深入地解读名著；原著精美段落以及段落中长难句的语法点分析，有助于读者从名著中最朴实、最基础的语言文字入手，快速学习经典段落、重难点语法，了解各种表达适用的语境。

什么是名著？名著就是指在世界范围内得到广泛认可和关注著作，其价值由于已经超越了时代本身而得以流传。名著拥有广泛的读者，通俗易懂的语言，富有教育意义的思想，和永不过时的真理。它是人类智慧的结晶，精神宝库中珍贵的财富。阅读名著，既能够陶冶情操，领悟人生真谛，也能够使读者跟从语言大师学习写作技巧，提高语言能力。英语是大多数国家大专院校都开设的必修课程，很多青少年从小就学习英语，随着我国对外开放的不断深入，科学技术不断进步，国际地位不断提高，迫切需要造就一大批精通外语的专门人才，而学英语这门语言，对于我们来说，大有裨益。

本书将名著和英语学习相结合，既继承了传统文化和精髓，又符合新时代对外语教学的要求。

首先，这本书是为广大的学生和教师写的。它解决了老师们苦于寻找能易适中的课外读物的难题，避免了老师自己花费大量的时间去收集资料编写材料。

其次，这本书也是为有英语基础的家长和英语爱好者写的。家长如果能和孩子一起利用本书，收获的也许不仅仅是孩子学习上的进步。同时它也可以作为工作之余消遣的休闲的读物。

本书精选了世界上各国的经典名著，清晰地反映了世界文学的发展历史。浓缩了名著的精华，提炼了作品的主旨，指导读者更好地学习和掌握世界名著，使读者能够从中领略到多部世界名著的风采，感受多元文化的魅力，并且近距离地接触文学大家，感受大家风范，汲取人生智慧，开阔文化视野，获得愉快的阅读体验，在阅读中轻松学习英语。

编者

2016 年 1 月

Contents
目录

001 Alice in Wonderland 爱丽丝漫游仙境

今日关键语导读 Today's Key Points

这是英国作家查尔斯·路德维希·道奇森以笔名路易斯·卡罗尔于1865年出版的儿童文学作品。故事叙述了一个名叫爱丽丝的女孩从兔子洞进入一个神奇国度，遇到许多会讲话的生物以及像人一般活动的纸牌，最后发现原来是一场梦。

障碍词先听为快 Words and Expressions

hatter ['hætə] n. 帽商；帽子制造者

dormouse ['dɔːmaus] n. 榛睡鼠；睡鼠

teapot ['tiːpɔt] n. 茶壶

curious ['kjuəriəs] adj. 好奇的，有求知欲的；古怪的；爱挑剔的

stupid ['stjuːpid] adj. 愚蠢的；麻木的；乏味的 n. 傻瓜，笨蛋

mushroom ['mʌʃrum] n. 蘑菇，伞菌；蘑菇形物体；暴发户 adj. 蘑菇的；蘑菇形的；迅速生长的 vi. 迅速增加；采蘑菇；迅速生长

strange [streindʒ] adj. 奇怪的；陌生的；外行的 adv. 奇怪地；陌生地，冷淡地

pour [pɔː,pɔə] vt. 灌，注；倒；倾泻；倾吐 vi. 倾泻；涌流；斟茶

crossly [krɒslɪ] adv. 横地；故意为难地；相反地；发怒地

"Two days slow! I told you that butter wasn't good for watches!" he said angrily to the March Hare.

"It was the best butter." said the March Hare sadly.

Alice was looking at the watch with interest. "It's a strange watch,"she said." It shows the day of the week, but not the time."

"But we know the time,"said the Hatter. "It's always six o'clock here."

Alice suddenly understood. "Is that why there are all these cups and plates?" she said. "It's always tea-time here, and you go on moving round the table. Is that right? But what happens when you come to the beginning again?"

"Don't ask questions,"said the March Hare crossly. "You must tell us a story now."

"But I don't know any stories." said Alice.

Then the March Hare and the Hatter turned to the Dormouse. "Wake up, Dormouse!" they shouted loudly in its ears. "Tell us a story."

"Yes, please do." said Alice.

The Dormouse woke up and quickly began to tell a story, but a few minutes later it was asleep again. The March Hare poured a little hot tea on its nose, and the Hatter began to look for a clean plate. Alice decided to leave and walked away into the wood. She looked back once, and the March Hare and the Hatter were trying to put the Dormouse into the teapot.

"Well, I won't go there again,"said Alice. "What a stupid tea-party it was!" Just then she saw a door in one of the trees. "How curious!" she thought." But everything is strange today. I think I'll go in."

So she went in. And there she was, back in the long room with the little glass table. At once, she picked up the gold key from the table, unlocked the little door into the garden, and then began to eat a piece of mushroom. When she was down to about thirty centimeters high, she walked through the door, and then, at last, she was in the beautiful garden with its green trees and bright flowers.

长难句解析

"Two days slow! I told you that butter wasn't good for watches!" he said angrily to the March Hare.

"It was the best butter." said the March Hare sadly.

"慢了两天！我告诉过你，黄油对钟表没好处。"他气哼哼地对三月兔说。

"这是最好的黄油。"三月兔失望地说。

be good for sb. 对什么有好处；sadly 副词，"失望地"用来修饰动词。

Alice suddenly understood. "Is that why there are all these cups and plates?" she said. "It's always tea-time here, and you go on moving round the table. Is that right? But what happens when you come to the beginning again?"

爱丽丝一下子明白了。“这就是为什么有杯子和盘子的原因吗？”她说，“这儿永远是喝茶的时间，你们就绕着桌子转。对不对？但当你们再次回到起点时会发生什么呢？”

when 引导时间状语从句，go on doing sth. 继续做某事。

Then the March Hare and the Hatter turned to the Dormouse. “Wake up, Dormouse!” they shouted loudly in its ears. “Tell us a story.”

“Yes, please do.” said Alice.

然后三月兔和制帽人转向睡鼠。“醒醒，睡鼠！”他们冲着它的耳朵喊起来，“给我们讲个故事。”

“对，请讲个故事吧。”爱丽丝说。

wake up 醒来，turn to sb. 转向某人。

The March Hare poured a little hot tea on its nose, and the Hatter began to look for a clean plate. Alice decided to leave and walked away into the wood. She looked back once, and the March Hare and the Hatter were trying to put the Dormouse into the teapot.

三月兔把热茶倒在睡鼠的鼻子上，制帽人开始找一个干净的盘子。爱丽丝决定离开，向小树林走去。她回头一看，三月兔和制帽人正在想办法把睡鼠塞到茶壶里去呢。

look for 寻找，寻求，指望。look back 回头；decide to do sth. 决定做某事。

002 Anna Karenina 安娜·卡列尼娜

今日关键语导读 Today's Key Points

《安娜·卡列尼娜》是俄国著名作家列夫·托尔斯泰的代表作品。本书通过女主人公安娜的爱情悲剧，和列文在农村面临危机而进行的改革与探索这两条线索，描绘了俄国从莫斯科到外省广阔而丰富多彩的图景，先后描写了150多个人物，是一部社会百科全书式的作品。

贵族妇女安娜追求爱情幸福，却在卡列宁的虚伪、渥伦斯基的冷漠和自私面前碰得头破血流，最终落得卧轨自杀、陈尸车站的下场。庄园主列文反对土地私有制，抵制资本主义制度，同情贫苦农民，却又因无法摆脱贵族习气而陷入无法解脱的矛盾之中。矛盾的时期、矛盾的制度、矛盾的人物、矛盾的心理，使全书在矛盾的漩涡中颠簸。这部小说是新旧交替时期紧张惶恐的俄国社会的写照。

障碍词先听为快 Words and Expressions

terror ['terə] n. 恐怖；恐怖的行为；令人讨厌的人

mingle ['miŋgl] vt. 使混合，使相混 vi. 混合，混淆

servant ['səːvənt] n. 仆人，佣人，雇工；[美] 奴仆，奴隶

quire ['kwaiə] n. 一刀（纸数量），（装订时）一折

honor ['ɔnə] n. 荣誉；信用；头衔 vt. 尊敬；给……以荣誉

sake [seik] n. 缘故；理由；目的

nursery ['nəːsəri] n. 婴儿室，临时托儿所，苗圃，滋生地
tangle ['tæŋgl] n. 纠缠，纠纷，混乱；争论

好英文娓娓动听 Beautiful stories

"He has gone! It is over!" Anna said to herself, standing at the window; and in answer to this statement the impression of the darkness when the candle had flickered out, and of her fearful dream mingling into one, filled her heart with cold terror.

"No, that cannot be!" she cried, and crossing the room she rang the bell. She was so afraid now of being alone, that without waiting for the servant to come in, she went out to meet him.

"I quire where the count has gone," she said. The servant answered that the count had gone to the stable.

"His honor left word that if you cared to drive out, the carriage would be back immediately."

"Very good. Wait a minute. I'll write a note at once. Send Mihail with the note to the stables. Make haste."

She sat down and wrote:

"I was wrong. Come back home; I must explain. For God's sake come! I'm afraid."

She sealed it up and gave it to the servant.

She was afraid of being left alone now; she followed the servant out of the room, and went to the nursery.

"Why, this isn't it, this isn't he! Where are his blue eyes, his sweet, shy smile?" was her first thought when she saw her chubby rosy little girl with her black, curly hair instead of Seryozha, whom in the tangle of her ideas she had expected to see in the nursery. The little girl sitting at the table was obstinately and violently battering on it with a cork, and staring aimlessly at her mother with her pitch-black eyes. Answering the English nurse that she was quite well, and that she was going to the country tomorrow, Anna sat down by the little girl and began spinning the cork to show her. But the child's loud, ringing laugh, and the motion of her eyebrows, recalled Vronsky so vividly that she got up hurriedly, restraining her sobs, and went away. "Can it be all over? No, it cannot be!" she thought. "He will come back. But how can he explain that smile, that excitement after he had been talking to her? But even if he doesn't explain, I will believe. If I don't believe, there's only one thing left for me, and I can't."

长难句解析

"Yes, I'm very much worried, and that's what reason was given me for, to escape; so then one must escape: why not put out the light when there's nothing more to look at, when it's sickening to look at it all? But how? Why did the conductor run along the foot board, why are they shrieking, those young men in that train? why are they talking, why are they laughing? It's all falsehood, all lying, all humbug, all cruelty!"

"是的，我苦恼万分，赋予我理智就是为了使我能够摆脱；因此我一定要摆脱。如果再也没有可看的，而且一切看起来都让人生厌的话，那么为什么不把蜡烛熄了呢？但是怎么办呢？为什么这个乘务员顺着栏杆跑过去？为什么下面那辆车厢里的那些年轻人在大声喊叫？为什么他们又说又笑？这全是虚伪的，全是谎话，全是欺骗，全是罪恶！……”

“...and that is what reason was...”,what 在这里引导名词性从句即表语从句；why not put... when there’s..., when it’s..., why引导原因状语从句，when 在这里引导时间状语从句。put out 译为“扑灭”的意思，还可以表示“生产，出版”的意思。

A peasant muttering something was working at the iron above her. And the light by which she had read the book filled with troubles, falsehoods, sorrow, and evil, flared up more brightly than ever before, lighted up for her all that had been in darkness, flickered, began to grow dim, and was quenched forever.

一个正在铁轨上干活的矮小的农民，嘟囔了句什么。那支蜡烛，她曾借着它的烛光浏览过充满了苦难、虚伪、悲哀和罪恶的书籍，比以往更加明亮地闪烁起来，为她照亮了以前笼罩在黑暗中的一切，然后蜡烛摇曳起来，开始昏暗下去，永远地熄灭了。

‘...And the light by which she had...’, which 在这里作关系代词，引导定语从句，先行词是light；...lighted up for her all that had been in...’ that 在这里引导定语从句。Be filled with 表示“充满着……，怀着……”。

Ever since, by his beloved brother's deathbed, Levin had first glanced into the questions of life and death in the light of these new convictions, as he called them, which had during the period from his twentieth to his thirty-fourth year imperceptibly replaced his childish and youthful beliefs--he had been stricken with horror, not so much of death, as of life, without any knowledge of when, and why, and how, and what it was.

自从列文看见他亲爱的垂死的哥哥那一瞬间，他第一次用他称为新的信念来看生死问题，这种信念在他二十岁到三十四岁之间不知不觉地代替了他童年和青年时代的信仰，——从那时起，死使他惊心动魄的程度还不如生那么厉害，他丝毫也不知道生从哪里来的，它为了什么目的，它如何来的，以及它究竟是什么。

ever since 副词短语，表示“从那时到现在，自从……，自……以后”；as“正如”，引导方式状语从句， which 在此句中引导非限定性定语从句；...without any knowledge of when and why and how and what...，when why how what 均引导宾语从句。

When Levin thought what he was and what he was living for, he could find no answer to the questions and was reduced to despair, but he left off questioning himself about it.

It seemed as though he knew both what he was and for what he was living, for he acted and lived resolutely and without hesitation. Indeed, in these latter days he was far more decided and unhesitating in life than he had ever been.

当列文想到他是什么和为什么活着的时候，他找不到答案，于是陷入悲观失望；但是当他不再问自己这些问题的时候，他反倒好像知道他是什么和为什么活着了，因为他坚决而明确地生活着和行动着；最近他甚至比以前更坚定明确得多了。

When Levin thought what he...，what引导的是宾语从句；It seems as though... 表示“看样子似乎是……”。Resolutely 表示“绝对地”，hesitation 译为“犹豫；踌躇”，far more... far在这里修饰形容词或副词的比较级。

读书笔记

003 Hans Andersen's Fairy Tales 安徒生童话

今日关键语导读 Today's Key Points

《安徒生童话》是丹麦作家兼诗人安徒生创作的家喻户晓的童话故事集，其中最著名的童话故事有《海的女儿》《小锡兵》《冰雪女王》等，这些脍炙人口的童话不仅是写给儿童的，也是写给成人的。天真是他童话的特点，但幽默才是这些故事真正的魅力所在。

障碍词先听为快 Words and Expressions

project ['prɔdʒekt] vt. 放映；计划；发射；展现，使突出 vi. 伸出，突出

penetrate ['penitreit] vt. 穿透，刺入；渗入；秘密潜入；洞悉，明了

illumination [iˌljuːmi'neiʃən] n. 照明；阐明，解释清楚

ornament ['ɔːnəmənt] v. 装饰；美化

stretch [stretʃ] vt. 伸展；张开

vanished ['vænɪʃ] adj. 消失了的

transparent [træns'pɛərənt] adj. 透明的；清澈的；易识破的；显而易见的

behold [bi'həuld] vt. 看到，注视；领悟

beam [biːm] vi. 发出光与热；面露喜色

immortal [i'mɔːtl] adj. 不死的；永恒的，不朽的；神的；流芳百世的

It was dreadfully cold, it was snowing fast, and almost dark; the evening—the last evening of the old year was drawing in. But, cold and dark as it was, a poor little girl, with bare head and feet, was still wandering about the streets. When she left her home she had slippers on, but they were much too large for her; indeed, properly, they belonged to her mother, and had dropped off her feet whilst she was running very fast across the road, to get out of the way of two carriages. One of the slippers was not to be found, the other had been snatched up by a little boy, who ran off with it thinking it might serve him as a doll's cradle.

So the little girl now walked on, her bare feet quite red and blue with the cold. She carried a small bundle of matches in her hand, and a good many more in her tattered apron. No one had bought any of them the live long day; no one had given her a single penny. Trembling with cold and hunger she walked on, the picture of sorrow: poor little child!

The snow-flakes fell on her long, fair hair, which curled in such pretty ringlets over her shoulders; but she thought not of her own beauty, or of the cold. Lights were glimmering through every window, and the savor of roast goose reached her from several houses; it was New Year's eve, and it was of this that she thought.

In a corner formed by two houses, one of which projected beyond the other. She sat down, drawing her little feet close under her, but in vain, she could not warm them. She dared not go home, she had sold no matches, earned not a single penny, and perhaps her father would beat her, besides her home was almost as cold as the street, it was an attic; and although the larger of the many chinks in the roof were stopped up with straw and rags. The wind and snow often penetrated through. Her hands were nearly dead with cold; one little match from her bundle would warm them. Perhaps, if she dared light it, she drew one out, and struck it against the wall, bravo! it was a bright, warm flame, and she held her hands over it. It was quite an illumination for that poor little girl; nay, call it rather a magic taper, for it seemed to her as though she was sitting before a large iron-stove with brass ornaments, so beautifully blazed the fire within! The child stretched out her feet to warm them also; alas, in an instant the flame had died away, the stove vanished, the little girl sat cold and comfortless, with the burnt match in her hand.

A second match was struck against the wall; it kindles and blazed, and wherever its light fell the wall became transparent as a veil. The little girl could see into the room within. She saw the table spread with a snow-white damask cloth, whereon were ranged shining china-dishes; the roast goose stuffed with apples and dried plums stood at one end, smoking hot, and which was pleasantest of all to see; the goose, with knife and fork still in her breast, jumped down from the dish, and waddled along the floor right up to the poor child. The match was burnt out, and only the thick, hard wall was beside her.

She kindled a third match. Again shot up the flame; and now she was sitting under a most beautiful Christmas tree, far larger, and far more prettily decked out, than the one she had seen last

Christmas eve through the glass doors of the rich merchant's house. Hundreds of wax-tapers lighted up the green branches, and tiny painted figures, such as she had seen in the shop-windows, looked down from the tree upon her. The child stretched out her hands towards them in delight, and in that moment the lights of the match warm quenched; still, however, the Christmas candles burned higher and higher, she beheld them beaming like stars in heaven; one of them fell, the lights streaming behind it like a long, fiery tail.

"Now some one is dying," said the little girl, softly, for she had been told by her old grandmother, the only person who had ever been kind to her, and who was now dead that whenever a star falls an immortal spirit returns to the God who gave it.

She struck yet another match against the wall; it flamed up, and surrounded by its light, appeared before her that same dear grandmother, gentle and loving as always, but bright and happy as she had never looked during her lifetime.

"Grandmother!" exclaimed the child, "Oh, take me with you! I know you will leave me as soon as the match goes out, you will vanish like the warm fire in the stove, like the splendid New Year's feast, like the beautiful large Christmas tree!" And she hastily lighted all the remaining matches in the bundle, last her grandmother should disappear. And the matches burned with such a blaze of splendor, that noon day could scarcely have been brighter. Never had the good old grandmother looked so tall and stately, so beautiful and kind; she took the little girl in her arms, and they both flew together-higher, till they were in that place where neither cold, nor hunger, nor pain, is ever known, they were in paradise.

But in the cold morning hour, crouching in the corner of the wall, the poor little girl was found: her cheeks glowing, her lips smiling, frozen to death on the last night of the old Year. The New Year's sun shone on the lifeless child; motionless she sat there with the matches in her lap, one bundle of them quite burnt out.

"She has been trying to warm herself, poor thing!" the people said, but no one knew of the sweet visions she had beheld, or how gloriously she and her grandmother were celebrating their New Year's festival.

长难句解析

But, cold and dark as it was, a poor little girl, with bare head and feet, was still wandering about the streets.

尽管天又黑又冷，一个贫穷的小女孩光着头，赤着脚仍徘徊在街头。

wander about 徘徊；cold and dark as it was，“cold and dark”表语提前表示强调。

Never had the good old grandmother looked so tall and stately, so beautiful and kind.

善良的老祖母从未像现在这样看上去这么高大，这么优雅，这么美丽和蔼。

never 置于句首，句子结构部分倒装。

It flamed up, and surrounded by its light, appeared before her that same dear grandmother, gentle and loving as always, but bright and happy as she had never looked during her lifetime.

在亮光里，她面前出现了那位亲爱的祖母。她依然是那么的慈爱和温和，然而那快活和幸福的样子却是她生前从未有过的。

be surrounded by 被……环绕，第一个 as 是介词，像……一样；第二个 as 是连词，引导原因状语从句。

Trembling with cold and hunger she walked on, the picture of sorrow: poor little child!

小女孩饥寒交迫，全身颤抖地朝前走着，一副愁苦的画面。

trembling 现在分词表伴随；walk on 前行。

读书笔记

004 Pride and Prejudice 傲慢与偏见

今日关键语导读 Today's Key Points

《傲慢与偏见》是简·奥斯汀的代表作，是一部描写爱情与婚姻的经典小说。作品以男女主人公达西和伊丽莎白由于傲慢和偏见而产生的爱情纠葛为线索，共写了四起姻缘：伊丽莎白与达西、简与宾利、莉迪亚与威克姆、夏洛蒂与柯林斯。傲慢的单身青年达西与怀有偏见的二小姐伊丽莎白、富裕的单身贵族宾利与贤淑的大小姐简之间的感情纠葛，充分表达了作者本人的婚姻观，强调经济利益对恋爱和婚姻的影响。小说情节富有喜剧性，语言机智幽默，是奥斯汀小说中最受欢迎的一部，并被多次改编成电影和电视剧。

障碍词先听为快 Words and Expressions

endeavour [in'devə] v. 努力；尽力

frequently ['friːkwəntli] adv. 频繁地；时常

extravagant [iks'trævəgənt] adj. 奢侈的；挥霍的

restoration ['restə'reiʃən] n. 恢复；复位

dismiss [dis'mis] vt. 解散；解雇

proceed [prə'siːd] vi. 开始；继续进行

mortified ['mɔːtifaid] adj. 窘迫的；受辱的

resentment [ri'zentmənt] n. 愤恨；怨恨

attentive [ə'tentiv] adj. 留意的；注意的

astonishment [əsˈtɔniʃmənt] *n.* 惊讶

好英文娓娓动听 Beautiful stories

As it happened that Elizabeth had much rather not, she endeavoured in her answer to put an end to every intreaty and expectation of the kind. Such relief, however, as it was in her power to afford, by the practice of what might be called economy in her own private expences, she frequently sent them. It had always been evident to her that such an income as theirs, under the direction of two persons so extravagant in their wants, and heedless of the future, must be very insufficient to their support; and whenever they changed their quarters, either Jane or herself were sure of being applied to for some little assistance towards discharging their bills. Their manner of living, even when the restoration of peace dismissed them to a home, was unsettled in the extreme. They were always moving from place to place in quest of a cheap situation, and always spending more than they ought. His affection for her soon sunk into indifference; her's lasted a little longer; and in spite of her youth and her manners, she retained all the claims to reputation which her marriage had given her.

Though Darcy could never receive him at Pemberley, yet, for Elizabeth's sake, he assisted him farther in his profession. Lydia was occasionally a visitor there, when her husband was gone to enjoy himself in London or Bath; and with the Bingleys they both of them frequently staid so long, that even Bingley's good humour was overcome, and he proceeded so far as to talk of giving them a hint to be gone.

Miss Bingley was very deeply mortified by Darcy's marriage; but as she thought it advisable to retain the right of visiting at Pemberley, she dropt all her resentment; was fonder than ever of Georgiana, almost as attentive to Darcy as heretofore, and paid off every arrear of civility to Elizabeth.

Pemberley was now Georgiana's home; and the attachment of the sisters was exactly what Darcy had hoped to see. They were able to love each other even as well as they intended. Georgiana had the highest opinion in the world of Elizabeth; though at first she often listened with an astonishment bordering on alarm at her lively, sportive, manner of talking to her brother. He, who had always inspired in herself a respect which almost overcame her affection, she now saw the object of open pleasantry. Her mind received knowledge which had never before fallen in her way. By Elizabeth's instructions, she began to comprehend that a woman may take liberties with her husband which a brother will not always allow in a sister more than ten years younger than himself.

长难句解析

As it happened that Elizabeth had much rather not, she endeavoured in her answer to put an end to every intreaty and expectation of the kind.

伊丽莎白果然不愿意讲，因此在回信中尽力打消她这种希望，断了她这一类的念头。

That引导宾语从句；had much rather not 指有很多不愿意，在此指“不愿意讲”；endeavour不及物动词，“竭力，试图”；put an end to结束。

Her mind received knowledge which had never before fallen in her way.

她以前无论如何也弄不懂的事，现在才恍然大悟了。

received knowledge 在这里表示恍然大悟；fall in one's way 被……得到；让遇到。整句的意思是：那些以前从来没有被她得到的知识、事情，现在她接受了。所以整句可以译作：她以前无论如何也弄不懂的事，现在才恍然大悟了。

He, who had always inspired in herself a respect which almost overcame her affection, she now saw the object of open pleasantry.

她一向尊敬哥哥，几乎尊敬得超过了手足的情份，想不到现在他竟成为公开打趣的对象。

who在定语从句中，用作限定关系代词表示“……的人”。which 指代respect，which 在从句中作主语，不能省略；inspired in在此表示“被激发的”。

Though Darcy could never receive him at Pemberley, yet, for Elizabeth's sake, he assisted him farther in his profession.

虽然达西再三不肯让韦翰到彭伯里来，但是看在伊丽莎白的面子上，他依旧帮助他找工作。

for one's sake 表示“……的缘故”，在此是“看在……的面子上”；yet区别于always，多用于否定句、疑问句，表示为“还、尚、迄今、到那时”，在此表示语气上的转折。

读书笔记

005 Around the World in 80 Days 八十天环游地球

今日关键语导读 Today's Key Points

这是凡尔纳一部著名的科幻小说，讲述的是英国绅士福格与朋友打赌两万英镑，要在80天内环游地球一周回到伦敦。但他不幸被误当作偷窃英格兰银行的大盗，被苏格兰警方追捕。随后他和仆人在路途中凭着机智与勇敢克服了艰难险阻，获得了胜利，而且抱得美人归——他在印度救出了一个殉葬的王公妻子（爱乌达）。

障碍词先听为快 Words and Expressions

transpire [træns'paiə] vt. 使蒸发；使排出 vi. 发生；蒸发；泄露

honourable ['ɔnərəbl] adj. 荣誉的；值得尊敬的；表示尊敬的；正直的

eccentric [ik'sentrik] n. 古怪的人 adj. 古怪的，反常的

resume [ri'zjuːm] n. 摘要；[管理] 履历，简历 vi. 重新开始，继续 vt. 重新开始，继续；恢复，重新占用

revive [ri'vaiv] vt. 使复兴；使苏醒；回想起；重演，重播 vi. 复兴；复活；苏醒；恢复精神

reappear ['riːə'piə] vi. 再出现

suspense [səs'pens] n. 悬念；悬疑；焦虑；悬而不决

despatch [dis'pætʃ] n. 派遣；发送（等于dispatch） v. 派遣；发送；匆匆吃下；匆匆离开

multitude ['mʌltitjuːd] n.群众；多数

impede [im'piːd] vt.阻碍；妨碍；阻止

pitch [pitʃ] n.沥青；音高；程度；树脂；球场 v.倾斜；投掷；搭帐篷；坠落；用沥青涂；扎营；向前倾跌

好英文娓娓动听 Beautiful stories

It is time to relate what a change took place in English public opinion, when it transpired that the real bank robber, a certain James Strand, had been arrested, on the 17th of December, at Edinburgh. Three days before, Phileas Fogg had been a criminal, who was being desperately followed up by the police; now he was an honourable gentleman, mathematically pursuing his eccentric journey round the world.

The papers resumed their discussion about the wager; all those who had laid bets, for or against him, revived their interest, as if by magic; the 'Phileas Fogg bends' again became negotiable, and many new wagers were made. Phileas Fogg's name was once more at a premium on 'Change.

His five friends of the Reform Club passed these three days in a state of feverish suspense. Would Phileas Fogg, whom they had forgotten, reappear before their eyes! Where was he at this moment? The 17th of December, the day of James Strand's arrest, was the seventy-sixth since Phileas Fogg's departure, and no news of him had been received. Was he dead? Had he abandoned the effort, or was he continuing his journey along the route agreed upon? And would he appear on Saturday, the 21st of December, at a quarter before nine in the evening, on the threshold of the Reform Club saloon?

The anxiety in which, for three days, London society existed, cannot be described. Telegrams were sent to America and Asia for news of Phileas Fogg. Messengers were despatched to the house in Saville Row morning and evening. No news. The police were ignorant what had become of the detective, Fix, who had so unfortunately followed up a false scent. Bets increased, nevertheless, in number and value. Phileas Fogg, like a racehorse, was drawing near his last turning-point. The bonds were quoted, no longer at a hundred below par, but at twenty, at ten, and at five; and paralytic old Lord Albemarle bet even in his favour.

A great crowd was collected in Pall Mail and the neighbouring streets on Saturday evening; it seemed like a multitude of brokers permanently established around the Reform Club. Circulation was impeded, and everywhere disputes, discussions, and financial transactions were going on. The police had great difficulty in keeping back the crowd, and as the hour when Phileas Fogg was due approached, the excitement rose to its highest pitch.

长难句解析

It is time to relate what a change took place in English public opinion.

现在我们应该来谈一谈这件事在英国社会上所引起的思想波动。

该句用了It is time to do sth.“是时候做某事”这个句型；take place 发生。

When it transpired that the real bank robber, a certain James Strand, had been arrested, on the 17th of December, at Edinburgh.

12月17日，在爱丁堡捕获了一个名叫杰姆·斯特朗的人。他才是那个真正盗窃英国国家银行的小偷。

when 引导的时间状语从句中又包含一个that引导的宾语从句，a certain James Strand在句中作为插入语。

Phileas Fogg had been a criminal, who was being desperately followed up by the police.

斐利亚·福格是一个被警察当局追捕的盗犯。

此句是who 引导定语从句；follow up，跟随。

The police were ignorant what had become of the detective, Fix, who had so unfortunately followed up a false scent.

警察厅也不知道那位白白盯着一个假小偷的费克斯警探到了哪儿了。

句中是由what引导的宾语补足语，对ignorant进行补充说明。

It seemed like a multitude of brokers permanently established around the Reform Club.

看来，那密密麻麻的一大群股票经纪人就好像在改良俱乐部附近生了根似的。

该句用了句型“It seems like...”好像……，似乎……。

读书笔记

006 The Hound of the Baskervilles 巴斯克维尔的猎犬

今日关键语导读 Today's Key Points

《巴斯克维尔的猎犬》是阿瑟·柯南·道尔最得意的长篇杰作之一，堪称福尔摩斯探案故事的代表作。讲述的是在巴斯克维尔家庭中，三百年来一直流传着的“魔鬼般的大猎狗”的神秘传说，像传说的那样，查尔兹爵士在离伦敦不远的一块沼泽地里死于非命。

障碍词先听为快 Words and Expressions

crouch ['krautʃ] v. 屈膝，蹲伏

emerge [i'məːdʒ] v. 出现，浮现；暴露；摆脱

exultant [ig'zʌltənt] adj. 狂喜的，欢欣鼓舞的

rigid ['ridʒid] adj. 严格的;僵硬的；（规则、方法等）死板的；刚硬的

paralyze ['pærəlaiz] v. 使瘫痪，使麻痹；使不能正常活动

smolder ['sməuldə] v. 用文火焖烧，熏烧，慢燃

delirious [di'liriəs] adj. 精神混乱的；非常激动的；极兴奋的，发狂的；神不守舍

savage ['sævidʒ] adj. 未开化的；野蛮的；凶猛的；残忍的

A sound of quick steps broke the silence of the moor. Crouching among the stones we stared intently at the silver-tipped bank in front of us. The steps grew louder, and through the fog, as through a curtain, there stepped the man whom we were awaiting. He looked round him in surprise as he emerged into the clear, starlit night. Then he came swiftly along the path, passed close to where we lay, and went on up the long slope behind us. As he walked he glanced continually over either shoulder, like a man who is ill at ease.

"Hist!" cried Holmes, and I heard the sharp click of a cocking pistol. "Look out! It's coming!"

There was a thin, crisp, continuous patter from somewhere in the heart of that crawling bank. The cloud was within fifty yards of where we lay, and we glared at it, all three, uncertain what horror was about to break from the heart of it. I was at Holmes's elbow, and I glanced for an instant at his face. It was pale and exultant, his eyes shining brightly in the moonlight. But suddenly they started forward in a rigid, fixed stare, and his lips parted in amazement. At the same instant Lestrade gave a yell of terror and threw himself face downward upon the ground. I sprang to my feet, my inert hand grasping my pistol, my mind paralyzed by the dreadful shape which had sprung out upon us from the shadows of the fog. A hound it was, an enormous coal-black hound, but not such a hound as mortal eyes have ever seen. Fire burst from its open mouth, its eyes glowed with a smoldering glare, its muzzle and hackles and dewlap were outlined in flickering flame. Never in the delirious dream of a disordered brain could anything more savage, more appalling, more hellish be conceived than that dark form and savage face which broke upon us out of the wall of fog.

长难句解析

Crouching among the stones we stared intently at the silver-tipped bank in front of us.

我们蹲在乱石之间，专心致志地盯着面前那段上缘呈银白色的雾墙。

crouching为v-ing形式，表伴随，stare at 凝视，in front of 在……前面。

The cloud was within fifty yards of where we lay, and we glared at it, all three, uncertain what horror was about to break from the heart of it.

那云状的浓雾距我们藏匿的地方不到五十码远，我们三个人都死死地朝那里瞪大眼睛，不知道那里将出现什么可怕的东西。

where引导地点状语从句，跟在介词后面作宾语，构成介宾短语；glare at 表示注视；be about to 将要……；the heart of... ……的心脏。

I sprang to my feet, my inert hand grasping my pistol, my mind paralyzed by the dreadful shape which had sprung out upon us from the shadows of the fog.

我跳了起来，我那已经变得不灵活的手紧抓着手枪。在雾影中向我们窜来的那形状可怕的东西吓得我魂飞魄散。

spring to sb.'s feet 表示跳跃；which引导定语从句，修饰前面的the dreadful shape；spring out，跳出、冲出、（从隐蔽处）突然冒出；the shadows of... ……的阴影。

A hound it was, an enormous coal-black hound, but not such a hound as mortal eyes have ever seen.

那确是一只猎狗，一只黑得像煤炭似的大猎狗，但并不是一只人们平常看到过的那种狗。

a hound it was 此句用了倒装句型，把名词（猎狗）放在be动词前面，表强调；such...as... 表示“和……一样”。

Never in the delirious dream of a disordered brain could anything more savage, more appalling, more hellish be conceived than that dark form and savage face which broke upon us out of the wall of fog.

像那个突然由雾障里向我们窜过来的黑色的躯体和狰狞的狗脸，就是疯子在最荒谬的梦里也不会看到比这家伙更凶恶、更可怕和更像魔鬼的东西了。

in the delirious dream of 表示“在最荒谬的梦里”，

dream前的形容词可以更换；never...could anything more than表比较，“再也没有什么可以比得过……”；后面的which引导定语从句，修饰savage face；the wall of fog表示“雾障”。

读书笔记

007 One Hundred Years of Solitude 百年孤独

今日关键语导读 Today's Key Points

小说以虚构中的市镇马康多的荣衰作为拉丁美洲百年沧桑的缩影。以诡异的手法反映了殖民、独裁、斗争和流血的历史，以及以往和孤独的主题。故事讲述了布恩迪亚家族在一百年间，六代人因权利与情欲的轮回上演的兴衰起落，第一代的老布恩迪亚在晚年被绑在树上过日子。欧苏拉是布恩迪亚家的女主人，一直在背后默默支持着家人，但她又充满正义感，她的孙子阿加底奥在马康多以暴力统治人民时，挺身而出为人民打抱不平。最后一个子孙——倭良诺的儿子在刚出生时被蚂蚁吃掉，倭良诺在看完遗稿后，随着马康多一起消失了。

障碍词先听为快 Words and Expressions

languid ['læŋgwid] adj. 倦怠的；呆滞的；软弱无力的

weepy ['wiːpi] a. 眼泪汪汪的；催人泪下的 n. 使人哭的小说；伤感的电影

conceal [kən'siːl] vt. 隐藏；隐瞒

mischievous ['mistʃivəs] adj. 淘气的；（人、行为等）恶作剧的；有害的

christening ['krisəniŋ] n. （基督教）洗礼；（基督教）洗礼仪式；命名典礼；v. 为……施洗礼（christen ['krisn]的ing形式）

respective [ris'pektiv] adj. 分别的，各自的

nevertheless [ˌnevəðə'les] adv. 然而，不过；虽然如此；conj. 然而，不过

intricate ['intrikit] adj. 复杂的；错综的，缠结的

coordinate [kəu'ɔːdinit] n. 坐标；同等的人或物；adj. 并列的；同等的；vt. 调整；整合

decisive [di'saisiv] adj. 决定性的；果断的，坚定的

好英文娓娓动听 Beautiful stories

Years later on his deathbed Aureliano Segundo would remember the rainy afternoon in June when he went into the bedroom to meet his first son. Even though the child was languid and weepy, with no mark of a Buendía, he did not have to think twice about naming him.

"We'll call him José Arcadio," he said.

Fernanda del Carpio, the beautiful woman he had married the year before, agreed. úrsula, on the other hand, could not conceal a vague feeling of doubt. Throughout the long history of the family the insistent repetition of names had made her draw some conclusions that seemed to be certain. While the Aureli-anos were withdrawn, but with lucid minds, the José Arcadios were impulsive and enterprising, but they were marked with a tragic sign. The only cases that were impossible to classify were those of José Arcadio Segun-do and Aureliano Segundo. They were so much alike and so mischievous during childhood that not even Santa Sofía de la Piedad could tell them apart. On the day of their christening Amaranta put bracelets on them with their respective names dressed them in different colored clothing marked with each one's initials, but when they began to go to school they decided to exchange clothing and bracelets and call each other by opposite names. The teacher, Melchor Escalona, used to knowing José Arcadio Segundo by his green shirt, went out of his mind when he discovered that the latter was wearing Aureliano Segundo's bracelet and that the otone said, nevertheless, that his name was Aureliano Segundo in spite of the fact that he was wearing the white shirt and the bracelet with José Arcadio Segundo's name. From then on he was never sure who was who. Even when they grew up and life made them different. úrsula still wondered if they themselves might not have made a mistake in some moment of their intricate game of confusion had become changed forever. Until the beginning of adolescence they were two synchronized machines. They would wake up at the same time, have the urge to go to the bathroom at the same time, suffer the same upsets in health, and they even dreamed about the same things. In the house, where it was thought that they coordinated their actions with a simple desire to confuse, no one realized what really was happening until one day when Santa Sofía de la Piedad gave one of them a glass of lemonade and as soon as he tasted it the other one said that it needed sugar. Santa Sofía de la Piedad, who had indeed forgotten to put sugar in the lemonade, told úrsula about it. "That's what they're all like," she said without surprise, "Crazy from birth." In time things became less disordered. The one who came out of the game of confusion with the name Aureliano Segundo grew to monumental size like his grandfathers, the one who kept the name of José Arcadio Segundo grew to be bony like the colonel, and the only thing they had in common was the family's solitary air. Perhaps it was that crossing of stature, names, and character that made úrsula suspect that they had been shuffled like a deck of cards since childhood.

The decisive difference was revealed in the midst of the war, when José Arcadio Segundo asked Colonel Geri-neldo Márquez to let him see an execution. Against úrsula's better judgment his wishes were satisfied. Aureliano Segundo, on the other hand, shuddered at the mere idea of witnessing an execution. He preferred to stay home. At the age of twelve he asked úrsula what was in the locked room. "Papers," she answered.

长难句解析

Years later on his deathbed Aureliano Segundo would remember the rainy afternoon in June when he went into the bedroom to meet his first son.

数年后当阿瑞利将要离开这个世界之时，他将想起六月的那个有雨的下午，那天，他走进了卧室与他的长子见了一面。

later on 稍后；when 引导时间状语从句。

Fernanda del Carpio, the beautiful woman he had married the year before, agreed.

去年他娶的那个漂亮妻子菲楠达同意了这个做法。

the beautiful woman 做Fernanda del Carpio 的同位语，he had... 作后置定语修饰woman.

They would wake up at the same time, have the urge to go to the bathroom at the same time, suffer the same upsets in health, and they even dreamed about the same things.

他们会在相同的时间醒来，在相同的时间去卧室，遭受相同的疾病，甚至会梦见相同的事物。

wake up醒来；at the same time同时；have the urge to 有做某事冲动；该句使用多个动词形成并列结构，构成排比。dream about梦见。

The one who came out of the game of confusion with the name Aureli-ano Segundo grew to monumental size like his grandfathers, the one who kept the name of José Arcadio Segundo grew to be bony like the colonel, and the only thing they had in common was the family's solitary air.

那个走出困惑的名叫阿瑞利的人逐渐成长为了如他祖父一样的不朽人物，那个叫做乔·阿卡多的人现今如上校般班瘦骨嶙峋，并且他们唯一的共同点在于家庭所具有的孤独气氛。

solitary表示孤独的，本句三个句子包含三个定语从句，who对the one进行修饰，only thing 前的that 省略了；in common 共用的，共有，共同。

008 Peter Pan 彼得潘

今日关键语导读 Today's Key Points

《彼得潘》是苏格兰小说家及剧作家詹姆斯·马修·巴利最为著名的剧作，主要讲述了彼得潘，一个会飞的拒绝长大的顽皮男孩在梦幻岛与温迪以及她的弟弟们所经历的各种历险故事。

障碍词先听为快 Words and Expressions

suspend [səs'pend] v. 延缓，推迟；是赞停；使悬浮

civil ['sivl] adj. 公民的；民间的；文职的；有礼貌的

marooner [mə'ruːnər] n. 野营旅行者

bask [baːsk] v. 晒太阳；取暖；愉快或舒适

irritate ['iriteit] v. 刺激，使兴奋；激怒

cheeky ['tʃiːki] adj. 无耻的；厚脸皮的

wail [weil] v. 哭泣；哭号

mortal ['mɔːtl] adj. 凡人的；致死的；终有一死的

interloper ['intələupə(r)] n. 闯入者；干涉他人事务者

glisten [glisn] v. 闪光，闪亮

好英文娓娓动听 Beautiful stories

If you shut your eyes and are a lucky one, you may see at times a shapeless pool of lovely pale colours suspended in the darkness;

then if you squeeze your eyes tighter, the pool begins to take shape, and the colours become so vivid that with another squeeze they must go on fire. But just before they go on fire you see the lagoon. This is the nearest you ever get to it on the mainland, just one heavenly moment; if there could be two moments you might see the surf and hear the mermaids singing.

The children often spent long summer days on this lagoon, swimming or the water, and so forth. You must not think from this that the mermaids were on friendly terms with them: on the contrary, it was among Wendy's lasting regrets that all the time she was on the island she never had a civil word from one of them. When she stole softly to the lagoon she might see them by the score, especially on Marooners'Rock, where they loved to bask, combing out their hair in a lazy way that quite irritated her; or she might even swim, on tiptoe as it were, probably splashing her with their tails, not by accident, but intentionally.

They treated all the boys in the same way, except of course Peter, who chatted with them on Marooner' Rock by the hour, and sat on their tails when they got cheeky. He gave Wendy one of their combs.

The most haunting time at which to see them is at the turn of the moon, when they utter strange wailing cries; but the lagoon is dangerous for mortals then, and until the evening of which we have now to tell, Wendy had never seen the lagoon by moonlight, less from fear, for of course Peter would have accompanied her, than because she had strict rules about every one being in bed by seven. She was often at the lagoon, however, on sunny days after rain, when the mermaids come up in extraordinary numbers to play with their bubbles. The bubbles of many colours made in rainbow water they treat as balls, hitting them gaily from one to another with their tails, and trying to keep the rainbow, and the keepers only are allowed to use their hands. Sometimes a dozen of these games will be going on in the lagoon at a time, and it is quite a pretty sight.

But the moment the children tried to join in they had to play by themselves, for the mermaids immediately disappeared. Nevertheless we have proof that they secretly watched the interlopers, and were not above taking an idea from them; for John introduced a new way of hitting the bubble, with the head instead of the hand, and the mermaids adopted it. This is the one mark that John has left on the Neverland.

It must also have been rather pretty to see the children resting on a rock for half an hour after their mid-day meal. Wendy insisted on their doing this, and it had to be a real rest even through the meal was make-believe. So they lay there in the sun, and their bodies glistened in it, while she sat beside them and looked important.

长难句解析

If you shut your eyes and are a lucky one, you may see at times a shapeless pool of lovely pale colours suspended in the darkness; then if you squeeze your eyes tighter, the pool begins to take shape, and the colours become so vivid that with another squeeze they must go on fire.

假若你闭上眼睛，运气足够好你会看到在黑暗中悬浮着一汪有各种浅灰色调的没有形状的漂亮水池；假若你把眼睛再迷一下，水池就开始生成形状来，颜色也变得鲜活明丽，再迷得紧些，这些颜色就红得像要着火了。

句中两个if分别引导两个条件状语从句。so...that...，如此……以致于……。

When she stole softly to the lagoon she might see them by the score, especially on Marooners'Rock, where they loved to bask, combing out their hair in a lazy way that quite irritated her; or she might even swim, on tiptoe as it were, probably splashing her with their tails, not by accident, but intentionally.

她轻手轻脚地走到泄湖边上时，也许会看到几十条美人鱼，尤其在海盗礁上。她们喜欢在那上面晒太阳，一边很懒散地梳着头发，这让她看了心痒痒的；她可以像之前踮着脚走路一样轻轻地游到她们附近，她们可能还会用尾巴溅她一身水，这不是碰巧，而是故意的。

句中when 引导时间状语从句；where 引导地点状语从句；that引导宾语从句 quite irritated her修饰way。

Wendy insisted on their doing this, and it had to be a real rest even through the meal was make-believe. So they lay there in the sun, and their bodies glistened in it, while she sat beside them and looked important.

温迪坚持要孩子们这样休息，即使午餐只是假的，午睡还得真睡。于是，他们就躺在太阳底下，阳光照得他们浑身油光发亮，而她则一脸庄重的神情坐在旁边守着。

句中even though 引导让步状语从句。insist on doing sth. 坚持做某事。

读书笔记

009 Tuck Everlasting
不老泉

今日关键语导读 Today's Key Points

娜塔莉·巴比特编著的《不老泉》讲述的是一名小女孩温妮梦幻般的被魔法所迷惑的故事。温妮向往着一种不受母亲控制的生活，当她在离家不远的森林里迷路的时候，偶然碰上了一位与她以前所遇见过的男孩感觉完全不一样的少年——塔克，并发现了塔克一家获得永恒生命的秘密。随着温妮被跟踪、遭“绑架”、被捕，故事开始复杂起来……

障碍词先听为快 Words and Expressions

beam [biːm] vi. 照射；堆满笑容

ceiling ['siːliŋ] n. 天花板；上限

melancholy ['melənkəli] adj. 忧郁的；使人悲伤的

tolerantly ['tɔlərəntli] adv. 宽容地，容忍地

twitch [twitʃ] vt. 使抽动；攫取；猛拉

vanish ['væniʃ] vt. 使不见，使消失

sigh [sai] vt. 叹息，叹气

brown [braun] adj. 棕色的；褐色的 n. 褐色；棕色 v. （使）变褐色

好英文娓娓动听 Beautiful stories

And so, at dawn, that day in the first week of August, Mae

Tuck woke up and lay for a while, beaming at the cobwebs on the ceiling. At last she said aloud, "The boys will be home tomorrow!"

Mae's husband, on his back beside her, did not stir. He was still asleep, and the melancholy creases that folded his daytime face were smoothed and slack. He snored gently, and for a moment the corners of his mouth turned upward in a smile. Tuck almost never smiled except in sleep.

Mae sat up in bed and looked at him tolerantly. "The boys will be home tomorrow," she said again, a little more loudly.

Tuck twitched and the smile vanished. He opened his eyes. "Why'd you have to wake me up?" he sighed. "I was having that dream again, the good one where we're all in heaven and never heard of Treegap."

Mae sat there frowning, a great potato of a woman with a round, sensible face and calm brown eyes. "It's no use having that dream," she said. "Nothing's going to change."

长难句解析

And so, at dawn, that day in the first week of August, Mae Tuck woke up and lay for a while, beaming at the cobwebs on the ceiling. At last she said aloud, "The boys' will be home tomorrow!"

那年八月第一个礼拜的某一天。天才亮，梅便醒了。她躺了一会儿，对着天花板上密密麻麻的蜘蛛网，静静地笑了好会儿。然后，她大声地说："孩子们明天就回来了！"

at dawn 黎明时，拂晓时；that day 那一天，后跟时间状语从句需用过去时态。

He snored gently, and for a moment the corners of his mouth turned upward in a smile. Tuck almost never smiled except in sleep.

他轻轻打着鼾，偶尔嘴角还微微掀着笑。除非是在梦中，平时塔克很少笑。

the corners of …的一角；in a smile，微笑、喜笑颜开；except 除了…以外。

Tuck twitched and the smile vanished. He opened his eyes. "Why'd you have to wake me up?" he sighed. "I was having that dream again, the good one where we're all in heaven and never heard of Treegap."

塔克的嘴角抽动了一下，笑意忽地不见了。他勉强睁开眼睛。"为什么又把我叫醒？"他叹了口气，"我又做了同样的梦，很美很美的梦，梦见我们一家都上了天堂，而且再也想不起树林村这个名字。"

Wake sb. up 弄醒某人；Where 引导地点状语从句；heard of 听说。

010 The Unquiet Grave 不平静的坟墓

今日关键语导读 Today's Key Points

死去的人并非总是安静地躺在坟墓里。有时他们在这个世界上还有没做完的事情或者想为自己所受的委屈报仇雪恨；或许生活中他们自己也作过恶，即使死了也不得安宁，所以他们一定要回来给活着的人带来麻烦和恐惧。

在本书的5个故事中，死者可能随时随地以最奇怪的方式到来——到牛津某一学院，威廉斯先生正在那儿饶有兴趣地看着一幅古旧的画作；或者光天化日之下来到年轻的汤姆森先生度假住的一家小旅馆。爱德华·邓宁先生的房间里灯灭了，他伸手去找火柴，黑暗中他的手触到的是什么？乡绅鲍尔斯的妻子和继子要问个问题，可只有鲍尔斯知道答案，你怎么去问一个躺在坟墓里的死人问题呢？当帕金斯教授吹起他拾到的一个很旧的口哨时，是只有风作答，还是有别的东西？一种你见不着、听不见却又难以想像有多么可怕的东西……

障碍词先听为快 Words and Expressions

arrange [ə'reindʒ] vi. 安排；排列；协商 vt. 安排；排列；整理

upstairs ['ʌp'stɛəz] n. 楼上 adj. 楼上的 adv. 在楼上，向楼上；上楼

luggage ['lʌgidʒ] n. 行李；皮箱

comfortable ['kʌmfətəbl] n. 盖被 adj. 舒适的，舒服的

scarecrow ['skeəkrəu] n. 稻草人，威吓物；衣衫褴褛的人

bony ['bəuni] adj. 骨的；多骨的；瘦骨嶙峋的；似骨的
faint [feint] n. adj. 模糊的；头晕的；虚弱的 vi. 昏倒
whisky ['(h)wiski] n. 威士忌酒 adj. 威士忌酒的
especially [is'peʃəli] adv. 特别；尤其；格外
innkeeper ['inkiːpə(r)] n. 客栈老板；旅馆主人

好英文娓娓动听 Beautiful stories

He made a simple plan. He would arrange to leave by an afternoon train and would have his luggage put on the cart for the station. Then, just before leaving, he would go back upstairs to make sure that he had not left anything behind. But, instead of going to his own room, he would go to the other. He put oil on the key to make it easier to open the door quietly.

His last day arrived. After lunch his luggage was taken downstairs and put on the cart for the station. Mr and Mrs Betts came to the front door to say goodbye. Thomson thanked them for making him so comfortable and they thanked him for staying with them. Then, as he had planned, Thomson said: "I'll just check that I haven't left a book or anything in my room. No, please don't worry, I can do it myself."

He hurried up the stairs to the locked room, turned the key quietly and opened the door. He almost laughed aloud. Leaning, or perhaps sitting, on the edge of the bed was —nothing more than an ordinary scarecrow! A scarecrow out of the garden, of course, just put away in the empty room...

Yes; but suddenly amusement stopped. Do scarecrows have

bony feet? Do their heads roll from side to side on their shoulders? Have they got heavy metal chains around their necks? Can they get up and move across the floor with rolling head and arms close at their sides...and shake with the cold?

Thomson shut the door with a bang, jumped down the stairs and fell in a faint at the door. When he became conscious again, Mr Betts was standing over him with a glass of whisky and a serious face.

"You shouldn't do it, sir," said Betts. "You shouldn't go looking into people's secrets, especially when they've done their best to make you comfortable."

Thomson said that he was very sorry but the innkeeper and his wife found it hard to accept his apologies.

长难句解析

Thomson thanked them for making him so comfortable and they thanked him for staying with them. Then, as he had planned...

汤姆森感谢他们让他如此舒适，也感谢他们可以一直陪伴他。然后，按照他的计划……

thank...for...因为……感谢……，as在此处引导定语从句。

He hurried up the stairs to the locked room, turned the key quietly and opened the door. He almost laughed aloud, leaning, or perhaps sitting, on the edge of the bed.

他快步上楼来到锁着的房间，轻轻转动钥匙打开了门。他几乎大笑起来，斜靠着或是坐在床的边缘 。

hurry up译为“急忙，赶紧”；leaning、sitting在此句中是现在分词表伴随状态。

Thomson shut the door with a bang, jumped down the stairs and fell in a faint at the door. When he became conscious again, Mr Betts was standing over him with a glass of whisky and a serious face.

汤姆森砰地把门关上了，然后从楼梯上跳下来，昏倒在门前。当他再次有意识的时候，贝茨先生拿着一瓶威士忌一脸严肃地站在他面前。

when在此句中引导时间状语从句，with表伴随。

You shouldn't go looking into people's secrets, especially when they've done their best to make you comfortable.

你不应该去窥探别人的秘密，尤其是当他们已经尽力使你感到自在。

look into 意思是“窥探”，do one's best to do...译为“尽某人最大努力去做……”，when在此处引导时间状语从句。

011 Lady Chatterley's Lover 查泰莱夫人的情人

今日关键语导读 Today's Key Points

《查泰莱夫人的情人》是英国作家劳伦斯最后一部长篇小说，也是西方十大情爱经典小说之一。小说中的康妮嫁给了贵族地主查泰莱为妻，但不久他便在战争中负伤，腰部以下终身瘫痪。在老家中，二人的生活虽无忧无虑，但却死气沉沉。庄园里的猎场守猎人重新燃起康妮的爱情之火及对生活的渴望，她经常悄悄来到他的小屋幽会。后来，康妮怀孕了，为掩人耳目到威尼斯度假。这时守猎人尚未离婚的妻子突然回来，暴露了他们之间的私情。巨大的社会差距迫使康妮为生下孩子先下嫁他人，让守猎人默默地等待孩子的降生。

障碍词先听为快 Words and Expressions

restlessness ['restləsnəs] n. 坐立不安；不安定

twitch [twitʃ] n. 抽搐；抽动；痉挛；阵痛 v. 抽搐；抽动；阵痛

prone [prəun] adj. 俯卧的；有……倾向的，易于……的

sanctuary ['sæŋktjuəri] n. 避难所；至圣所；耶路撒冷的神殿

void [vɔid] adj. 空的；无效的；无人的 n. 空虚；空间；空隙 vt. 使无效；排放

vaguely ['veigli] adv. 含糊地；暧昧地；茫然地

revulsion [ri'vʌlʃən] n. 剧变；厌恶；强烈反感；抽搐

juncture ['dʒʌŋktʃə] n. 接缝；连接；接合

imperious [im'piəriəs] adj. 专横的；迫切的；傲慢的

monument ['mɔnjumənt] n. 纪念碑；历史遗迹；不朽的作品 vt. 为……树碑

好英文娓娓动听 Beautiful stories

Connie was aware, however, of a growing restlessness. Out of her disconnexion, a restlessness was taking possession of her like madness. It twitched her limbs when she didn't want to twitch them, it jerked her spine when she didn't want to jerk upright but preferred to rest comfortably. It thrilled inside her body, in her womb, somewhere, till she felt she must jump into water and swim to get away from it; a mad restlessness. It made her heart beat violently for no reason. And she was getting thinner.

It was just restlessness. She would rush off across the park, abandon Clifford, and lie prone in the bracken. To get away from the house...she must get away from the house and everybody. The work was her one refuge, her sanctuary.

But it was not really a refuge, a sanctuary, because she had no connexion with it. It was only a place where she could get away from the rest. She never really touched the spirit of the wood itself...if it had any such nonsensical thing.

Vaguely she knew herself that she was going to pieces in some way. Vaguely she knew she was out of connexion: she had lost touch with the substantial and vital world. Only Clifford and his books, which did not exist...which had nothing in them! Void to void. Vaguely she knew. But it was like beating her head against a stone.

Her father warned her again: "Why don't you get yourself a beau, Connie? Do you all the good in the world."

That winter Michaelis came for a few days. He was a young Irishman who had already made a large fortune by his plays in America. He had been taken up quite enthusiastically for a time by smart society in London, for he wrote smart society plays. Then gradually smart society realized that it had been made ridiculous at the hands of a down-at-heel Dublin street-rat, and revulsion came. Michaelis was the last word in what was caddish and bounderish. He was discovered to be anti-English, and to the class that made this discovery this was worse than the dirtiest crime. He was cut dead, and his corpse thrown into the refuse can.

Nevertheless Michaelis had his apartment in Mayfair, and walked down Bond Street the image of a gentleman, for you cannot get even the best tailors to cut their low-down customers, when the customers pay.

Clifford was inviting the young man of thirty at an inauspicious moment in the young man's career. Yet Clifford did not hesitate. Michaelis had the ear of a few million people, probably; and, being a hopeless outsider, he would no doubt be grateful to be asked down to Wragby at this juncture, when the rest of the smart world was cutting him. Being grateful, he would no doubt do Clifford `good' over there in America. Kudos! A man gets a lot of kudos, whatever that may be, by being talked about in the right way, especially `over there'. Clifford was a coming man; and it was remarkable what a sound publicity instinct he had. In the end

Michaelis did him most nobly in a play, and Clifford was a sort of popular hero. Till the reaction, when he found he had been made ridiculous.

Connie wondered a little over Clifford's blind, imperious instinct to become known: known, that is, to the vast amorphous world he did not himself know, and of which he was uneasily afraid; known as a writer, as a first-class modern writer. Connie was aware from successful, old, hearty, bluffing Sir Malcolm, that artists did advertise themselves, and exert themselves to put their goods over. But her father used channels ready-made, used by all the other R. A.s who sold their pictures. Whereas Clifford discovered new channels of publicity, all kinds. He had all kinds of people at Wragby, without exactly lowering himself. But, determined to build himself a monument of a reputation quickly, he used any handy rubble in the making.

长难句解析

Connie was aware, however, of a growing restlessness.

然而，康妮日益感觉到一些坐立不安。

however 表示转折

It was only a place where she could get away from the rest.

这是她能够远离他人得以清静的唯一的地方。

where 引导的状语从句修饰place；the rest 表示其他的人，其他的事。

He was a young Irishman who had already made a large fortune by his plays in America.

他是一个年轻的爱尔兰人，并且他早已在美国发了一笔大财。

who 引导的定语从句修饰a young Irishman；make a fortune 表示发财的意思。

Clifford was inviting the young man of thirty at an inauspicious moment in the young man's career.

克里佛德邀请那个三十岁的年轻人的时候，那个年轻人正处于事业的低谷。

sb. of thirty（岁数）某人多少岁；in one's career 在某人的职业生涯中。

读书笔记

012 The Lady of the Camellias 茶花女

今日关键语导读 Today's Key Points

《茶花女》是法国的著名作家小仲马的代表作，文章讲述了著名交际花玛格丽特凭借自己的美貌出入上层社会的热闹场合，迫于生计出卖自己的尊严和肉体。在阿尔芒的追求下，两人相爱却遭到阿尔芒父亲的阻碍，迫于无奈离开阿尔芒，最终因患上肺病离开人世的爱情悲剧。

障碍词先听为快 Words and Expressions

elapse [iˈlæps] vi. 消逝；时间过去 n. 流逝；时间的过去

tangible [ˈtændʒəbl] adj. 有形的；切实的；可触摸的 n. 有形资产

auction [ˈɔːkʃən] vt. 拍卖；竞卖 n. 拍卖

mistress [ˈmistris] n. 情妇；女主人；主妇；女教师；女能人

brain [brein] n. 头脑，智力；脑袋 vt. 猛击……的头部

好英文娓娓动听 Beautiful stories

A considerable time elapsed without my hearing a word about Armand, but on the other hand the subject of Marguerite had come up a great deal.

I do not know if you have noticed, but it only takes the name of someone who should in all likelihood have remained unknown or at least of no particular interest to you, to be pronounced once in your hearing, for all sorts of details to collect round that name, and for you then to have all your friends speak about a subject of which they had never spoken to you before. Next thing, you discover that the person in question was there, just out of range, all the while. You realize that your paths have crossed many times without your noticing, and you find in the events which others recount some tangible link or affinity with certain events in your own past. I had not quite reached that point with Marguerite, since I had seen her, met her, knew her by her face and habits. Yet ever since the auction, her name had cropped up so frequently in my hearing and, in the circumstances which I have related in the previous chapter, her name had become associated with sorrow so profound, that my surprise had gone on growing and my curiosity had increased.

The result was that now I never approached any friends, with whom I had never spoken of Marguerite, without saying:

"Did you know someone called Marguerite Gautier?"

"The Lady of the Camellias?"

"That's her."

"Rather!"

These "Rather!" sometimes came with smiles which left no possible doubt as to their meaning.

"Well, what kind of girl was she?" I would go on.

"A very decent sort."

"Is that all?"

"Heavens! I should hope so. A few more brains and perhaps a bit more heart than the rest of them."

"But you know nothing particular about her?"

"She ruined Baron de G."

"Anyone else?"

"She was the mistress of the old Duke de."

"Was she really his mistress?"

"That's what they say: at any rate, he gave her a great deal of money."

Always the same general details.

But I would have been interested to learn a little about the affair between Marguerite and Armand.

One day, I chanced upon one of those men who live habitually on intimate terms with the most notorious courtesans. I questioned him.

"Did you know Marguerite Gautier?"

The answer was that same "Rather!"

"What sort of girl was she?"

"A fine-looking, good-hearted type. Her death was a great sadness to me."

"She had a lover called Armand Duval, didn't she?"

"Tall chap with fair hair?"

"That's him."

"Yes, she did."

"And what was this Armand like?"

"A young fellow who threw away the little he had on her, I believe, and was forced to give her up. They say it affected his reason."

"What about her?"

"She loved him very much too, they also say, but as girls of her sort love. You should never ask more of them than they can give."

"What became of Armand?"

"Couldn't say. We didn't know him all that well. He stayed five or six months with Marguerite, in the country. When she came back to town, he went off somewhere."

"And you haven't seen him since?"

"Never."

I had not seen Armand again either. I had begun to wonder if, the day he called on me, the recent news of Marguerite's death had not exaggerated the love he had once felt for her and therefore his grief, and I told myself that perhaps, in forgetting the dead girl, he had also forgotten his promise to return to see me.

长难句解析

I do not know if you have noticed, but it only takes the name of someone who should in all likelihood have remained unknown or at least of no particular interest to you, to be pronounced once in your hearing, for all sorts of details to collect round that name, and for you then to have all your friends speak about a subject of which they had never spoken to you before.

我不知道您可曾有过这样的感觉：一个看来跟您素不相识或者至少是毫无关系的人，一旦有人在您面前提到他的姓名，跟这个人有关的各种琐闻就会慢慢地汇集拢来，您的三朋四友也都会来和您谈起他们从来也没有跟您谈过的事，您几乎就会觉得这个人仿佛就在您的身边。

if引导条件状语从句；who引导定语从句；at least 至少；all sorts of 各种各样的……；which引导定语从句。

These "Rather!" sometimes came with smiles which left no possible doubt as to their meaning.

"熟悉得很！"他们说这句话的时候，有时脸上还带着那种含义显而易见的微笑。

with 表伴随；which引导定语从句；as to 至于，关于。

That's what they say: at any rate, he gave her a great deal of money.

大家都是这么说的，不管怎么说，那老公爵给过她很多钱。

what 引导的从句在原句中做表语；at any rate 表示无论如何，不管怎样；a great deal of 大量。

One day, I chanced upon one of those men who live habitually on intimate terms with the most notorious courtesans.

一天，我遇到了一个人。这个人和那些风月场中的名媛来往甚密。

who 引导的定语从句修饰前面的men；chance upon sb 遇见某人。

I had begun to wonder if, the day he called on me, the recent news of Marguerite's death had not exaggerated the love he had once felt for her and therefore his grief, and I told myself that perhaps, in forgetting the dead girl, he had also forgotten his promise to return to see me.

我甚至在寻思，他来我家，是不是因为他知道了玛格丽特刚才死去的消息而勾起了旧情，因此才格外悲伤。我思忖他也许早就把再来看我的诺言随同死者一起抛到九霄云外去了。

wonder 后面if 引导条件状语从句；call on sb 表示拜访某人。

读书笔记

013 Daddy Long-Legs 长腿叔叔

今日关键语导读 Today's Key Points

《长腿叔叔》作者简·韦伯斯特，通过书信的形式向读者展现了一个孤女四年多的学习和生活。主人公朱蒂从小在孤儿院长大，在她十八岁那年，得到一位“长腿叔叔”的资助而上了大学。从此，在长达四年的时间里，她一直给这位素未谋面的叔叔写信。朱蒂非常独立、自尊心很强，虽然得到了别人的帮助，但是她仍然努力学习，获得学校颁发的奖学金，并立志成为一个作家。同时，她还利用暑假给低年级的学生做家教。在这个过程中，她也得到了两位男性朋友的青睐。最后才发现原来在这两位男性朋友中，有一位正是她一直给她写信的“长腿叔叔”。

障碍词先听为快 Words and Expressions

institution [ˌinsti'tjuːʃən] n. 机构；制度；院校；院；学会

originality [ˌəridʒi'næliti] n. 独创性；创造性；创造力；新颖

numb [nʌm] v. 呆住；知觉麻木；变得麻木不仁

superintend [ˌsjuːpərin'tend] v. 监督；主管；管理；主持；指挥

outfit ['autfit] n. 装备；准备；设备；团体；装置 v. 装备；配备；准备；供给

correspond [kɔris'pɔnd] v. 对应；相应；通信；符合；一致

detest [di'test] v. 憎恶；憎恨；恨；嫌；深恶；嫌恶；厌恨；恨之入骨；深恨

platitude ['plætitjuːd] n. 陈词滥调；老生常谈；单调

tentative ['tentətiv] adj. 实验性的；不确定的；尝试的 n. 实验；尝试；试探

befall [bi'fɔːl] v. 降临；遭遇；发生；碰到；遇到

好英文娓娓动听 Beautiful stories

"It seemed to me that you showed little gratitude in holding up to ridicule the institution that has done so much for you. Had you not managed to be funny I doubt if you would have been forgiven. But fortunately for you, Mr—, that is, the gentleman who has just gone—appears to have an immoderate sense of humour. On the strength of that impertinent paper, he has offered to send you to college."

"To college?" Jerusha's eyes grew big. Mrs. Lippett nodded.

"He waited to discuss the terms with me. They are unusual. The gentleman, I may say, is erratic. He believes that you have originality, and he is planning to educate you to become a writer."

"A writer?" Jerusha's mind was numbed. She could only repeat Mrs. Lippett's words.

"That is his wish. Whether anything will come of it, the future will show. He is giving you a very liberal allowance, almost, for a girl who has never had any experience in taking care of money, too liberal. But he planned the matter in detail, and I did not feel free to make any suggestions. You are to remain here through the summer, and Miss Pritchard has kindly offered to superintend your outfit. Your board and tuition will be paid directly to the college, and you will receive in addition during the four years you are there, an allowance of thirty-five dollars a month. This will enable you to enter on the same standing as the other students. The money will be sent to you by the gentleman's private secretary once a month, and in return, you will write a letter of acknowledgment once a month. That is—you are not to thank him for the money; he doesn't care to have that mentioned, but you are to write a letter telling of the progress in your studies and the details of your daily life. Just such a letter as you would write to your parents if they were living.

"These letters will be addressed to Mr. John Smith and will be sent in care of the secretary. The gentleman's name is not John Smith, but he prefers to remain unknown. To you he will never be anything but John Smith. His reason in requiring the letters is that he thinks nothing so fosters facility in literary expression as letter-writing. Since you have no family with whom to correspond, he desires you to write in this way; also, he wishes to keep track of your progress. He will never answer your letters, nor in the slightest particular take any notice of them. He detests letter-writing and does not wish you to become a burden. If any point should ever arise where an answer would seem to be imperative—such as in the event of your being expelled, which I trust will not occur—you may correspond with Mr. Griggs, his secretary. These monthly letters are absolutely obligatory on your part; they are the only payment that Mr. Smith requires, so you must be as punctilious in sending them as though it were a bill that you were paying. I hope that they will always be respectful in tone and will reflect credit on your training. You must remember that you are writing to a Trustee of the John Grier Home."

Jerusha's eyes longingly sought the door. Her head was in a whirl of excitement, and she wished only to escape from Mrs. Lippett's platitudes and think. She rose and took a tentative step backwards. Mrs. Lippett detained her with a gesture; it was an oratorical opportunity not to be slighted.

"I trust that you are properly grateful for this very rare good fortune that has befallen you? Not many girls in your position ever have such an opportunity to rise in the world. You must always remember."

"I—yes, ma'am, thank you. I think, if that's all, I must go and sew a patch on Freddie Perkins's trousers."

The door closed behind her, and Mrs. Lippett watched it with dropped jaw, her peroration in mid-air.

The Letters of Miss Jerusha Abbott to Mr. Daddy-Long-Legs Smith

长难句解析

It seemed to me that you showed little gratitude in holding up to ridicule the institution that has done so much for you.

在我听起来你在嘲笑着这个把你养大，为你做了这么多的孤儿院，并且没有表示出一点感激。

it 引导的条件状语从句，在此句中“it”做形式主语而“that”引导的从句做真正的主语。

He is giving you a very liberal allowance, almost, for a girl who has never had any experience in taking care of money, too liberal.

他会给你足够多的零用钱，对一个从没理过财的女孩子来说这实在是太多了。

who 引导定语从句；take care of 关心、照料。

His reason in requiring the letters is that he thinks nothing so fosters facility in literary expression as letter-writing.

他要求你写信的原因是他认为没有什么比写信更能培养写作技巧。

that引导宾语从句；nothing so...as...，没有……比……更……

Since you have no family with whom to correspond, he desires you to write in this way; also, he wishes to keep track of your progress.

由于你没有家人可联络，他才希望你写这样信给他；另一方面他也想随时知道你的学习状况。

since 引导的原因状语从句；desire to do sth. 希望做某事，keep track of 与……保持联系。

If any point should ever arise where an answer would seem to be imperative—such as in the event of your being expelled, which I trust will not occur—you may correspond with Mr. Griggs, his secretary. These monthly letters are absolutely obligatory on your part; they are the only payment that Mr. Smith requires, so you must be as punctilious in sending them as though it were a bill that you were paying.

如果有任何紧急事件需要回复的，比如你要被退学啦，这我相信应该不会发生的，你可以跟他的秘书，格利兹先生联络。这些每个月的书信是你绝对要遵守的义务，这也是史密斯先生唯一的要求，所以你一定要一丝不苟地写信，就当做你在付帐单一样。

If 引导条件状语从句；which 引导非限制性定语从句。

读书笔记

014 The Boy in the Striped Pyjamas 穿条纹睡衣的男孩

今日关键语导读 Today's Key Points

二战期间，八岁的布鲁诺是集中营中德国司令官的儿子，他与集中营围栏的另一边的一个犹太男孩结下了友谊，从而发生了许多令人意料不到的事情。

障碍词先听为快 Words and Expressions

wardrobe ['wɔːdrəub] n. 衣柜；行头；全部戏装

crate [kreit] n. 板条箱；篓

muster ['mʌstə] vi. 召集；聚集

respectful [ris'pektful] adj. 恭敬的；有礼貌的

staircase ['steəkeis] n. 楼梯

previous ['priːvjəs] adj. 以前的；早先的；过早的

chaos ['keiɔs] n. 混沌，混乱

pack [pæk] vt. 包装；压紧；捆扎；挑选；塞满

twist [twist] vt. 捻；拧；扭伤；编织；使苦恼

好英文娓娓动听 Beautiful stories

One afternoon, when Bruno came home from school, he was surprised to find Maria, the family's maid—who always kept her head bowed and never looked up from the carpet— standing in his bedroom, pulling all his belongings out of the wardrobe and packing them in four large wooden crates, even the things he'd hidden at the back that belonged to him and were nobody else's business.

"What are you doing?" he asked in as polite a tone as he could muster, for although he wasn't happy to come home and find someone going through his possessions, his mother had always told him that he was to treat Maria respectfully and not just imitate the Way Father spoke to her. "You take your hands off my things."

Maria shook her head and pointed towards the staircase behind him, where Bruno's mother had just appeared. She was a tall woman with long red hair that she bundled into a sort of net behind her head, and she was twisting her hands together nervously as if there was something she didn't want to have to say or something she didn't want to have to believe.

"Mother," said Bruno, marching towards her, "what's going on? Why is Maria going through my things?"

"She's packing them," explained Mother.

"Packing them?" he asked, running quickly through the events of the previous few days to consider whether he'd been particularly naughty or had used those words out loud that he wasn't allowed to use and was being sent away because of it. He couldn't think of anything though. In fact, over the last few days he had behaved in a perfectly decent manner to everyone and couldn't remember causing any chaos at all. "Why?" he asked then. "What have I done?"

Mother had walked into her own bedroom by then but Lars,

the chaos, was in there, packing her things too. She sighed and threw her hands in the air in frustration before marching back to the staircase, followed by Bruno, who wasn't going to let the matter drop without an explanation.

"Mother," he insisted. "What's going on? Are we moving?"

"Come downstairs with me," said Mother, leading the way towards the large dining room where the Fury had been to dinner the week before. 'We'll talk down there.'

长难句解析

"Mother," said Bruno, marching towards her, "what's going on? Why is Maria going through my things?"

"妈妈，"布鲁诺说，一边走向她，"怎么回事啊？为什么马瑞在检查我的东西？"

go through 经历，检阅；march 行军，走向。

In fact, over the last few days he had behaved in a perfectly decent manner to everyone and couldn't remember causing any chaos at all.

实际上，在过去的几天里他对每个人都很有礼貌，并且认为并没有造成过任何的麻烦。

chaos 混乱，麻烦；decent 正派的，得体的，相当好的；not ...at all 一点也不。

She sighed and threw her hands in the air in frustration before marching back to the staircase, followed by Bruno, who wasn't going to let the matter drop without an explanation.

她叹了口气，在回楼梯之前沮丧地将双手挥向天空，后面跟着布鲁诺，布鲁诺并不打算让问题就这样无声无息地得到解决。

followed by过去分词做后置定语；who 引导非限制性定语从句；in frustration 沮丧地。

读书笔记

015 The Da Vinci Code 达·芬奇密码

今日关键语导读 Today's Key Points

《达·芬奇密码》是美国作家丹·布朗创作的侦探小说。小说主人公，哈佛大学的符号学专家罗伯特·兰登在法国巴黎出差期间的一个午夜接到一个紧急电话，得知卢浮宫博物馆年迈的馆长被人杀害在卢浮宫的博物馆里，人们在他的尸体旁边发现了一个难以捉摸的密码。兰登发现一连串的线索就隐藏在达芬奇的艺术作品当中，以及由此拉开的一系列对真相的探索。

障碍词先听为快 Words and Expressions

enthusiast [in'θjuːziæst] n. 热情者，热心者；热衷于……的人；入迷者，狂热者；尤指热烈支持者；忠于（原则、事业、信仰等）的人

outline ['əutlain] n. 轮廓；大纲；概要；略图 vt. 概述；略述；描画……轮廓

scandalous ['skændələs] adj. 可耻的；诽谤性的

academic [ˌækə'demik] adj. 学术的；理论的；学院的 n. 大学生，大学教师；学者

anticipation [ˌæntisi'peiʃən] n. 希望；预感；先发制人；预支

shrug [ʃrʌg] vt. 耸肩，耸肩表示 n. 耸肩 vi. 耸肩

quotation [kwəu'teiʃən] n. [贸易] 报价单；引用语；引证

speculation [ˌspekju'leiʃən] n. 投机；推测；思索；投机买卖

delusion [di'luːʒən] n. 迷惑，欺骗；错觉；幻想

好英文娓娓动听 Beautiful stories

Langdon winced, glancing at Sophie. "Virgin is the term Grail enthusiasts use to describe anyone who has never heard the true Grail story."

Teabing turned eagerly to Sophie. "How much do you know, my dear?"

Sophie quickly outlined what Langdon had explained earlier—the Priory of Sion, the Knights Templar, the Sangreal documents, and the Holy Grail, which many claimed was not a cup... but rather something far more powerful.

"That's all?" Teabing fired Langdon a scandalous look. "Robert, I thought you were a gentleman. You've robbed her of the climax!"

"I know, I thought perhaps you and I could..." Langdon apparently decided the unseemly metaphor had gone far enough.

Teabing already had Sophie locked in his twinkling gaze. "You are a Grail virgin, my dear. And trust me, you will never forget your first time."

Seated on the divan beside Langdon, Sophie drank her tea and ate a scone, feeling the welcome effects of caffeine and food. Sir Leigh Teabing was beaming as he awkwardly paced before the open fire, his leg braces clicking on the stone hearth.

"The Holy Grail," Teabing said, his voice sermonic. "Most people ask me only where it is. I fear that is a question I may never answer." He turned and looked directly at Sophie. "However... the far more relevant question is this: What is the Holy Grail?"

Sophie sensed a rising air of academic anticipation now in both of her male companions.

"To fully understand the Grail," Teabing continued, "we must first understand the Bible. How well do you know the New Testament?"

Sophie shrugged. "Not at all, really. I was raised by a man who worshipped Leonardo da Vinci."

Teabing looked both startled and pleased. "An enlightened soul. Superb! Then you must be aware that Leonardo was one of the keepers of the secret of the Holy Grail. And he hid clues in his art."

"Robert told me as much, yes."

"And Da Vinci's views on the New Testament?"

"I have no idea."

Teabing's eyes turned mirthful as he motioned to the bookshelf across the room. "Robert, would you mind? On the bottom shelf. La Storia di Leonardo."

Langdon went across the room, found a large art book, and brought it back, setting it down on the table between them. Twisting the book to face Sophie, Teabing flipped open the heavy cover and pointed inside the rear cover to a series of quotations. "From Da Vinci's notebook on polemics and speculation," Teabing said, indicating one quote in particular. "I think you'll find this relevant to our discussion."

Sophie read the words.

Many have made a trade of delusions

and false miracles, deceiving the stupid multitude.

—LEONARDO DA VINCI

"Here's another," Teabing said, pointing to a different quote.

Blinding ignorance does mislead us.

O! Wretched mortals, open your eyes!

—LEONARDO DA VINCI

Sophie felt a little chill. "Da Vinci is talking about the Bible?"

Teabing nodded. "Leonardo's feelings about the Bible relate directly to the Holy Grail. "In fact, Da Vinci painted the true Grail, which I will show you momentarily, but first we must speak of the Bible." Teabing smiled. "And everything you need to know about the Bible can be summed up by the great canon doctor Martyn Percy." Teabing cleared his throat and declared, "The Bible did not arrive by fax from heaven."

"I beg your pardon?"

"The Bible is a product of man, my dear. Not of God. The Bible did not fall magically from the clouds. Man created it as a historical record of tumultuous times, and it has evolved through countless translations, additions, and revisions. History has never had a definitive version of the book."

长难句解析

Sophie quickly outlined what Langdon had explained earlier—the Priory of Sion, the Knights Templar, the Sangreal documents, and the Holy Grail, which many claimed was not a cup... but rather something far more powerful.

索菲把兰登早些时候告诉她的一些东西简要地说了一下：从隐修会到圣殿武士团，从圣杯文件到圣杯女神的传说，它不只是个杯子，而是具有神力的圣杯。

what引导的宾语从句，had done过去完成时，表示过去一动作从过去某一时间开始，并对现在产生了影响；which引导非限制性定语从句。

Seated on the divan beside Langdon, Sophie drank her tea and ate a scone, feeling the welcome effects of caffeine and food. Sir Leigh Teabing was beaming as he awkwardly paced before the open fire, his leg braces clicking on the stone hearth.

索菲靠着兰登坐在沙发上，喝着茶，吃着烤饼，享用着美味的食物，雷·提彬爵士微笑着，在炉火前面笨拙地踱来踱去，假肢敲在地面上，发出吱吱的响声。

be seated on 坐在某地，v-ing作伴随状语表状态，feel the welcome effects of sth.原义为感受令人满意的效果，在此译为享受……。click on 是敲击的意思。

Teabing's eyes turned mirthful as he motioned to the bookshelf across the room. "Robert, would you mind? On the bottom shelf. La Storia di Leonardo."

提彬开心地指着对面的书架，说道："罗伯特，请从书架的底层把那本《达·芬奇的故事》拿过来。"

as 引导时间状语从句，表示“当……时候”，would you mind在此有请求的意思，意思是“你介意……吗？”mind的用法：1）+ doing sth.（动名词，用于mind的主语与doing的逻辑主语一致时）2）+ one's doing sth.（动名词的复合结构，用于mind的主语与doing的逻辑主语不一致时）3）+ if clause（if引导的宾语从句）

Twisting the book to face Sophie, Teabing flipped open the heavy cover and pointed inside the rear cover to a series of quotations. "From Da Vinci's notebook on polemics and speculation," Teabing said, indicating one quote in particular. "I think you'll find this relevant to our discussion."

提彬把书转过来朝着索菲，翻开沉重的封面，指着封底上的几行引言说道：“这些摘自达·芬奇所作的有关辩论术和思考方法的笔记。”他又指着其中的一行说道，“我想你会发现这一行跟我们讨论的话题有关。”

a series of 一系列，twisting动名词做主语表伴随；in particular尤其；be relevant to与……相关

"In fact, Da Vinci painted the true Grail, which I will show you momentarily, but first we must speak of the Bible." Teabing smiled. "And everything you need to know about the Bible can be summed up by the great canon doctor Martyn Percy." Teabing cleared his throat and declared, "The Bible did not arrive by fax from heaven."

“实际上，达·芬奇画出了真正的圣杯，一会儿我就拿给你看。不过，我们必须先讲一下《圣经》。”提彬停了一下，然后微笑着说道：“你对《圣经》所需了解的一切可以用伟大的教会医生马丁·珀西的一句话来概括。”提彬清了清喉咙，大声说道：“《圣经》不是来自天堂的传真。”

in fact 事实上，实际上；which引导定语从句，修饰前面的the true Grail；speak of 谈论；know about了解；sum up 总结，概括；clear one’s throat 清嗓子

读书笔记

016 David Copperfield 大卫·科波菲尔

今日关键语导读 Today's Key Points

《大卫·科波菲尔》是英国作家狄更斯创作的他生平最喜爱的一部小说。故事讲述了主人公大卫尚未出生时，父亲就去世了。不久，母亲改嫁，继父常常虐待他。母亲去世后，继父把不足10岁的他送去当童工。他历经艰辛，最后找到了姨婆贝西小姐。贝西收留了大卫，让他上学深造。大卫求学期间寄宿在姨婆的律师威克菲尔家里，并与威克菲尔的女儿安妮丝结下了深厚的情谊。大卫中学毕业后，在斯本罗律师事务所做实习生时，爱上了斯本罗律师的女儿朵拉，但二人婚后并不幸福。大卫最终成了一名作家，朵拉却患上了重病，后来离开了人世。大卫满怀悲痛地出国旅行散心，期间，安妮丝始终与他保持联系。当他三年后返回英国时，才发觉安妮丝一直爱着他。

障碍词先听为快 Words and Expressions

industrious [in'dʌstriəs] adj. 勤奋的，勤劳的

afterwards ['ɑːftəwədz] adv. 后来；然后

murmur ['məːmə] vi. 低声说；私下抱怨；发出轻柔持续的声音

edification [ˌedifi'keiʃən] n. 启迪；教诲；精神修养

bestow [bi'stəu] vt. 使用；授予；放置

immense [i'mens] adj. 巨大的，广大的；无边无际的；非常好的

pounce [pauns] vt. 扑过去抓住 vi. 突袭，猛扑

bundle ['bʌndl] n. 束；捆
transport [træns'pɔːt] vt. 运输；流放；使狂喜
explode [iks'pləud] vt. 使爆炸；爆炸；推翻

好英文娓娓动听 Beautiful stories

"Please let me hold the pens", said Dora. "I want to have something to do with all those many hours when you are so industrious. May I hold the pens?" The remenberance of her pretty joy when I said Yes, brings tears to my eyes. The next time I sat down to write, and regularly afterwards, she sat in her old place, with a spare bundle of pens at her side. Her triumph in this connection with my work, and her delight when I wanted a new pen —which I very often feigned to do— suggested to me a new way of pleasing my child-wife.

......

Dora would not allow me, for a long time, to remove the handkerchief. She sat sobbing and murmuring behind it, that, if I was uneasy, why had I ever been married? Why hadn't I said, even the day before we went to church, that I knew I should be uneasy, and I would rather not? If I couldn't bear her, why didn't I send her away to her aunts at Putney, or to Julia Mills in India? Julia would be glad to see her, and would not call her a transported page.

......

I pressed Traddles into the service without his knowledge; and whenever he came to see us, exploded my mines upon him for the edification of Dora at second hand. The amount of practical wisdom I bestowed upon Traddles in this manner was immense, and of the best quality; but it had no other effect upon Dora than to depress her spirits, and make her always nervous with the dread that it would be her turn next. I found myself in the condition of a schoolmaster, a trap, a pitfall; of always playing spider to Dora's fly, and always pouncing out of my hole to her infinite disturbance.

长难句解析

She sat in her old place, with a spare bundle of pens at her side.

她总是坐在那里，旁边放着一大把准备好的钢笔。

a spare bundle of 一大把…；at one's side 在…旁边。

Her triumph in this connection with my work, and her delight when I wanted a new pen —which I very often feigned to do.

她从这点联系中得到的快乐，以及每次我想要一支笔时她都很开心——我经常假装这样。

when引导时间状语从句；句中的which引导的是一个非限制的定语从句，修饰前面的整个句子。

She sat sobbing and murmuring behind it.

她哭着低声说。

句中的sobbing and murmuring 是现在分词作状语表伴随，修饰sat这个动词。表明动作的持续性和状态。

I pressed Traddles into the service without his knowledge.

我在特拉德尔不知情的情况下，把他拉进了我的计划。

without his knowledge 做宾语补足语。

Whenever he came to see us, exploded my mines upon him for the edification of Dora at second hand.

每次他来看我们的时候，我都把自己从朵拉那里受到的启发统统灌输给他。

whenever引导时间状语从句；the edification of 教导、启发、熏陶；at second hand间接地，用过的，二手的。

读书笔记

017 The Cat in the hat
戴帽子的猫

今日关键语导读 Today's Key Points

作者西多·苏思·吉赛尔，是儿童文学作家及艺术家，绰号“苏士博士”。这本书内容诙谐有趣，情节简单，语言像诗一般琅琅上口，深受每一代儿童的喜爱。故事主要讲了妈妈有事外出，被迫窝在家里的康拉德和小妹妹萨莉正在发愁如何才能捱过无聊之极的一天，就在此时，一只戴帽子、会说美语的猫到访，之后他们之间发生了一系列有趣的事情。

障碍词先听为快 Words and Expressions

step [step] n. 步，脚步；步骤；步伐；梯级

mat [mæt] n. 垫；垫子；衬边

trick [trik] n. 把戏；窍门；花招

mind [maind] vi. 介意；注意

fear [fiə] n. 害怕；恐惧；敬畏；担心

bump [bʌmp] vt. 碰，撞；颠簸

stand [stænd] vt. & vi. 站立，（使）直立，站着

好英文娓娓动听 Beautiful stories

The sun did not shine.
It was too wet to play,
so we sat in the house
all that cold, cold, wet day.

I sat there with Sally.
We sat there, we two.
And I said, "How I wish
we had something to do!"
Too wet to go out
and too cold to play ball.

So we sat in the house.
We did nothing at all.
So all we could do was to
sit!
Sit!
Sit!
Sit!
And we did not like it.
Not one little bit.
And then
something went BUMP!
How that bump made us jump!
We looked!
Then we saw him step in on the
mat!
We looked!
And we saw him!
The Cat in the hat!
And he said to us,
"Why do you sit there like
that?"
"I know it is wet
and the sun is not sunny.
But we can have
lots of good fun that is funny!"
"I know some good games we
could play,"
said the cat.
"I know some new tricks,"
said the Cat in the Hat.
"A lot of good tricks.
I will show them to you.
Your mother
will not mind at all if I do."

Then Sally and I
did not know what to say.
Our mother was out of the
house
for the day.
But our fish said, "No! No!
Make the cat go away!
Tell that cat go away!
Tell that cat in the Hat
you do Not want to play.
He should not be there.
He should not be about.
He should not be here
when your mother is out!"
"Now! Now! Have no fear.
Have no fear!" said the cat.
"My tricks are not bad,"
Said the Cat in the Hat."

"Why, we can have
lots of good fun, if you wish,
with a game that I call
UP-UP-UP with a fish!"
"Put me down!" said the fish.
"This is no fun at all!
Put me down!" said the fish.
"I do Not wish to fall!"

"Have no fear!" said the cat.
"I will not let you fall.
I will hold you up high
as I stand on a ball.
With a book on one hand!
And a cup on my hat!
But that is not All I can do!"
said the cat...

长难句解析

"I know it is wet and the sun is not sunny. But we can have lots of good fun that is funny!"

"我知道今天太阳没有出来天气很湿润，但是我们有很多好玩的事情可以做啊！"

that 引导定语从句，修饰lots of good fun。

"A lot of good tricks. I will show them to you. Your mother will not mind at all if I do." Then Sally and I did not know what to say.

"很多好玩的花样，我将会展示给你们看，你们的妈妈一点也不会介意我这样做"然后我和萨莉不知道该说什么了。

a lot of 大量，许多；not...at all 一点也不。

"Put me down!" said the fish. "This is no fun at all! Put me down!" said the fish. "I do Not wish to fall!"

“把我放下来！”这条鱼说道，“这一点儿也不好玩！把我放下来！我不想掉下去！”

put sb. down，把某人放下。

读书笔记

018 The Picture of Dorian Gray 道林·格雷的画像

今日关键语导读 Today's Key Points

《道林·格雷的画像》是英国作家奥斯卡·王尔德的著作，天生漂亮异常的道林·格雷因见了画家霍华德给他画的真人一样大的肖像，发现了自己惊人的美，又听信了亨利爵士的吹嘘，开始为自己韶华易逝、美貌难久感到痛苦，表示希望那幅肖像能代替自己承担岁月和心灵的负担，而让自己永远保持青春貌美。他这个不切实际的愿望后来却莫名其妙地实现了。他开始无所顾忌，不恶不作，最后这幅肖像却成为了记录恶行的证据，他因肖像而生也因肖像而死。

障碍词先听为快 Words and Expressions

scarlet ['skaːlit] adj. 深红的；鲜红色的

candor ['kændə] n. 坦白；直率

unspotted ['ʌn'spɔtid] adj. 清白的；无瑕疵的；无污点的

philanthropy [fi'lænθrəpi] n. 博爱，慈善；慈善事业

divan [di'væn] n. （无扶手和靠背的）长沙发椅

sulky ['sʌlki] adj. 生气的；阴沉的

whim [(h)wim] n. 奇想；一时的兴致；怪念头；幻想

horribly ['hɔrəbli] adv. 可怕地；非常地

oblige [ə'blaidʒ] vt. 赐，施恩惠

tedious ['tiːdiəs] adj. 沉闷的；冗长乏味的

Lord Henry looked at him. Yes, he was certainly wonderfully handsome, with his finely-curved scarlet lips, his frank blue eyes, his crisp gold hair. There was something in his face that made one trust him at once. All the candor of youth was there, as well as all youth's passionate purity. One felt that he had kept himself unspotted from the world. No wonder Basil Hallward worshipped him. He was made to be worshipped.

"You are too charming to go in for philanthropy, Mr. Gray—far too charming." And Lord Henry flung himself down on the divan, and opened his cigarette-case.

Hallward had been busy mixing his colors and getting his brushes ready. He was looking worried, and when he heard Lord Henry's last remark he glanced at him, hesitated for a moment, and then said, "Harry, I want to finish this picture today. Would you think it awfully rude of me if I asked you to go away?"Lord Henry smiled, and looked at Dorian Gray. "Am I to go, Mr. Gray?" he asked. "Oh, please don't, Lord Henry. I see that Basil is in one of his sulky moods, and I can't bear him when he sulks. Besides, I want you to tell me why I should not go in for philanthropy."

"I don't know that I shall tell you that, Mr. Gray. But I certainly will not run away, now that you have asked me to stop. You don't really mind, Basil, do you? You have often told me that you liked your sitters to have some one to chat to."

Hallward bit his lip. "If Dorian wishes it, of course you must stay. Dorian's whims are laws to everybody, except himself."

Lord Henry took up his hat and gloves. "You are very pressing,

Basil, but I am afraid I must go. I have promised to meet a man at the Orleans. Good-bye, Mr. Gray. Come and see me some afternoon in Curzon Street. I am nearly always at home at five o'clock. Write to me when you are coming. I should be sorry to miss you."

"Basil," cried Dorian Gray, "if Lord Henry goes I shall go, too. You never open your lips while you are painting, and it is horribly dull standing on a platform and trying to look pleasant. Ask him to stay. I insist upon it."

"Stay, Harry, to oblige Dorian, and to oblige me," said Hallward, gazing intently at his picture. "It is quite true, I never talk when I am working, and never listen either, and it must be dreadfully tedious for my unfortunate sitters. I beg you to stay."

"But what about my man at the Orleans?"

Hallward laughed. "I don't think there will be any difficulty about that. Sit down again, Harry. And now, Dorian, get up on the platform, and don't move about too much, or pay any attention to what Lord Henry says. He has a very bad influence over all his friends, with the exception of myself."

长难句解析

Lord Henry looked at him. Yes, he was certainly wonderfully handsome, with his finely-curved scarlet lips, his frank blue eyes, his crisp gold hair.

亨利勋爵打量着他。不错，他确实长得漂亮无比，红红的、曲线柔和的嘴唇，直率的蓝眼睛，鬈曲的金发。

look at sb. 看着某人；finely-curved 为复合词

He was looking worried, and when he heard Lord Henry's last remark he glanced at him, hesitated for a moment, and then said, "Harry, I want to finish this picture today. Would you think it awfully rude of me if I asked you to go away?" Lord Henry smiled, and looked at Dorian Gray. "Am I to go, Mr. Gray?" he asked.

他看上去心事重重，听了亨利勋爵的最后一句话，他瞥了他一眼，犹豫了一下，随后说："亨利，我想今天完成这幅画，要是我请你离开的话，你会认为我没有礼貌吗？"亨利勋爵微微一笑，瞧了瞧道林·格雷："我得走吗，格雷先生？"

when引导时间状语从句 glance at sb.；瞥某人一眼 for a moment 一会儿

if 引导条件状语从句；go away 离开；looked at 注视

"If Dorian wishes it, of course you must stay. Dorian's whims are laws to everybody, except himself."

要是道林希望你留下，你当然得留下。道林的随心所欲约束着我们每个人，除了他自己。"

if 引导条件状语从句；except"除……之外"；of course 当然。

It is quite true, I never talk when I am working, and never listen either, and it must be dreadfully tedious for my unfortunate sitters.

确实如此，工作的时候我从来不说话，也不听人家说话。不幸的模特，一定觉得枯燥得可怕。

when引导时间状语从句；it must be...表肯定推测“那一定是……”。

读书笔记

019 Sons and lovers 儿子与情人

今日关键语导读 Today's Key Points

《儿子与情人》是英国作家劳伦斯的成名作。小说讲述了一个经典爱情故事。书中的第一代是沃尔特·莫雷尔和格特鲁德夫妇。沃尔特原本充满了活力，乐观、讨人喜欢。后来脾气却变坏，酗酒打人，对丈夫失望的妻子遂将希望寄托在儿子身上。但是她钟爱的长子威廉不幸早夭，随之对次子保罗产生了强烈的感情。而保罗的两个女朋友却有不同的爱情观，让他无所适从。母亲去世后，保罗决定离开家乡，到城市去。

障碍词先听为快 Words and Expressions

erect [i'rekt] vt. 使竖立；建造；安装

vigorous ['vigərəs] adj. 有力的；精力充沛的

animation [ˌæni'meiʃən] n. 活泼，生气；激励；卡通片绘制

grotesque [grəu'tesk] n. 奇异风格；怪异的东西 adj. 奇形怪状的

intellectual [ˌinti'lektjuəl] adj. 智力的；聪明的；理智的

subdued [sʌb'djud] adj. 减弱的；被制服的；被抑制的

ornament ['ɔːnəmənt] n. 装饰；装饰物；教堂用品 vt. 装饰，修饰

candour ['kændə] n. 正直，公正；直率；洁白

refugee [ˌrefju(ː)'dʒiː] n. 难民，避难者；流亡者，逃亡者

sensuous ['sensjuəs] adj. 感觉上的，依感观的；诉诸美感的

When she was twenty-three years old, she met, at a Christmas party, a young man from the Erewash Valley. Morel was then twenty-seven years old. He was well set-up, erect, and very smart. He had wavy black hair that shone again, and a vigorous black beard that had never been shaved. His cheeks were ruddy, and his red, moist mouth was noticeable because he laughed so often and so heartily. He had that rare thing, a rich, ringing laugh. Gertrude Coppard had watched him, fascinated. He was so full of colour and animation, his voice ran so easily into comic grotesque, he was so ready and so pleasant with everybody. Her own father had a rich fund of humour, but it was satiric. This man's was different: soft, non-intellectual, warm, a kind of gambolling.

She herself was opposite. She had a curious, receptive mind which found much pleasure and amusement in listening to other folk. She was clever in leading folk to talk. She loved ideas, and was considered very intellectual. What she liked most of all was an argument on religion or philosophy or politics with some educated man. This she did not often enjoy. So she always had people tell her about themselves, finding her pleasure so.

In her person she was rather small and delicate, with a large brow, and dropping bunches of brown silk curls. Her blue eyes were very straight, honest, and searching. She had the beautiful hands of the Coppards. Her dress was always subdued. She wore dark blue silk, with a peculiar silver chain of silver scallops. This, and a heavy brooch of twisted gold, was her only ornament. She was still perfectly intact, deeply religious, and full of beautiful candour.

Walter Morel seemed melted away before her. She was to the miner that thing of mystery and fascination, a lady. When she spoke to him, it was with a southern pronunciation and a purity of English which thrilled him to hear. She watched him. He danced well, as if it were natural and joyous in him to dance. His grandfather was a French refugee who had married an English barmaid—if it had been a marriage. Gertrude Coppard watched the young miner as he danced, a certain subtle exultation like glamour in his movement, and his face the flower of his body, ruddy, with tumbled black hair, and laughing alike whatever partner he bowed above. She thought him rather wonderful, never having met anyone like him. Her father was to her the type of all men. And George Coppard, proud in his bearing, handsome, and rather bitter; who preferred theology in reading, and who drew near in sympathy only to one man, the Apostle Paul; who was harsh in government, and in familiarity ironic; who ignored all sensuous pleasure: —he was very different from the miner. Gertrude herself was rather contemptuous of dancing; she had not the slightest inclination towards that accomplishment, and had never learned even a Roger de Coverley. She was puritan, like her father, high-minded, and really stern. Therefore the dusky, golden softness of this man's sensuous flame of life, that flowed off his flesh like the flame from a candle, not baffled and gripped into incandescence by thought and spirit as her life was, seemed to her something wonderful, beyond her.

长难句解析

Walter Morel seemed melted away before her. She was to the miner that thing of mystery and fascination.

沃尔特·莫雷尔似乎对她很着迷，她对于矿工来说是神秘和充满吸引力的。

melt away融化，逐渐消失；（使）着迷，神魂颠倒。

He was so full of colour and animation, his voice ran so easily into comic grotesque, he was so ready and so pleasant with everybody.

他充满着奇思妙想和活力，他的思绪很容易跑到荒谬的漫画中，他和每个人相处得都很愉快。

be full of 充满；run into 跌入。

When she spoke to him, it was with a southern pronunciation and a purity of English which thrilled him to hear.

当她跟他说话的时候，她的南方口音和一口纯正的英语让他心潮澎湃。

when引导时间状语从句；a purity of 纯正的……；which引导定语从句。

His grandfather was a French refugee who had married an English barmaid—if it had been a marriage.

他身为一个法国难民的祖父娶了一个英国的酒吧女招待员，如果这也算婚姻的话。

who引导定语从句；if引导条件状语从句。

What she liked most of all was an argument on religion or philosophy or politics with some educated man.

她最喜欢的是和一些受过教育的人讨论宗教，哲学，政治问题。

what引导主语（名词性）从句。

读书笔记

020 How the Steel Was Tempered
钢铁是怎样炼成的

今日关键语导读 Today's Key Points

《钢铁是怎样炼成的》是前苏联作家尼古拉·奥斯特洛夫斯基所著的一部长篇小说，于1933年写成。小说通过记叙保尔·柯察金的成长道路告诉人们，一个人只有在革命的艰难困苦中战胜敌人也战胜自己，只有在把自己的追求和祖国、人民的利益联系在一起的时候，才会创造出奇迹，才会成长为钢铁战士。

障碍词先听为快 Words and Expressions

provincial [prə'vinʃəl] *adj.* 省的；领地的；地方的，乡下的

depression [di'preʃən] *n.* 沮丧；下陷处；衰弱

ordeal [ɔː'diːl,ɔː'diːəl] *n.* 严峻的考验；苦难的经验；折磨

scarecrow ['skeəkrəu] *n.* 稻草人

possession [pə'zeʃən] *n.* 所有，拥有；领地；财产

respect [ris'pekt] *n.* *v.* 尊重

remove [ri'muːv] *vt.* 开除；去除；脱掉，拿下；迁移

cut off 切断，隔绝

left alone 不干涉，让……什么独自

every moment of life 寸寸光阴

This quiet provincial town whose streets he now roamed filled him with a vague feeling of depression. He was not surprised that he felt a stranger here now. Even to take a stroll through the town in daytime had become an ordeal. Passing by the gossiping housewives sitting on their stoops, he could not help overhearing their idle chatter.

"Now who could that scarecrow be?"

"Looks like he had the consumption, lung trouble, that is."

"A fine jacket he's got on. Stolen, I'll be bound."

And plenty more in the same vein. Pavel was disgusted with it all.

He had torn himself away from all this long ago. He felt a far closer kinship now with the big city to which he was bound by the strong, vitalizing bonds of comradeship and labor.

By now he had reached the pine woods, and he paused a moment at the road fork. To his right stood the old prison cut off from the woods by a high spiked fence and beyond it the white buildings of the hospital.

It was here on this broad common that the hangman's noose had choked the warm life out of Valya and her comrades. Pavel stood in silence on the spot where the gallows had been, then walked over to the bluff and down to the little cemetery where the victims of the White guard terror lay in their common graves. Loving hands had laid spruce branches on the graves and built a neat green fence around the graveyard. The pines grew straight and slender on the top of the bluff and the young grass spread a silky green carpet over the slopes.

There was a melancholy hush here on the outskirts of the town. The trees whispered gently and the fresh scent of spring rose from the regenerated earth. On this spot Pavel's comrades had gone bravely to their deaths that life might be beautiful for those born in poverty.

Slowly Pavel raised his hand and removed his cap, his heart filled with sadness.

Man's dearest possession is life. It is given to him but once, and he must live it so as to feel no torturing regrets for wasted years, never know the burning shame of a mean and petty past; so live that, dying, he might say: all my life, all my strength were given to the finest cause in all the world — the fight for the Liberation of Mankind. And one must make use of every moment of life, lest some sudden illness or tragic accident cut it short.

With these reflections, Korchagin turned away from the cemetery.

At home his mother was unhappily preparing for her son's departure. Watching her, Pavel saw that she was hiding her tears from him.

"Perhaps you'll stay, Pavel dear?" she ventured. "It's hard for me to be left alone in my old age. It doesn't matter how many children you have, they all grow up and leave you. Why must you run off to the city? You can live here just as well. Or perhaps some bob-haired magpie there has caught your fancy? You boys never tell your old mother anything. Artem went and got married without a word to me and you're worse than him in that respect. I only see you when you get yourself crippled," his mother grumbled softly as she packed his meagre belongings into a clean bag.

Pavel took her by the shoulders and drew her towards him.

"No magpies for me, Mother! Don't you know that birds choose mates of their own species? And would you say I was a magpie?"

长难句解析

This quiet provincial town whose streets he now roamed filled him with a vague feeling of depression. He was not surprised that he felt a stranger here now. Even to take a stroll through the town in daytime had become an ordeal.

在这个僻静的小城里，保尔漫步街头，心里却有一种难言的怅惘。难怪保尔觉得这个小城变得陌生和无聊了。连白天出去散散步，都会惹得人心里不痛快。

whose 引导定语从句；He was not surprised that 中that引导的是一个宾语从句。

Passing by the gossiping housewives sitting on their stoops, he could not help overhearing their idle chatter. "Now who could that scarecrow be?"

当他从那些坐在台阶上闲扯的长舌妇跟前走过的时候，常常听到她们急促地这样议论："瞧，姐妹们，哪儿来的这么个丑八怪？"

sitting，v-ing作伴随状语；could not help doing something 情不自禁做某事。

There was a melancholy hush here on the outskirts of the town. The trees whispered gently and the fresh scent of spring rose from the regenerated earth. On this spot Pavel's comrades had gone bravely to their deaths that life might be beautiful for those born in poverty.

这里是小城的边缘，寂静而冷清。松林在低语，春天的大地在复苏，散发着潮湿的泥土气息。同志们就是在这里英勇就义的。他们为那些出生即贫贱、落地便为奴的人能过上美好的生活，献出了自己的生命。

此处是一个there be 句型，that引导一个定语从句，those后面省略了关系代词who。

Man's dearest possession is life. It is given to him but once, and he must live it so as to feel no torturing regrets for wasted years, never know the burning shame of a mean and petty past; so live that, dying, he might say: all my life, all my strength were given to the finest cause in all the world— the fight for the Liberation of Mankind. And one must make use of every moment of life, lest some sudden illness or tragic accident cut it short.

人最宝贵的是生命。生命每个人只有一次。人的一生应当这样度过：回首往事，他不会因为虚度年华而悔恨，也不会因为卑鄙庸俗而羞愧；临终之际，他能够说：“我的整个生命和全部精力，都献给了世界上最壮丽的事业——为解放全人类而斗争。”要抓紧时间赶快生活，因为一场莫名其妙的疾病，或者一个意外的悲惨事件，都会使生命中断。

so as to 引导目的状语从句；regret for为……后悔；make use of充分利用。

It doesn’t matter how many children you have, they all grow up and leave you. Why must you run off to the city? You can live here just as well.

不管养多少孩子，长大就都飞了。那个城市有什么可留恋的呢？这儿一样可以过日子嘛。

It doesn’t matter. 没关系；grow up 长大；run off 逃跑；as well 在此处译成“也、还是、一样”。

“I only see you when you get yourself crippled,” his mother grumbled softly as she packed his meagre belongings into a clean bag.

“总要等你们生病了，受伤了，我才能见到你们。”妈妈一面低声诉说着，一面把儿子的几件简单衣物装到一个干净的袋子里。

when 引导时间状语从句；as引导时间状语从句，表示当……时候。

---

021 Gulliver's Travels 格列佛游记

今日关键语导读 Today's Key Points

《格列佛游记》是乔纳森·斯威夫特所著的一部杰出的游记体讽刺小说。小说描述了一个酷爱航海旅行的英国人格列佛，年青时学医，后来在海轮上担任外科医生，四处周游世界，经历了大大小小惊险而有趣的奇遇。

障碍词先听为快 Words and Expressions

obtain [əb'tein] vt. 获得

liberty ['libəti] n. 自由；许可；冒失

metropolis [mi'trɔpəlis] n. 大都市；首府；重要中心

inhabitants [ɪn'hæbɪtənt] n. 居民；居住者

proclamation [prɔklə'meiʃ(ə)n] n. 公告；宣布；宣告；公布

encompass [in'kʌmpəs] vt. 包含；包围，环绕；完成

principal ['prinsəp(ə)l,'prinsip(ə)l] adj. 主要的；资本的

circumspection [ˌsəːkəm'spekʃən] n. 慎重；细心

straggler ['strægglə] n. 流浪者；落伍的士兵；离群的动物；[植] 蔓生的枝叶

provide [prə'vaid] vt. 提供；规定；准备

The first request I made, after I had obtained my liberty, was, that I might have license to see Mildendo, the metropolis; which the emperor easily granted me, but with a special charge to do no hurt either to the inhabitants or their houses. The people had notice, by proclamation, of my design to visit the town. The wall which encompassed it is two feet and a half high, and at least eleven inches broad, so that a coach and horses may be driven very safely round it; and it is flanked with strong towers at ten feet distance. I stepped over the great western gate, and passed very gently, and sidling, through the two principal streets, only in my short waistcoat, for fear of damaging the roofs and eaves of the houses with the skirts of my coat. I walked with the utmost circumspection, to avoid treading on any stragglers who might remain in the streets, although the orders were very strict, that all people should keep in their houses, at their own peril. The garret windows and tops of houses were so crowded with spectators, that I thought in all my travels I had not seen a more populous place. The city is an exact square, each side of the wall being five hundred feet long. The two great streets, which run across and divide it into four quarters, are five feet wide. The lanes and alleys, which I could not enter, but only view them as I passed, are from twelve to eighteen inches. The town is capable of holding five hundred thousand souls: the houses are from three to five stories: the shops and markets well provided.

长难句解析

The first request I made, after I had obtained my liberty, was that I might have license to see Mildendo, the metropolis.

在我获得自由后做的第一个请求就是让我有机会去看看首都米敦都。

after 是连词，连接一个句子，表示在……之后；that 引导一个表语从句。

The wall which encompassed it is two feet and a half high, and at least eleven inches broad, so that a coach and horses may be driven very safely round it.

被两英尺半高，和至少11英寸宽的墙包围着，可以使得马车和马很安全地通过。

which引导定语从句；at least 至少；so that 表示以至于，引导结果状语从句。

I stepped over the great western gate, and passed very gently.

我走过大西门并且轻轻地穿过去了。

step over 表示跨过；gently 是副词，温和地、轻轻地，修饰pass这个动词。

The two great streets, which run across and divide it into four quarters, are five feet wide.

这两条大街各宽五英尺，十字交错将它分为四个部分。

which引导非限制性定语从句；divide into 表示将……划分成……；feet 为英尺，也是foot (脚)的复数形式。

The town is capable of holding five hundred thousand souls.

这个镇上有五十万人。

be capable of doing sth. 表示有能力做某事；five hundred thousand 表示五十万。

读书笔记

022 Harry Potter 哈利·波特

今日关键语导读 Today's Key Points

本书是英国女作家J·K·罗琳所著的系列魔幻文学作品，本系列共有七本，描写的是主人公哈利·波特在霍格沃茨魔法学校七年的学习生活与冒险故事。本书被翻译成六十二种语言，总销量为三亿本。主要讲了哈利波特在一岁时失去了父母，之后便到了姨父家，在那里哈利波特饱受痛苦度过了十年。但是十一岁生日那天一切都发生了变化：信使猫头鹰带来了一封神秘的信，邀请哈利去一个神秘的魔法学校，在那里他不仅找到了朋友，更学会了许多魔法。

障碍词先听为快 Words and Expressions

chatter ['tʃætə] n. 唠叨；饶舌；潺潺流水声 vt. 喋喋不休地说；使咔嗒咔嗒作声 vi. 唠叨；喋喋不休；（动物等）吱吱叫

corridor ['kɔridɔː] n. 走廊

in midair n. 半空中

portrait ['pɔːtrit] n. 肖像；描写；半身雕塑像 n. 人名；（法）波雷特

poltergeist ['pəultəgaist] n. 敲击作响闹恶作剧的鬼

zoom [zuːm] n. 急剧上升；嗡嗡；变焦摄影 vi. 急剧上升；摄像机移动 vt. 使摄像机移动

scramble ['skræmbl] n. 抢夺，争夺；混乱，混乱的一片；爬行 vt. 爬行，攀登；不规则的生长；仓促行动 vi. 攀登；使混杂；仓促凑成；扰乱
squashy ['skwɔʃi] adj. 熟透的；柔软的；容易压坏的；又湿又软的
spiral staircase n. 螺旋梯

好英文娓娓动听 Beautiful stories

The Gryffindor first years followed Percy through the chattering crowds, out of the Great Hall, and up the marble staircase. Harry's legs were like lead again, but only because he was so tired and full of food. He was too sleepy even to be surprised that the people in the portraits along the corridors whispered and pointed as they passed, or that twice Percy led them through doorways hidden behind sliding panels and hanging tapestries. They climbed more staircases, yawning and dragging their feet, and Harry was just wondering how much farther they had to go when they came to a sudden halt.

A bundle of walking sticks was floating in midair ahead of them, and as Percy took a step toward them they started throwing themselves at him.

"Peeves," Percy whispered to the first years. "A poltergeist." He raised his voice, "Peeves — show yourself."

A loud, rude sound, like the air being let out of a balloon, answered.

"Do you want me to go to the Bloody Baron?"

There was a pop, and a little man with wicked, dark eyes and a wide mouth appeared, floating cross-legged in the air, clutching the walking sticks.

"Oooooooh!" he said, with an evil cackle. "Ickle Firsties! What fun!"

He swooped suddenly at them. They all ducked.

"Go away, Peeves, or the Baron'll hear about this, I mean it!" barked Percy.

Peeves stuck out his tongue and vanished, dropping the walking sticks on Neville's head. They heard him zooming away, rattling coats of armor as he passed.

"You want to watch out for Peeves," said Percy, as they set off again.

"The Bloody Baron's the only one who can control him, he won't even listen to us prefects. Here we are."

At the very end of the corridor hung a portrait of a very fat woman in a pink silk dress.

"Password?" she said.

"Caput Draconis," said Percy, and the portrait swung forward to reveal a round hole in the wall. They all scrambled through it — Neville needed a leg up — and found themselves in the Gryffindor common room, a cozy, round room full of squashy armchairs.

Percy directed the girls through one door to their dormitory and the boys through another. At the top of a spiral staircase — they were obviously in one of the towers — they found their beds at last: five four-posters hung with deep red, velvet curtains. Their trunks had already been brought up. Too tired to talk much, they pulled on their pajamas and fell into bed.

"Great food, isn't it?" Ron muttered to Harry through the hangings. "Get off, Scabbers! He's chewing my sheets."

Harry was going to ask Ron if he'd had any of the treacle tart, but he fell asleep almost at once.

Perhaps Harry had eaten a bit too much, because he had a very strange dream. He was wearing Professor Quirrell's turban, which kept talking to him, telling him he must transfer to Slytherin at once, because it was his destiny. Harry told the turban he didn't want to be in Slytherin; it got heavier and heavier; he tried to pull it off but it tightened painfully — and there was Malfoy, laughing at him as he struggled with it — then Malfoy turned into the hook-nosed teacher, Snape, whose laugh became high and cold — there was a burst of green light and Harry woke, sweating and shaking.

He rolled over and fell asleep again, and when he woke next day, he didn't remember the dream at all.

长难句解析

There was a pop, and a little man with wicked, dark eyes and a wide mouth appeared, floating cross-legged in the air, clutching the walking sticks.

一个长着淘气的黑眼睛和大嘴巴的小矮人出现了。他盘着腿飘浮在空中，手中握着那捆拐杖。

clutch 表示紧紧抓住，clutching 一句做伴随状语

Peeves stuck out his tongue and vanished, dropping the walking sticks on Neville's head. They heard him zooming away, rattling coats of armor as he passed.

皮皮鬼吐出舌头做个鬼脸，把拐杖丢在纳威头上便消失了。孩子们听见他飞过的声音，连忙举起盔甲保护自己。

stick out 醒目、显眼，这里是“突出”的意思 ；vanish 表示销声匿迹，无影无踪；dropping 一句做伴随状语。

He was wearing Professor Quirrell's turban, which kept talking to him, telling him he must transfer to Slytherin at once, because it was his destiny.

他正戴着奇洛教授的无边帽，那顶帽子一直不停地跟他讲话，要他必须马上转到斯莱特林去，还说这是他的命运决定的。

which 引导定语从句，指代前面的turban；keep doing sth. 一直做某事；at once 立刻，马上。

He tried to pull it off but it tightened painfully — and there was Malfoy, laughing at him as he struggled with it — then Malfoy turned into the hook-nosed teacher, Snape, whose laugh became high and cold — there was a burst of green light and Harry woke, sweating and shaking.

他拼命想挣脱它，可它偏偏越勒越紧，令哈利痛苦不已。正当他挣扎的时候，马尔福出现了，不停地嘲笑着哈利，接着马尔福摇身一变，成了鹰钩鼻子的斯内普教授，笑声也越来越尖，越来越冷。一道绿光闪过，哈利被吓醒了，浑身是汗，全身发抖。

laughing 现在分词作伴随状语；whose 引导定语从句；a burst of 爆发，闪现；sweating and shaking 作伴随状语。

读书笔记

023 The Shell Seekers 海边拾贝人

今日关键语导读 Today's Key Points

佩妮洛普·基琳在63岁时得了轻微的心脏病，但她不愿屈服于命运的安排。病还没有完全康复，她就向医院保证责任自负，然后便回家休养。可她的子女担心母亲的身体状况，试图替她包办一切琐事。他们还想说服她，叫她把一批珍藏的古画（包括一副“寻贝壳者”）卖掉换钱……子女的自私心态让老人寒心，而佩妮洛普只想在这些古画中寻求往昔的回忆。眼前唾手可得的利益真的能换来家庭亲情吗？究竟哪样更重要？茫然之间，她到了老家的海边，只有在这儿她才能真正感到心灵的释放。

障碍词先听为快 Words and Expressions

polish ['pəuliʃ] v. 擦光；磨光；修改；润色

parlourmaid ['pɑːləmeɪd] n. （侍候用餐，负责应门等的）客厅女侍

meager ['miːgə(r)] adj. 瘦的；粗劣的；不足的；贫乏的

seamanlike ['siːmənlaik] adj. 熟练水手似的；海员般的

parade [pə'reid] n. 检阅；游行；一系列；炫耀

square [skwεə] n. 正方形；广场；平方；方格

council ['kaunsil] n. 委员会；（郡、镇等）政务会

squad [skwɔd] n. 班；小队

ceremony ['seriməni] n. 典礼；礼节；客套

requisition [ˌrekwiˈziʃən] vt. 征用；申请领取

snowdrop [ˈsnəudrɔp] n. 雪花莲

好英文娓娓动听 Beautiful stories

"I don't want it cut off."

"Well... make some sort of effort. Try to get the hang of a neat little bun."

"Oh. Yes. All right."

"Off you go then."

She went. "Goodbye." The door half closed behind her and then opened again. "Ma'am."

She was drafted to the Royal Naval Gunnery School, HMS Excellent, at Whale Island. She was a Steward, but, perhaps because she "spoke proper", was made an Officer's Steward, which meant that she worked in the Wardroom: laying up tables, serving drinks, telling people they were wanted on the telephone, polishing silver and waiting at meals. As well, before darkness fell, she had to go around all the cabins and do the black-out, knocking on doors, and, if there was someone inside, saying "Permission to darken ship, sir." She was, in fact, a glorified parlourmaid, and was paid a parlourmaid's wages, thirty shillings a fortnight. Every two weeks, she had to attend pay parade, lining up until it was time to salute the sour-faced Pay Commander —who looked as though he hated women and probably did—say her name, and be handed the meagre buff envelope.

Asking permission to darken ship was just part of a whole

new language she had had to learn, and she had spent a week at a training depot doing this. A bedroom was a cabin; the floor, the deck; when she went to work, she was going on board; a Make and Mend was a half day; and if you had a row with your friend it was called Parting Brass Rags, but as she didn't have a friend to have a row with, the occasion to use this seamanlike expression never arose.

Whale Island really was an island, and you had to cross a bridge to get there, which was quite exciting and made it seem like going on board a ship even if you weren't. A very long time ago it had started life as a mudbank in the middle of Portsmouth Harbour, but by now was a large and important Naval Training Establishment, with a parade ground and a drill-shed and a church, and jetties, and huge batteries where the men did their training. Administrative offices and accommodation were housed in a lot of neat red brick blocks and buildings. The lower deck quarters were square and plain, like council houses, but the Wardroom was quite grand, a country manor with the football field as its estate.

The noise was incessant. Bugles blew and pipes sounded and daily orders came crackling out over the Tannoy system. Men in training went everywhere at the double, their boots going thump-thump-thump on the tarmac. On the Parade Ground, Chief Petty Officers screamed themselves into apoplexy at squads of terrified young seamen doing their best to master the complexities of Close Order Drill. Each morning, the ceremony of Captain's Divisions and Colours took place, with the Royal Marine Band blasting out "Braganza" and "Hearts of Oak". If you were caught out of doors while the White Ensign climbed the flagpole, you had to face the quarterdeck and stand to attention, saluting, until it was all over.

The Wrens Quarters, where Penelope was sent to live, were in a requisitioned hotel at the north end of the town. Here, she shared a cabin with five other girls, all sleeping in double-decker bunks. One of the girls had dreadful BO, but as she never washed, this was hardly surprising. The Quarters were two miles from Whale Island, and as no naval transport was provided and there were no buses, Penelope put through a telephone call to Sophie to ask Sophie to send her old school bicycle. Sophie promised to do this. She would put it on a train, and Penelope would duly collect it from Portsmouth Station.

"And how are you, my darling?"

"All right." It was horrible to hear Sophie's voice and not be with her. "How are you? How's Papa?"

"Miss Pawson has taught him to use a stirrup-pump."

"And Doris, and the boys?"

"Ronald has got into the football team. And we think that Clark has measles. And I have snowdrops in the garden."

"Already?" She wanted to see them. She wanted to be there. It was horrible to think of them all at Carn Cottage and not to be with them. To think of her own darling private bedroom, with the curtains stirring in the sea breeze and the beams of the lighthouse crossing the walls.

长难句解析

Every two weeks, she had to attend pay parade, lining up until it was time to salute the sour-faced Pay Commander.

每两周，她就要去参加游行，跟着队伍去向愁眉苦脸的指挥官致敬。

lining up表示“排队”，v-ing表伴随；It was ...commander一句中it是形式主语，指代to...commander的内容。

She was a Steward, but, perhaps because she “spoke proper”, was made an Officer’s Steward, which meant that she worked in the Wardroom: laying up tables, serving drinks, telling people they were wanted on the telephone, polishing silver and waiting at meals.

她曾是一个管家，但是怎么说呢，也许是因为她“说话得体”——这是某个军官的管家的评价，这就意味着她在为军官工作：将桌子摆放整齐，准备好饮料，在电话里告诉别人他们需要的东西，把银制器皿擦亮以及准备饭菜。

which引导非限制性定语从句，代指前面整句的内容，that 引导宾语从句。后面的v-ing并列结构表伴随。

A bedroom was a cabin; the floor, the deck; when she went to work, she was going on board; a Make and Mend was a half day.

卧室就是一个小船舱：有地板、桌子；当她要工作时，她就去甲板上，制造和修理就要耗去半天。

when 引导时间状语，board 含义较广，作名词有“甲板、董事会、膳食”等含意，动词有“上（船、车或飞机）、搭伙、寄宿”等含义。

One of the girls had dreadful BO, but as she never washed, this was hardly surprising.

其中一个女孩有严重的狐臭，但由于她从来都不洗澡，这倒也是不足为奇。

BO= Body Odor（狐臭）；as在这里引导原因状语从句。hardly为频率副词，“几乎不”。

"Already?" She wanted to see them. She wanted to be there. It was horrible to think of them all at Carn Cottage and not to be with them. To think of her own darling private bedroom, with the curtains stirring in the sea breeze and the beams of the lighthouse crossing the walls.

“已经准备好了？”她想要见见他们，想要跟他们呆在一起。想到他们都在康恩小屋而自己没有跟他们一起，这种感觉很糟糕。那里有属于她自己温馨的卧室，里面有被海风吹起的窗帘，以及穿过墙壁来自灯塔的光。

It was中的it 是一个形式主语，真正的主语是“to think of them all at Carn Cottage and not to be with them”，后面with介词短语表状态。

024 Heidi 海蒂

今日关键语导读 Today's Key Points

《海蒂》是瑞士作家约翰娜·斯比丽著名的作品之一。该书讲述了天真善良、聪明可爱的8岁小姑娘海蒂被姨妈送到山上，跟性情古怪的爷爷住在一起。但很快，她爱上了山上的一切，爷爷也渐渐喜欢上了这个活泼可爱的小女孩。可没过多久姨妈又把她送到城里的一户人家去陪伴有残疾的克莱拉小姐一起学习。那里虽然衣食无忧，但女管家对她非常严厉，女仆也瞧不起她，最主要的是没有大山和自由，海蒂由此患上了思乡病。 最后，海蒂终于又回到山上，在她的感染与鼓励下，她双腿残疾的好朋友克莱拉也重新从轮椅上站了起来。

障碍词先听为快 Words and Expressions

steeply [stiːplɪ] adv. 陡峭地；险峻地

wayfarer ['weɪfeərə(r)] n. 旅人，徒步旅行者

grazing ['greiziŋ] v. 擦过；抓伤（graze的现在分词）

shawl [ʃɔːl] n. 围巾，长方形披巾

hut [hʌt] n. 小屋；临时营房

prominent ['prɔminənt] adj. 突出的，显著的；杰出的；卓越的

spacious ['speiʃəs] adj. 宽敞的，广阔的；无边无际的

hay [hei] n. 干草

loiter ['lɔitə] vt. 虚度；闲荡；混

The little old town of Mayenfeld is charmingly situated. From it a footpath leads through green, well-wooded stretches to the foot of the heights which look down imposingly upon the valley. Where the footpath begins to go steeply and abruptly up the Alps, the heath,with its short grass and pungent herbage, at once sends out its soft perfume to meet the wayfarer.

One bright sunny morning in June, a tall, vigorous maiden of the mountain region climbed up the narrow path, leading a little girl by the hand. The youngster's cheeks were in such a glow that it showed even through her sun-browned skin. Small wonder though! For in spite of the heat, the little one, who was scarcely five years old, was bundled up as if she had to brave a bitter frost. Her shape was difficult to distinguish, for she wore two dresses, if not three, and around her shoulders a large red cotton shawl. With her feet encased in heavy hob-nailed boots, this hot and shapeless little person toiled up the mountain.

The pair had been climbing for about an hour when they reached hamlet half-way up the great mountain named the Alm. This hamlet was called "Im Dirfli"or "The Little Village". It was the elder girl's home town, and therefore she was greeted from nearly every house; people called to her from windows and doors, and very often from the road. But, answering questions and calls as she went by, the girl did not loiter on her way and only stood still when she reached the end of the hamlet. There a few cottages lay scattered about, from the furthest of which a voice called out to her through an open door: "Deta, please wait one moment! I am coming with you, if you are going further up."

When the girl stood still to with, the child instantly let go her hand and promptly sat down on the ground.

"Are you tired, Heidi?" Deta asked the child.

"No, but hot," she replied.

"We shall be up in an hour, if you take big steps and climb with all your little might!"Thus the elder girl tried to encourage her small companion.

A stout, pleasant-looking woman stepped out of the house and joined the two. The child had risen and wandered behind the old acquaintances, who immediately started gossiping about their friends in the neighborhood and the people of the hamlet generally.

"Where are you taking the child, Deta?"asked the newcomer. "Is she the child your sister left?"

"Yes."Deta assured her;" I am taking her up to the Alm-Uncle and there I want her to remain."

"You can't really mean to take her there Deta. You must have lost your senses, to go to him. I am sure the old man will show you the door and won't even listen to what you say."

"Why not? As he's her grandfather, it is high time he should do something for the child. I have taken care of her until this summer and now a good place has been offered to me. The child shall not hinder me from accepting it, I tell you that!"

长难句解析

One bright sunny morning in June, a tall , vigorous maiden of the mountain region climbed up the narrow path , leading a little girl by the hand .

六月的一个清晨，阳光灿烂，一个身材高大、结实的女人领着一个小女孩，正在这条路上走着。

lead+ing. 做主语，非谓语动词用法，表伴随。

With her feet encased in heavy hob-nailed boots.

她的脚上穿着笨重的靴子。

with作伴随状语，修饰her feet。

"Yes." Deta assured her; I am taking her up to the Alm-Uncle and there I want her to remain."

"对"蒂缇回答说，"所以我要送她到阿鲁姆大叔那儿"。

take sb. up 把某人送走，将某人带走。

---

025 The Big Friendly Giant 好心眼儿巨人

今日关键语导读 Today's Key Points

《好心眼儿巨人》的作者是英国著名儿童文学作家达尔，书讲的是一个女孩和一个巨人的故事。在达尔笔下，好心眼儿巨人具有人类最美好的特质：善良、好学、爱心、平和等等。这本著作曾获英国儿童图书奖、德国青少年文学奖等诸多大奖。有评价称，凡是读过达尔所著书籍的孩子全都情不自禁迷倒在他创造的奇幻的魔力世界中，无人能够幸免。

障碍词先听为快 Words and Expressions

shadowy ['ʃædəui] adj. 朦胧的；有阴影的；虚无的；暗黑的

spurt [spəːt] n. 冲刺；喷涌 v. 喷射；喷出

tremble ['trembl] vi. 发抖；战栗；焦虑；摇晃

obviously ['ɔbviəsli] adv. 明显地

definitely ['definitli] adv. 清楚地，当然；明确地，肯定地

unscrew ['ʌn'skruː] vt. 旋开；旋松；从……旋出螺丝

straighten ['streitn] vt. 整顿；使……改正；使……挺直；使……好转

carefully ['keəfuli] adv. 小心地

pavement ['peivmənt] n. 人行道

misty ['misti] adj. 模糊的；有雾的

The tall black figure was coming her way. It was keeping very close to the houses across the street, hiding in the shadowy places where there was no moonlight. On and on it came, nearer and nearer. But it was moving in spurts. It would stop, then it would move on, then it would stop again. But what on earth was it doing? Ah-ha! Sophie could see now what it was up to. It was stopping in front of each house. It would stop and peer into the upstairs window of each house in the street. It actually had to bend down to peer into the upstairs windows. That's how tall it was. It would stop and peer in. Then it would slide on to the next house and stop again, and peer in, and so on all along the street. It was much closer now and Sophie could see it more clearly. Looking at it carefully, she decided it had to be some kind of person. Obviously it was not a human. But it was definitely a person. A giant person, perhaps. Sophie stared hard across the misty moonlit street. The Giant (if that was what he was) was wearing a long black cloak. In one hand he was holding what looked like a VERY LONG; THIN TRUMPET. In the other hand, he held a large suitcase. The Giant had stopped now right in front of Mr and Mrs Goochey's house. The Goocheys had a greengrocers shop in the middle of the High Street, and the family lived above the shop. The two Goochey children slept in the upstairs front room, Sophie knew that. The Giant was peering through the window into the room where Michael and Jane Goochey were sleeping. From across the street, Sophie watched and held her breath. She saw the Giant step back a pace and put the suitcase down on the pavement. He bent over and opened the suitcase. He took something out of it. It looked like a glass jar, one of those square ones with a screw top. He unscrewed the top of the jar and poured what was in it into the end of the long thing. Sophie watched, trembling. She saw the Giant straighten up again and she saw him poke the trumpet in through the open upstairs window of the room where the Goochey children were sleeping. She saw the Giant take a deep breath and whoof, he blew through the trumpet. No noise came out, but it was obvious to Sophie that whatever had been in the jar had now been blown through the trumpet into the Goochey children's bedroom.

长难句解析

It was keeping very close to the houses across the street, hiding in the shadowy places where there was no moonlight.

房间离街对面的房子很近，藏在没有月光的阴影处。

where引导定语从句。

Looking at it carefully, she decided it had to be some kind of person.

仔细看了看后，她确定它应该是人类。

v-ing做伴随状语；some kind of 某种。

He unscrewed the top of the jar and poured what was in it into the end of the long trumpet thing.

他拧开瓶盖，将里面的东西倒进了那个长长的像喇叭一样的物体里。

the top of ……的顶部；what引导宾语从句；the end of...的末端。

No noise came out, but it was obvious to Sophie that whatever had been in the jar had now been blown through the trumpet into the Goochey children's bedroom.

没有任何声音，但苏菲清楚地知道不管盖子里面有什么，现在都通过喇叭吹向古雪家孩子们的房间。

that 引导宾语从句；blow sth into sth. 将……吹进……里面；whatever引导的主语从句。

读书笔记

026 Heart of Darkness 黑暗的心

今日关键语导读 Today's Key Points

《黑暗的心》是美国作家约瑟夫·康拉德的一部现代主义小说，它记录了船长马洛在一艘停靠于伦敦外的海船上所讲的刚果河的故事。马洛的故事除了涉及马洛自己年轻时的非洲经历之外，还讲述了他在非洲期间所认识的一个叫库尔兹的白人殖民者——一个矢志将“文明进步”带到非洲的理想主义者，后来堕落成贪婪的殖民者的经过。

障碍词先听为快 Words and Expressions

cruising ['kruːziŋ] adj. 巡航的

flutter ['flʌtə] n. 摆动；鼓翼；烦扰

interminable [in'təːminəbl] adj. 冗长的；无止尽的

luminous ['ljuːminəs] adj. 发光的；明亮的；清楚的

vanishing ['væniʃiŋ] adj. 消失的

conviction [kən'vikʃən] n. 证明有罪的；定罪；说服；深信

dominoe ['dɒmɪnəʊ] n. 多米诺骨牌；牙齿；骰子

ascetic [ə'setik] adj. 苦行的；禁欲主义的

unstained ['ʌn'steind] adj. 没有沾污的；清白的

diaphanous [dai'æfənəs] adj. 透明的；精致的；模糊的

The Nelie, a cruising yawl, swung to her anchor without a flutter of the sails, and was at rest. The flood had made, the wind was nearly calm, and being bound down the river, the only thing for it was to come to and wait for the turn of the tide.

The sea-reach of the Thames stretched before us like the beginning of an interminable waterway. In the offing the sea and the sky were welded together without a joint, and in the luminous space the tanned sails of the barges drifting up with the tide seemed to stand still in red clusters of canvas sharply peaked, with gleams of varnished sprits. A haze rested on the low shores that ran out to sea in vanishing flatness. The air was dark above Gravesend, and farther back still seems condensed into a mournful gloom, brooding motionless over the biggest, and the greatest, town on earth.

The Director of Companies was our captain and our host. We four affectionately watched his back as he stood in the bows looking to seaward. On the whole river there was nothing that looked half so nautical. He resembled a pilot, which to a seaman is trustworthiness personified. It was difficult to realize his work was not out there in the luminous estuary, but behind him, within the brooding gloom.

Between us there was, as I have already said somewhere, the bond of the sea. Besides holding our hearts together through long periods of separation, it had the effect of making us tolerant of each other's yarns—and even convictions. The Lawyer—the best of old fellows—had, because of his many years and many virtues, the only cushion on deck, and was lying on the only rug. The Accountant had brought out already a box of dominoes, and was toying architecturally with the bones. Marlow sat cross-legged right aft, leaning against the mizzen-mast. He had sunken cheeks, a yellow complexion, a straight back , an ascetic aspect, and, with his arms dropped, the palms of hands outwards, resembled an idol. The Director, satisfied the anchor had good hold, made his way aft and sat down amongest us. We exchanged a few words lazily. Afterwards there was slience on board the yacht. For some reason or other we did not begin that game of dominoes. We felt meditative, and fit for nothing but placid staring. The day was ending in a serenity of still and exquisite brilliance. The water shone pacifically; the sky, without a speck, was a benign immensity of unstained light; the very mist on the Essex marshes was like a gauzy and radiant fabric, hung from the wooded rises inland, and draping the low shores in diaphanous fold. Only the gloom to the west, brooding over the upper reaches, became more somber every minute, as if angered by the approach of the sun.

长难句解析

The Nelie, a cruising yawl, swung to her anchor without a flutter of the sails, and was at rest. The flood had made, the wind was nearly calm, and being bound down the river, the only thing for it was to come to and wait for the turn of the tide.

“奈丽”号小艇摇晃几下后抛锚停船，船上的风帆纹丝不动。潮水已经涨高，大风也已平息。船正沿江而下，现在只好停泊等待退潮。

句中anchor 一词不仅有“锚”的意思还经常用作“新闻节目主播”“靠山”。

He resembled a pilot, which to a seaman is trustworthiness personified. It was difficult to realize his work was not out there in the luminous estuary, but behind him, within the brooding gloom.

他酷似一位领航员，而在海员眼里，领航员就是诚实的化身。很难意识到他的工作并不是在那发光的河口，而是在他身后，伴随着阴霾。

which引导非限制性定语从句；固定句式：It is+adj+to do sth. 做某事怎么样。

Marlow sat cross-legged right aft, leaning against the mizzen-mast. He had sunken cheeks, a yellow complexion, a straight back, an ascetic aspect, and, with his arms dropped, the palms of hands outwards, resembled an idol.

马洛盘腿坐在船尾，背倚着桅杆。他两腮下陷，面色发黄，腰板挺得笔直，显出一副苦行僧的样子。两条胳膊垂着，手掌心朝外，就像一座神像。

lean against 靠在……上；Leaning一句中v –ing 形式表伴随状态。

027 Black Beauty 黑美人

今日关键语导读 Today's Key Points

《黑美人》是英国作家安娜休厄之作，书中描写了十九世纪英格兰地区一名叫“黑骏马”的马及其朋友悲欢离合的故事。“黑骏马”天资聪颖，多次救主人于危难之中，但是后来仍然遭受厄运。“黑骏马”受过良好的训练，它知道它永不能踢、咬或是逃跑，永远都得服从命令，不管多累多饿。它总是举止得体，但是当它从一个主人被卖到另一个主人，它懂得了一匹马的一生是多么困难，某一些人又是多么愚蠢和冷酷。成年后，几经易主，历经磨难，最终在与死神擦肩而过后重获新生。书中揭示人性的善恶美丑，表达了希望人们善待动物的美好愿望。

障碍词先听为快 Words and Expressions

courage ['kʌridʒ] n. 勇气；胆量

often ['ɔ(ː)fn,'ɔːftən] adv. 经常，常常；往往，在许多场合

sociable ['səuʃəbl] adj. 社交的；好交际的；友善的

luggage ['lʌgidʒ] n. 行李；皮箱

gentle ['dʒentl] adj. 温和的；文雅的

shelter ['ʃeltə] vi. 躲避，避难

footpath ['futpaːθ] n. 人行道；小路；小径

gallop ['gæləp] vt. 使飞跑；迅速运输

enemies ['enəmɪz] n. 敌人；对某种主张、事业等怀有敌意的人

（enemy的复数形式）

forelock ['fɔːlɔk] n. 额发，额毛；栓

好英文娓娓动听 Beautiful stories

We had both the same sort of courage at our work, and John had oftener to hold us in than to urge us forward; he never had to use the whip with either of us; then our paces were much the same, and I found it very easy to keep step with her when trotting, which made it pleasant, and master always liked it when we kept step well, and so did John. After we had been out two or three times together we grew quite friendly and sociable, which made me feel very much at home.

Our master had two other horses that stood in another stable. One was Justice, a roan cob, used for riding or for the luggage cart; the other was an old brown hunter, named Sir Oliver; he was past work now, but was a great favorite with the master, who gave him the run of the park; he sometimes did a little light carting on the estate, or carried one of the young ladies when they rode out with their father, for he was very gentle and could be trusted with a child as well as Merrylegs.

For three years and a half of my life I had had all the liberty I could wish for; but now, week after week, month after month, and no doubt year after year, I must stand up in a stable night and day except when I am wanted, and then I must be just as steady and quiet as any old horse who has worked twenty years. Straps here and straps there, a bit in my mouth, and blinkers over my eyes.

Now, I am not complaining, for I know it must be so. I only mean to say that for a young horse full of strength and spirits, who has been used to some large field or plain where he can fling up his head and toss up his tail and gallop away at full speed, then round and back again with a snort to his companions

There was no kind master like yours to look after me, and talk to me, and bring me nice things to eat. The man that had the care of us never gave me a kind word in my life. I do not mean that he ill-used me, but he did not care for us one bit further than to see that we had plenty to eat, and shelter in the winter. A footpath ran through our field, and very often the great boys passing through would fling stones to make us gallop. I was never hit, but one fine young colt was badly cut in the face, and I should think it would be a scar for life. We did not care for them, but of course it made us more wild, and we settled it in our minds that boys were our enemies. We had very good fun in the free meadows, galloping up and down and chasing each other round and round the field; then standing still under the shade of the trees. But when it came to breaking in, that was a bad time for me; several men came to catch me, and when at last they closed me in at one corner of the field, one caught me by the forelock, another caught me by the nose and held it so tight I could hardly draw my breath; then another took my under jaw in his hard hand and wrenched my mouth open, and so by force they got on the halter and the bar into my mouth; then one dragged me along by the halter, another flogging behind, and this was the first experience I had of men's kindness; it was all force. They did not give me a chance to know what they wanted.

长难句解析

Then our paces were much the same, and I found it very easy to keep step with her when trotting, which made it pleasant, and master always liked it when we kept step well, and so did John.

之后我们的速度几乎一样，我发现小跑的时候跟上她的脚步很简单，这让小跑变得很愉快，当我们步伐一致的时候，主人总是很喜欢，约翰也一样。

find it +adj.+to do sth.意为“发现做某事很……”；“it”为形式主语；so +助动词/be动词，意为“……也一样”；when引导时间状语从句，which引导定语从句；so did John 表示约翰也一样，注意与so John did 这一强调句区分。

He was past work now, but was a great favorite with the master, who gave him the run of the park.

他现在已经老得无法工作了，但主人依然还是很喜欢他，允许他到处跑。

who引导定语从句。

Now, I am not complaining, for I know it must be so. I only mean to say that for a young horse full of strength and spirits, who has been used to some large field or plain where he can fling up his head and toss up his tail and gallop away at full speed.

现在，我不再抱怨，因为我知道这是注定了的。我的意思是，对于一个充满了力量和精神的，以前常常在广阔田地上摇头摆尾、全力飞奔的年轻的马来说。

for意为“因为”；mean to do意为“计划做某事”；has been done为现在完成时；where引导地点状语从句。fling up放弃，使（某物）出现，使注意（某事），向上抛（某物）；toss up向上掷，向上扬；at full speed 飞速。

We had very good fun in the free meadows, galloping up and down and chasing each other round and round the field; then standing still under the shade of the trees.

我们在宽广的草地上非常开心，跳上跳下，互相围着草地追赶，然后站在树荫下。

have fun意为“玩得开心”，galloping和chasing为现在分词作状语，表伴随。

But when it came to breaking in, that was a bad time for me; several men came to catch me, and when at last they closed me in at one corner of the field.

但说到训练，对我来说，那是一段糟糕的时光，有几个人过来抓住我，最后他们把我关在牧场的某一个角落。

when it comes to...意为“当谈到……”；break in有“打断；闯入；训练；使逐渐习惯”等意思。

---

028 Scarlet and Black 红与黑

今日关键语导读 Today's Key Points

《红与黑》是法国小说家弗雷德里克·司汤达长篇小说的代表作，小说通过对主人公于连的个人奋斗及两次爱情经历的描写，揭示了复辟王朝时期的波澜的阶级大博斗，反映了政治黑暗、教会腐败，贵族反动和资产阶级利欲熏心的生活画面。

障碍词先听为快 Words and Expressions

appease [ə'piːz] vt. 使平息；使满足；使和缓；对……让步

wretched ['retʃid] adj. 可怜的；卑鄙的

hypocrisy [hi'pɔkrəsi] n. 虚伪；伪善

sublimity [sə'blimiti] n. 崇高；庄严；气质高尚

humble ['hʌmbl] adj. 谦逊的；简陋的

fainting ['feintiŋ] n. 昏晕；不省人事

convulsive [kən'vʌlsiv] adj. 抽搐的；惊厥的

multitude ['mʌltitjuːd] n. 群众；多数

bundle ['bʌndl] n. 束；捆

misery ['mizəri] n. 痛苦，悲惨；不幸

dreadful ['dredful] adj. 可怕的；糟透的

"I beg you," said Julien, whenever they were alone, "say nothing to anyone. Let me be the sole confidant of your pain. If you still love me, don't speak: all your words can't take away our Stanislas's fever."

But this was cold comfort and had no effect. He had no idea if Madame de Rênal had gotten it into her head that, to appease the anger of a jealous God, she either had to hate Julien or see her child die. Her inability to hate her lover, which she knew she could not do, was what made her so wretched.

"Go away from me," she said to Julien one day. "In the name of God, leave this house. It's your presence here that is killing my son.

"God is punishing me," she added in a low voice. "He is just. I worship His justice. My sins are frightful, and I have been living without remorse! All this was the first sign of God turning away from me: I need to be doubly punished."

Julien was deeply moved. There was no hypocrisy in her, no exaggeration. "She believes that, in loving me, she is killing her child, and yet the miserable woman loves me more than she does the child. No question, I cannot doubt it: remorse is killing her, and thus the sublimity of her emotions. But how could I have inspired such a love—me, so poor, so badly raised, so ignorant, sometimes so clumsy and so inept?"

One night, the child grew still sicker. At about two in the morning, Monsieur de Rênal came to see him. Consumed by fever, the child was severely flushed and did not recognize his father. Suddenly Madame de Rênal threw herself at her husband's feet: Julien saw that she meant to tell him everything and ruin herself forever.

Luckily, her strange behavior annoyed Monsieur de Rênal.

"Good-bye! Good-bye!" he said, starting to walk away.

"No, listen to me," his wife cried, on her knees in front of him, trying to hold him back. "Hear the whole truth. I'm the one who's killing my son. I gave him life and I'm taking it away from him. Heaven is punishing me, in the eyes of God I am guilty of murder. I must abandon myself, I must humble myself. Perhaps this sacrifice will appease the Lord."

If Monsieur de Rênal had been a man of any imagination, he would have known everything.

"Romantic notions," he exclaimed, pulling away from his wife, who was trying to wrap her arms around his knees. "All that is just romantic gush. Julien, the moment it's light outside, call the doctor."

And he retired to his bed. Madame de Rênal dropped back on her knees, half fainting, and pushed Julien away with a convulsive movement, when he tried to help her. Julien stood there, stunned.

So here's the adulteress!" he said to himself. "Could it be possible that these tricky priests...might be right? Those who commit a multitude of them, may earn the true comprehension of sin? How incredible!..."

For twenty minutes after Monsieur de Rênal left, Julien watched the woman he loved, her head resting on the child's little bed; she was completely motionless and virtually unconscious.

"Here's a woman of superior intellect reduced to a bundle of misery, and all because," he told himself, "she's come to know me."

Time sped by. "What can I do for her?" He had to make up his mind. "It's not a question, anymore, just about me. What do people and their dull affectations mean to me? What can I do for her?... leave her? But I'd be leaving her alone, and in the grip of the most dreadful grief.

长难句解析

But this was cold comfort and had no effect. He had no idea if Madame de Rênal had gotten it into her head that, to appease the anger of a jealous God, she either had to hate Julien or see her child die. Her inability to hate her lover, which she knew she could not do, was what made her so wretched.

但是这心寒的安慰并没有奏效。他不知她是否已经知道瑞娜夫人了，但是为了平息那嫉妒的主麾下的天使，她不得不去恨于连，或者看到她的孩子去死。她没有办法去恨她所爱，当然她自己也知道，这件事情本身使得她这么的糟糕。

have no effect"没有效果，不起作用"；if引导条件状语从句；that引导宾语从句；either...or，表示"要么……要么"；which引导定语从句，指代前面整个句子，后面的what引导一个表语从句。

"Go away from me," she said to Julien one day. "In the name of God, leave this house. It's your presence here that is killing my son.

“离我远点”，她那天对着于连说道：“以上帝的名义，离开这座房子，你出现在这里完全是在折磨我儿子。”

It's...that...是一个强调句型，强调的是your presence（你的出现）；go away from sb，远离某人；in the name of 以……之名；kill的现在进行时引申为折磨。

"Romantic notions," he exclaimed, pulling away from his wife, who was trying to wrap her arms around his knees. "All that is just romantic gush. Julien, the moment it's light outside, call the doctor."

“浪漫的想法，”他大喊到，同时也逃离了他的妻子，那个曾经试图用她的手臂温暖他的膝盖的人：“所有的这些仅仅只是浪漫的涌动。于连，这个时候已经天亮了，去叫医生。”

who引导定语从句；pull away from表示“逃离、脱离”；try to do sth.“尽力做某事”，the moment，表示“……的时刻”。

Consumed by fever, the child was severely flushed and did not recognize his father. Suddenly Madame de Rênal threw herself at her husband's feet: Julien saw that she meant to tell him everything and ruin herself forever.

正在被发烧所煎熬的孩子，脸颊极端发红，同时也没有认出他的爸爸。突然，瑞纳女士跪在她丈夫的脚下：于连终于理解了她正在试图告诉他的所有事情，并且也知道她已经不可挽回地毁了自己。

consumed by fever的主语和主句的主语child一致，故省去，that引导宾语从句。

For twenty minutes after Monsieur de Rênal left, Julien watched the woman he loved, her head resting on the child's little bed; she was completely motionless and virtually unconscious.

瑞纳先生离开20分钟之后，于连看着那个他曾经爱过的女人，她的头靠在孩子睡的小床上；她一动不动，几乎感觉不到任何事情。

he loved作后置定语，修饰woman。

读书笔记

029 The Scarlet Letter 红字

今日关键语导读 Today's Key Points

红字是美国作家霍桑的长篇小说。《红字》讲述了发生在北美殖民时期的恋爱悲剧。女主人公海丝特嫁给了医生奇灵渥斯，他们之间却没有爱情。在孤独中海丝特与牧师丁梅斯代尔相恋并生下女儿珠儿。海丝特被当众惩罚，戴上标志“通奸”的红字示众。然而海丝特坚贞不屈，拒不说出孩子的父亲，最终海丝特因为不断热心接济和帮助别人，赢得了人们的尊敬，使胸前那本来代表耻辱的红字变成了美好善良德行的象征。

障碍词先听为快 Words and Expressions

worship ['wəːʃip] v. 崇拜；尊敬；爱慕

property ['prɔpəti] n. 性质，性能；财产；所有权

mysterious [mis'tiəriəs] adj. 神秘的；不可思议的；难解的

scarlet ['skaːlit] adj. 深红的；鲜红色的；罪孽深重的；淫荡的

remainder [ri'meində] n. 余数，残余，剩余物；其余的人

fanciful ['fænsiful] adj. 想象的；稀奇的

sin [sin] n. 罪孽；罪恶；过失

passionate ['pæʃənit] adj. 热情的；热烈的，激昂的；易怒的

assure [ə'ʃuə] v. 保证；担保；使确信；弄清楚

eternal [i(ː)'təːnl] adj. 永恒的；不朽的

After Mr.Dimmesdale's death, no one changed more in appearance than the old man known as Roger Chillingworth. All his strength and energy had been used to harm his patient. Soon enough, the man disappeared from the town, and was never heard from again. This unhappy man had made his aim in life to add to the suffering of the young minister. When the evil old ma no longer had such a purpose, the devil took him back to hell. It is a curious subject of observation, however, whether hatred and love are not of the same place. Each takes a great deal of emotion from a person. The two feelings seem basically the same, except that one is smiled upon by God, while the other is worshipped by the devil.

When the old man, Roger Chillingworth died, which took place within the year, he left all his property and fortune to little Pearl, the daughter of Hester Prynne.

So Pearl, the strange little child, became the richest young lady in America. After that time, the town came to greatly respect the mysterious little girl and her mother. Perhaps if little Pearl would have remained In New England, she would have married a son of a great Puritan family, but her mother took her back to England, and the townspeople no longer saw the bright scarlet letter and the strange little child always nearby. For many years, the story of the scarlet letter was told to the young children of the town, and the story became famous. One afternoon, many years later, some children were playing near the old cottage where Hester and her little Pearl lived long before. The children saw that a woman in an old gray dress was coming to the cottage. Near the doorway to the cottage, she turned around to see the children, and for one moment, the children saw the bright red and gold of the scarlet letter on her chest.

And Hester Prynne had returned to her shame! But where was little Pearl? If still alive, she must now be a beautiful young woman. Through the remainder of Hester's life, she would often receive small packages or would be seen doing fanciful needlework for a small child. Many had heard that Pearl was alive and happily married.

But there was a more real life for Hester Prynne here in New England than in that unknown place where Pearl had found a home. Here had been her sin; here,her sadness; and here was yet her punishment. She had returned, therefore, and continued her life of shame, although no town ruler would have forced the holy woman to continue with her public punishment. Never afterwards did that scarlet letter leave her chest. The towns people no longer views the letter as a punishment, however, but rather as representing Hester's great strength and bravery. Women would often go to her for help in questions of love and passion. The women respected her to advise them, as they understood that she, too, had had such passionate feeling before. Hester comforted and advised them, as best she could. She assured them, too, that one day, they would find happiness with one man, as she had.

And, after many, many years, a new tomb was set right next to her minster's. One the tombstone for the two eternal lover's, was written:

"On a field, a deep-colored letter A shines brightly."

长难句解析

After Mr. Dimmesdale's death, no one changed more in appearance than the old man known as Roger Chillingworth. All his strength and energy had been used to harm his patient.

丁梅斯代尔先生死后，变化最大的是老人罗杰·齐灵渥斯。他所有的力量和精力都用来迫害他的病人了。

more ...than... 比……更多；in appearance 在外表上，appearance一词除了有“外表”的意思外，还可以指（在公共活动或广播中的）露面或（尤指出人意料地）出现。

When the old man, Roger Chilling worth died, which took place within the year, he left all his property and fortune to little Pearl, the daughter of Hester Prynne.

不到一年，老人罗杰·齐灵渥斯就去世了，他把自己所有的财产都留给了海斯特·白兰的女儿，小珠儿。

句中when引导时间状语从句，which引导非限制性定语从句，指代整件事。take place 发生。

Here had been her sin; here,her sadness; and here was yet her punishment. She had returned, therefore, and continued her life of shame, although no town ruler would have forced the holy woman to continue with her public punishment.

这里有她犯下的罪过，有她的忧伤，还有她的惩罚。所以，她回来了，继续过着耻辱的生活，但是镇上的长官们再不会逼这个神圣的女人当众接受惩罚了。

here 表地点的小副词放句首，句子用倒装；句中 although 引导让步状语从句；force sb. to do sth.，逼迫某人做某事。

读书笔记

030 The Monkey's Paw 猴爪

今日关键语导读 Today's Key Points

《猴爪》是英国著名短篇小说作家雅各布斯的一篇短篇小说。《猴爪》在欧美读者中一直盛誉不衰，是英国惊险小说中的典范之作。作者极力渲染猴爪在人们心理上造成的阴森恐怖气氛，令人看后不寒而栗。直到故事结束，作者也没说出是什么可怕的东西等候在门前，给读者留下了悬念和回味。

障碍词先听为快 Words and Expressions

window ['windəu] n. 窗；窗口；窗户

breakfast ['brekfəst] n. 早餐；早饭

paw [pɔː] n. 爪子；手

pound [paund] n. 英镑；重击，重击声；兽栏；拘留所

quietly ['kwaiətli] adv. 安静地；秘密地；平稳地

perhaps [pə'hæps] adv. 也许；可能

postman ['pəustmən] n. 邮递员；邮差

happily ['hæpili] adv. 快乐地；幸福地；幸运地；恰当地

suddenly ['sʌdənli] adv. 突然地；忽然

好英文娓娓动听 Beautiful stories

The next morning the winter sun came through the window

and the house felt nice and warm again. Mr White felt better and he smiled at his wife and son. The family sat down to have breakfast and they began to talk about the day. The monkey's paw was on a little table near the window, but nobody looked at it and nobody thought about it. "I'm going to the shops this morning," Mrs White said. "I want to get something nice for dinner. Are you going to come with me?" she asked her husband. "No, I'm going to have a quiet morning. I'm going to read," her husband answered. "Well, I'm not going to go out this evening," Herbert said, "so we can go to bed early tonight. We were very late last night. And we aren't going to have stories about monkey's paws!" Mrs White said. She was angry. "Why did we listen to your friend?" she asked her husband. "A monkey's paw can't give you things!" she stopped but the two mendid not answer her. "Thirty thousand pounds!" she said quietly. "We needed that money." Just then Herbert looked at the clock and stood up. "I'm going to work," he said. "Perhaps the postman has got the money for you in a letter. Remember, I want some of it too!" Herbert laughed and his mother laughed too. "Don't laugh, son," Mr White said. "Tom Morris is an old friend and he thinks the story is true. Perhaps it is." "Well, leave some of the money for me," Herbert laughed again. His mother laughed too and she went to the door with him. "Goodbye, Mother," Herbert said happily. "Get some thing nice for dinner this evening at the shops. I'm always hungry after a day at work.'' "I know you are!" Mrs White answered. Herbert left the house and walked quickly down the road. His mother stood at the door for some time and watched him. The winter sun was warm, but suddenly she felt very cold.

长难句解析

The next morning the winter sun came through the window and the house felt nice and warm again.

第二天早上，冬天的太阳透过窗户，屋里感觉舒适又温暖。

come through 表示穿过，照过；and连接两个并列的句子。

The monkey's paw was on a little table near the window, but nobody looked at it and nobody thought about it.

猴子的爪子放在一张小桌子在窗户附近，但是没有人看到它，没人想到它。

on 是介词，表示放在……地方；but是表示转折的意思，and连接两个并列的句子。

I want to get something nice for dinner. Are you going to come with me?

我想去买一些好吃的东西做晚餐，你想跟我一起去吗?

want to do sth. 想要做某事；something nice 表示一些好的东西，形容词修饰something要放在后面；be going to do sth. 表示打算做某事；come with sb. 和某人一起。

Herbert left the house and walked quickly down the road. His mother stood at the door for some time and watched him.

赫伯特离开家，走得很快。他的母亲站在门口看着他有一段时间了。

leave the house 离开家；quickly 是副词，修饰walk，表示走得快。

The winter sun was warm, but suddenly she felt very cold.

冬天的太阳是温暖的，但是她突然感到很冷。

warm 表示温暖的，是形容词；suddenly 是副词，表示突然地；feel cold 表示感到寒冷。

读书笔记

031 Wuthering Heights 呼啸山庄

今日关键语导读 Today's Key Points

《呼啸山庄》是英国女作家勃朗特姐妹之一艾米莉·勃朗特的作品，是19世纪英国文学的代表作之一。小说描写吉卜赛弃儿希斯克利夫被山庄老主人收养后，因受辱和恋爱不遂离家，回来后对与其女友凯瑟琳结婚的地主林顿及其子女进行报复的故事。全篇充满反对压迫、争取幸福的斗争精神，又始终笼罩着离奇、紧张的超现实气氛，带有部分哥特文学的奇幻恐怖色彩。

障碍词先听为快 Words and Expressions

solitary ['sɔlitəri] adj. 孤独的；独居的 n. 独居者；隐士

withdraw [wið'drɔː] vt. 撤退；收回；撤消；拉开 vi. 撤退；离开

resolution [ˌrezə'ljuːʃən] n. 分辨率；决议；解决；决心

perseverance [ˌpəːsi'viərəns] n. 坚持不懈；不屈不挠

occupation [ˌɔkju'peiʃən] n. 职业；占有；消遣；占有期

interrupted [ˌintə'rʌptid] adj. 中断的；被打断的；不规则的 vt. 打断；中断（interrupt的过去分词）

sentiment ['sentimənt] n. 感情，情绪；情操；观点；多愁善感

circumstance ['səːkəmstəns] n. 环境，情况；事件；境遇

reserved [ri'zəːvd] adj. 保留的，预订的；缄默的，冷淡的；包租的 v. 保留（reserve的过去分词）

invitation [ˌinvi'teiʃən] n. 邀请；引诱

1801.I have just returned from a visit to my landlord—the solitary neighbour that I shall be troubled with. This is certainly a beautiful country! In all England, I do not believe that I could have fixed on a situation so completely removed from the stir of society. A perfect misanthropist 's heaven:

Mr Heathcliff and I are such a suitable pair to divide the desolation between us. A capital fellow! He little imagined how my heart warmed towards him when I beheld his black eyes withdraw so suspiciously under their brows, as I rode up, and when his fingers sheltered themselves, with a jealous resolution, still farther in his waistcoat, as I announced my name.

"Mr Heathcliff!" I said.

A nod was the answer.

"Mr Lockwood, your new tenant, sir. I do myself the honour of calling as soon as possible after my arrival, to express the hope that I have not inconvenienced you by my perseverance in soliciting the occupation of Thrushcross Grange: I heard yesterday you had had some thoughts..."

"Thrushcross Grange is my own, sir," he interrupted, wincing. "I should not allow anyone to inconvenience me, if I could hinder it—walk in!"

The "walk in" was uttered with closed teeth, and expressed the sentiment, `Go to the deuce': even the gate over which he leant manifested no sympathizing movement to the words; and I think that circumstance determined me to accept the invitation: I felt interested in a man who seemed more exaggeratedly reserved than myself.

长难句解析

I have just returned from a visit to my landlord—the solitary neighbour that I shall be troubled with. This is certainly a beautiful country!

我刚刚拜访过我的房东回来——就是那个将要给我惹麻烦的孤独的邻居。这儿可真是一个美丽的乡间！

return from从某处返回；that引导定语从句；be troubled with 与……产生麻烦事，相当于I shall be troubled with the solitary neighbour。

He little imagined how my heart warmed towards him when I beheld his black eyes withdraw so suspiciously under their brows, as I rode up, and when his fingers sheltered themselves, with a jealous resolution, still farther in his waistcoat, as I announced my name.

在我骑着马走上前去时，看见他的黑眼睛缩在眉毛下猜忌地瞅着我。而在我通报自己姓名时，他把手指深藏到背心袋里，完全是一副不信任我的样子。刹那间，我对他产生了亲切之感，而他却根本未察觉到。

这句的主干是he little imagined...，后面的全部内容做imagined的宾语；when引导时间状语从句。

"Mr Lockwood, your new tenant, sir. I do myself the honour of calling as soon as possible after my arrival, to express the hope that I have not inconvenienced you by my perseverance in soliciting the occupation of Thrushcross Grange: I heard yesterday you had had some thoughts..."

"先生，我是洛克乌德，您的新房客。我一到这儿就尽可能马上来向您表示敬意，希望我坚持要租画眉田庄没什么使您不方便。昨天我听说您想……"。

the honour of...的荣誉；as soon as possible 尽可能……；that引导定语从句；the occupation of，属于某人的。

"Thrushcross Grange is my own, sir,"he interrupted, wincing. "I should not allow anyone to inconvenience me, if I could hinder it—walk in!"

"画眉田庄是我自己的，先生。"他打断了我的话，闪避着："只要是我能够阻止，我不会允许任何人给我带来什么不方便的。进来吧！"

allow sb. to do sth. 允许某人做某事；if引导条件状语从句。

---

032 Brokeback Mountain 断背山

今日关键语导读 Today's Key Points

《断背山》是美国著名作家安妮·普劳克斯的短篇小说，最初于1997年10月13日发表在《纽约客》杂志上,第二年即获欧·亨利短篇小说奖和全美杂志奖。

整本小说集亦获纽约客最佳小说奖等三项大奖。描写怀俄明州残酷艰难的自然环境下，命运多舛的角色，从其人生历练中出的令人不寒而栗、倍感神圣庄严之美。

障碍词先听为快 Words and Expressions

pile up 积累，堆放起来

move off 离开；出发，走掉

press on 强加于；向前推进

flickering ['flikəriŋ] adj. 闪烁的，忽隐忽现的；摇曳的

pickup ['pikʌp] n. 收集，整理；小卡车；拾起；搭车者；偶然结识者

squint [skwint] v. 眯眼看；斜视；窥视；偏移

come up 走近；发生；开始；被提出

wear off 磨损；逐渐消逝

fecundity [fi'kʌndəti] n. 繁殖力；多产；肥沃

livestock ['laivstɔk] n. 牲畜；家畜

The first snow came early, on August thirteenth, piling up a foot, but was followed by a quick melt. The next week Joe Aguirre sent word to bring them down —another, bigger storm was moving in from the Pacific — and they packed in the game and moved off the mountain with the sheep, stones rolling at their heels, purple cloud crowding in from the west and the metal smell of coming snow pressing them on. The mountain boiled with demonic energy, glazed with flickering broken-cloud light, the wind combed the grass and drew from the damaged krummholz and slit rock a bestial drone. As they descended the slope Ennis felt he was in a slow-motion, but headlong, irreversible fall.

Joe Aguirre paid them, said little. He had looked at the milling sheep with a sour expression, said, "Some of these never went up there with you." The count was not what he'd hoped for either. Ranch stiffs never did much of a job.

"You go again this next summer?" said Jack to Ennis in the street, one leg already up in his green pickup. The wind was gusting hard and cold.

"Maybe not." A dust plume rose and hazed the air with fine grit and he squinted against it. "Like I said, Alma and me is getting married in December. Try to get something on a ranch. You?" He looked away from Jack's jaw, bruised blue from the hard punch Ennis had thrown him on the last day.

"If nothing better comes along. Thought some about going back up to my daddy's place, give him a hand over the winter, then maybe head out for Texas in the spring. If the draft don't get me."

"Well, see you around, I guess." The wind tumbled an empty feed bag down the street until it fetched up under his truck.

"Right," said Jack, and they shook hands, hit each other on the shoulder, then there was forty feet of distance between them and nothing to do but drive away in opposite directions. Within a mile Ennis felt like someone was pulling his guts out hand over hand a yard at a time. He stopped at the side of the road and, in the whirling new snow, tried to puke but nothing came up. He felt about as bad as he ever had and it took a long time for the feeling to wear off.

In December Ennis married Alma Beers and had her pregnant by mid-January. He picked up a few short-lived ranch jobs, then settled in as a wrangler on the old Elwood Hi-Top place north of Lost Cabin in Washakie County. He was still working there in September when Alma Jr., as he called his daughter, was born and their bedroom was full of the smell of old blood and milk and baby and the sounds were of squalling and sucking and Alma's sleepy groans, all reassuring of fecundity and life's continuance to one who worked with livestock.

长难句解析

The first snow came early, on August 13th, piling up a foot, but was followed by a quick melt.

八月十三日，山里的第一场雪早早地降临了。雪积了一尺多高，但很快又融化了。

piling up为动词现在分词表伴随，表示积雪的状态；be followed by被追随。

Joe Aguirre paid them, said little. He had looked at the milling sheep with a sour expression, said, "Some of these never went up there with you." The count was not what he'd hoped for either. Ranch stiffs never did much of a job.

乔·安奎尔付了他们工钱，没说太多。不过他看过那些满地乱转的羊后，面露不悦地说道："这里头有些羊可没跟你们上山。"而羊的数量，也没有剩到他原先希望的那么多。农场的人干活永远不上心。

look at 注视；hope for 希望，期待；either两者中的一个或另一个，注意与neither 区分。

"If nothing better comes along. Thought some about going back up to my daddy's place, give him a hand over the winter, then maybe head out for Texas in the spring. If the draft don't get me."

"如果没有更好的差事，这个冬天我打算去我爸那儿给他搭把手。要是一切顺利，春天的时候我也许会去德州。"

come along出现；一起来；though放在句首引导让步状语从句，相当于although，注意不能与but同时出现在一个句中；give sb. a hand over sth. 表示在某事上帮某人；head out 离去；启程，出海；if引导条件状语从句，表假设。

He stopped at the side of the road and, in the whirling new snow, tried to puke but nothing came up. He felt about as bad as he ever had and it took a long time for the feeling to wear off.

他在路边停下车，在漫天席卷的雪花中，想吐但是什么都吐不出来。他从来没有这么难受过，这种情绪过了很久才平息下来。

at the side of 在……的一边；try to do sth. 表示尽力做某事，try doing sth. 尝试做某事；come up 出现；as...as 像……一样；wear off 磨损；逐渐消逝。

In December Ennis married Alma Beers and had her pregnant by mid-January. He picked up a few short-lived ranch jobs, then settled in as a wrangler on the old Elwood Hi-Top place north of Lost Cabin in Washakie County.

十二月，埃尼斯和阿尔玛·比尔斯完婚，一月中旬，阿尔玛怀孕了。埃尼斯先后在几个农场打零工，后来去了沃什基郡罗斯特凯宾北部的老爱尔伍德西塔帕，当了一名牧马人。

pick up捡起；获得；收拾；不费力地学会；settle in安顿下来，适应于新家；wrangler（尤指放马的）牧人；牛仔，也可指“争执人；在争吵的人”。

033 Dr Jekyll and Mr Hyde 化身博士

今日关键语导读 Today's Key Points

《化身博士》出自英国著名作家史蒂文森笔下，书中讲述杰克喝了一种试验用的药剂，在晚上化身成邪恶的海德先生四处作恶，他终日徘徊在善恶之间，其内心的内疚和犯罪的快感不断冲突，令他饱受折磨。这种貌似荒诞无稽的故事，其实蕴含了最深刻的人性命题：人，到底是黑白分明，一成不变的非善即恶，还是既善亦恶，时善时恶？

障碍词先听为快 Words and Expressions

companionable [kəm'pænjənəb(ə)l] adj. 友善的；好交往的

mysterious [mis'tiəriəs] adj. 神秘的；不可思议的

fetch [fetʃ] vt. 取来；卖得；给（某人）一击

bleach [bli:tʃ] n. 漂白剂；漂白

cheque [tʃek] n. 支票=check(美)

cruel ['kruəl] adj. 残酷的；残忍的；引起痛苦的

generous ['dʒenərəs] adj. 慷慨的；宽宏大量的；丰厚的；丰盛的；味浓的

criminal ['kriminl] n. 罪犯

violent ['vaiələnt] adj. 猛烈的；强烈的；暴力的；极端的

Mr Utterson the lawyer was a quiet, serious man. He was shy with strangers and afraid of showing his feelings. Among friends, however, his eyes shone with kindness and goodness. And, although this goodness never found its way into his conversation, it showed itself in his way of life. He did not allow himself many enjoyable things in life. He ate and drank simply and, although he enjoyed the theater, he had not been to a play for twenty years. However, he was gentler towards other men's weaknesses, and was always ready to help rather than blame them. As a lawyer, he was often the last good person that evil-doers met on their way to prison, or worse. These people often carried with them memories of his politeness and fairness. Mr Utterson's best friend was a distant cousin called Richard Enfield, who was well known as a fun-loving "man about town". Nobody could understand why they were friends, as they were different from each other in every way. They often took long walks together, however, marching through the streets of London in companionable silence. One of these walks used to take them down a narrow side street in a busy part of London. It was a clean, busy, friendly street with bright little shops and shiny doorknockers. Near the end of this street, however, stood a dark, mysterious, windowless building. The door had neither bell nor knocker and looked dusty and uncared for. Dirty children played fearlessly on the doorstep, and nobody ever opened the door to drive them away. One day, as Mr Enfield and his friend passed the building, Mr Enfield pointed to it. "Have you ever noticed that place?" he asked. "It reminds me of a very strange story." "Really?" said Mr Utterson. "Tell me." "Well, began Enfield I was coming home about three o'clock on a black winter morning, when suddenly I saw two people. The first was a short man who was walking along the street, and the second was a little girl who was running as fast as she could. Well, the two bumped into each other and the child fell down. Then a terrible thing happened. The man calmly walked all over the child's body with his heavy boots, and left her screaming on the ground. It was an inhuman thing to do. I ran after the man, caught him and fetched him back. There was already a small crowd around the screaming child. The man was perfectly cool, but he gave me a very evil look, which made me feel sick in my stomach. The child's family then arrived, and also a doctor. The child had been sent to fetch the doctor for a sick neighbor, and was on her way home again." "The child is more frightened than hurt," said the doctor—and that, you would think, was the end of the story. But, you see, I had taken a violent dislike to the short man. So had the child's family—that was only natural. But the doctor, who seemed a quiet, kindly man, was also looking at our prisoner with murder in his eyes. "The doctor and I understood each other perfectly. Together we shouted at the man, and told him we would tell this story all over London so that his name would be hated." He looked back at us with a proud, bleach look. "Name your price," he said. "We made him agree to a hundred pounds for the child's family. With another black look, the man led us to that door over there. He took out a key and let himself into the building. Presently he came out and handed us ten pounds in gold and a cheque for ninety pounds from Coutts's Bank. The name on the cheque was a well-known one." "See here," said the doctor doubtfully, "it isn't usual for a man to walk into an empty house at four in the morning and come out with another man's cheque for nearly a hundred pounds." "Don't worry," said the man with an ugly look, "I'll stay with you until the banks open, and change the cheque myself." "So we all went off, the doctor and the prisoner and myself, and spent the rest of the night at my house. In the morning we went together to the bank. Sure enough, the cheque was good, and the money was passed to the child's family." "Well, well," said Mr Utterson. "Yes," said Enfield, "it's a strange story. My prisoner was clearly a hard, cruel man. But the man whose name was on the cheque was well known all over London for his kind and generous acts. Why would a man like that give his cheque to a criminal?" "And you don't know if the writer of the cheque lives in that building?" asked Mr Utterson. "I don't like to ask," said his friend. "In my experience, it's not a good idea to ask too many questions, in case the answers are ugly, violent ones. But I've studied the place a little. It doesn't seem like a house. There's no other door, and the only person who uses that door is the man I've just described to you. There are three windows on the side of the house, which look down onto a small courtyard. The windows are shut, but they're always clean. There's a chimney too, which is usually smoking. So somebody must live there." The two men continued on their walk. Then Utterson broke the silence. "Enfield," he said, "you're right about not asking too many questions. However, I want to ask the name of the man who walked over the child." "Very well," said

Enfield. "He told us his name was Hyde." "What does he look like?" "He's not easy to describe, although I remember him perfectly. He's a strange-looking man. He's short, but has a strong, heavy body. There's something wrong with his appearance, something ugly and unpleasing—no, something hateful. I disliked him at once." Mr Utterson thought deeply. "Are you sure he used a key?" he asked. "What do you mean?" Asked Enfield in surprise. "I know it must seem strange," said his friend. "But you see, if I don't ask you the name on the cheque, it's because I know it already..." "Well, why didn't you tell me?" said his friend rather crossly. "Anyway, he did have a key, and he still has it. I saw him use it only a week ago." Mr Utterson looked at him thoughtfully, but said nothing more.

长难句解析

Mr Utterson's best friend was a distant cousin called Richard Enfield, who was well known as a fun-loving "man about town". Nobody could understand why they were friends, as they were different from each other in every way.

厄特森先生最好的朋友是他的一个远房表亲，叫理查德·恩菲尔德。这个人是城里出名的热闹分子。谁也搞不明白他们为何是朋友，因为他们无论在从哪个方面都极不相同。

who引导定语从句；be well known 著名的；why引导原因状语从句；as引导原因状语，有“由于”之意；be different from 与……不同。

Near the end of this street, however, stood a dark, mysterious, windowless building. The door had neither bell nor knocker and looked dusty and uncared for. Dirty children played fearlessly on the doorstep, and nobody ever opened the door to drive them away.

在街道的尽头，有一幢阴暗、神秘、没有窗户的楼房，门上既没有铃也没门环，到处是灰，想必是无人问津。脏兮兮的孩子们在门前的阶梯上无所畏惧地疯闹着，也从未有人开门轰他们走。

the end of，在……的尽头；stood a dark...特殊倒装结构；neither...or...，既不……也不……；drive sb. away，把……带走。

Together we shouted at the man, and told him we would tell this story all over London so that his name would be hated. He looked back at us with a proud, bleach look. "Name your price," he said.

我和医生一起冲着那人大声喊，并声称要让整个伦敦都知道这事，让人人都唾弃他的名字。他回头瞪了我们一眼，一副不可一世的样子："开个价吧。"他说。

together位于句首，加强语气；shout at sb. 朝某人大喊；so that 以至于，表结果。

In my experience, it's not a good idea to ask too many questions, in case the answers are ugly, violent ones. But I've studied the place a little. It doesn't seem like a house. There's no other door, and the only person who uses that door is the man I've just described to you.

根据我的经验，问太多的问题可不是个好主意。万一得到的答案既令人厌恶又十分凶残，那该如何是好？但我还是稍微研究了一下那个地方。它看起来并不像一所房子，没别的门，唯一使用那扇门的人就是我刚才和你描述的那个人。

in case，“万一”，可用于倒装句who引导定语从句；I've just described to you，为后置定语修饰the man。

The first was a short man who was walking along the street, and the second was a little girl who was running as fast as she could. Well, the two bumped into each other and the child fell down. Then a terrible thing happened.

头一个是个矮个子，正沿着街边走，第二个是个小姑娘，跑得特别快。两个人一下撞到了一起，小孩儿摔倒了。然后，可怕的事发生了。

who 引导定语从句；“the first...the second...”，第一……第二……；bump into 相撞。

034 The Count of Monte Cristo 基督山伯爵

今日关键语导读 Today's Key Points

《基督山伯爵》是法国著名作家大仲马的代表作。故事讲述19世纪法国皇帝拿破仑“百日王朝”时期，法老号大副爱德蒙·唐泰斯受船长委托，为拿破仑党人送了一封信，却遭到两个卑鄙小人和法官的陷害，被打入黑牢。狱友法利亚神甫向他传授各种知识，并在临终前把埋于基督山岛上的一批宝藏的秘密告诉了他。唐泰斯越狱后找到了宝藏，成为巨富，从此化名基督山伯爵，经过精心策划，报答了恩人，惩罚了仇人的故事。

障碍词先听为快 Words and Expressions

prophet ['prɔfit] n. 先知；预言者；提倡者

counterpart ['kauntəpɑːt] n. 副本；配对物；极相似的人或物

monarchy ['mɔnəki] n. 君主政体；君主国；君主政治

totter ['tɔtə] v. 摇晃，摇动，摇摆；摇摇欲坠

divulge [dai'vʌldʒ] v. 泄漏（秘密等），揭露

imperial [im'piəriəl] adj. 帝国的；皇帝的

reenter [ˌriː'entə(r)] v. 重新入内，重返

rekindle ['riː'kindl] v. 重新点燃

magistrate ['mædʒistrit,'mædʒistreit] n. 地方法官；文职官员；治安推事

tremble ['trembl] v. 发抖；战栗；焦虑；摇晃

The Hundred Days.

Mr. Noirtier was a true prophet, and things progressed rapidly, as he had predicted. Every one knows the history of the famous return from Elba, a return which was unprecedented in the past, and will probably remain without a counterpart in the future.

Louis XVIII made but a faint attempt to parry this unexpected blow; the monarchy he had scarcely reconstructed tottered on its precarious foundation, and at a sign from the emperor the incongruous structure of ancient prejudices and new ideas fell to the ground. Villefort, therefore, gained nothing save the king's gratitude (which was rather likely to injure him at the present time) and the cross of the Legion of Honor, which he had the prudence not to wear, although M. de Blacas had duly forwarded the brevet.

Napoleon would, doubtless, have deprived Villefort of his office had it not been for Noirtier, who was all powerful at court, and thus the Girondin of 1793 and the Senator of 1806 protected him who so lately had been his protector.

All Villefort's influence barely enabled him to stifle the secret Dantes had so nearly divulged. The king's procureur alone was deprived of his office, being suspected of royalism.

However, scarcely was the imperial power established — that is, scarcely had the emperor reentered the Tuileries and begun to issue orders from the closet into which we have introduced our readers, — he found on the table there Louis XVIII's half-filled snuff-box, — scarcely had this occurred when Marseilles began, in spite of the authorities, to rekindle the flames of civil war, always smouldering in the south, and it required but little to excite the populace to acts of far greater violence than the shouts and insults with which they assailed the royalists whenever they ventured abroad.

Owing to this change, the worthy shipowner became at that moment — we will not say all powerful, because Morrel was a prudent and rather a timid man, so much so, that many of the most zealous partisans of Bonaparte accused him of "moderation" — but sufficiently influential to make a demand in favor of Dantes.

Villefort retained his place, but his marriage was put off until a more favorable opportunity. If the emperor remained on the throne, Gerard required a different alliance to aid his career; if Louis XVIII returned, the influence of M. de Saint-Meran, like his own, could be vastly increased, and the marriage be still more suitable. The deputy-procureur was, therefore, the first magistrate of Marseilles, when one morning his door opened, and M. Morrel was announced.

Any one else would have hastened to receive him; but Villefort was a man of ability, and he knew this would be a sign of weakness. He made Morrel wait in the ante-chamber, although he had no one with him, for the simple reason that the king's procureur always makes every one wait, and after passing a quarter of an hour in reading the papers, he ordered M. Morrel to be admitted.

Morrel expected Villefort would be dejected; he found him as he had found him six weeks before, calm, firm, and full of that glacial politeness, that most insurmountable barrier which separates the well-bred from the vulgar man.

He had entered Villefort's office expecting that the magistrate would tremble at the sight of him; on the contrary, he felt a cold shudder all over him when he saw Villefort sitting there with his elbow on his desk, and his head leaning on his hand. He stopped at the door; Villeffort gazed at him as if he had some difficulty in recognizing him; then, after a brief interval, during which the honest ship owner turned his hat in his hands.

长难句解析

Mr. Noirtier was a true prophet, and things progressed rapidly, as he had predicted. Every one knows the history of the famous return from Elba, a return which was unprecedented in the past, and will probably remain without a counterpart in the future.

诺瓦蒂埃先生真是一个预言家，事态的发展正如他所说的那样。谁都知道从艾尔巴岛卷土重来的这次著名的历史事件，——那次奇妙的回归，不仅是史无前例，而且大概也会后无来者。

as正如……一样；the history of，……的历史；which引导定语从句；in the future 在未来。

Napoleon would, doubtless, have deprived Villefort of his office had it not been for Noirtier, who was all powerful at court, and thus the Girondin of 1793 and the Senator of 1806 protected him who so lately had been his protector.

诺瓦蒂埃当时成了显赫一时的人物，要不是为了他，拿破仑无疑早就把维尔福免职了。这个1973年的吉伦特党人和1806年的上议院保护了这个不久前保护他的人。

who引导定语从句；had it not been for，倒装，表虚拟，意为“要不是”。

All Villefort's influence barely enabled him to stifle the secret Dantes had so nearly divulged. The king's procureur alone was deprived of his office, being suspected of royalism.

维尔福的全部力量都用在封住那几乎被唐太斯所泄露的秘密上。只有检察官被免了职，因为他有效忠于王室的嫌疑。

being引导的句子做原因；procureur 属于法语单词，意为检察官。

读书笔记

035 The Giver 记忆传授人

今日关键语导读 Today's Key Points

《记忆传授人》是洛伊丝·劳里的一部科幻小说，描写的故事发生在一个乌托邦世界里。在这个世界里，一切事情都在精确的控制之中，人们安居乐业，衣食无忧，也没有战争或痛苦的感觉．大家所要做的事情早在一开始就被确定好，没有改变的可能。孩子们都在规定好的统一模式里长大。当12岁的乔纳思成为新任的“记忆传授人”之后，他却陡然发现支撑这个社会的不过是谎言，而人们也在这样的环境下变得越来越冷漠，越来越残酷。于是他决定要改变一切……

障碍词先听为快 Words and Expressions

subsided [səb'saɪd] v. （土地）下陷（因在地下采矿）（subside的过去式和过去分词）；减弱；下降至较低或正常水平；一下子坐在椅子等上

gnawing ['nɔːiŋ] adj. 痛苦的，苦恼的 v. 咬（gnaw的现在分词）；（长时间）折磨某人；（使）苦恼；（长时间）危害某事物

emptiness ['emptinis] n. 空虚；空腹；无知；无能

grimly [grɪmlɪ] adv. 可怕地；严肃地；坚强地；讨厌地

chastised [tʃæ'staɪz] v. 严惩（某人）（尤指责打）（chastise的过去式）

community [kə'mjuːniti] n. 社区；社会团体；共同体 [生态] 群落

yearned [jɜːnd] v. 渴望，切盼，向往（yearn的过去式和过去分词）
encountering [in'kauntərɪŋ] v. 遇到（encounter的现在分词）；遭遇；偶然碰到；与（人、部队）冲突
sprained [spreɪnd] v. 扭伤（关节）（sprain的过去式和过去分词）
throbbed [θrɔbd] v. 抽痛（throb的过去式和过去分词）；（心脏、脉搏等）跳动

好英文娓娓动听 Beautiful stories

But when the memory glimpses subsided, he was left with the gnawing, painful emptiness. Jonas remembered, suddenly and grimly, the time in his childhood when he had been chastised for misusing a word. The word had been "starving." You have never been starving, he had been told. You will never be starving.

Now he was hungry. If he had stayed in the community, he would not be. It was as simple as that. Once he had yearned for choice. Then, when he had had a choice, he had made the wrong one: the choice to leave. And now he was starving.

But if he had stayed... His thoughts continued. If he had stayed, he would have starved in other ways. He would have lived a life hungry for feelings, for color, for love.

And Gabriel? For Gabriel there would have been no life at all. So there had not really been a choice.

It became a struggle to ride the bicycle as Jonas weakened from lack of food, and realized at the same time that he was encountering something he had for a long time yearned to see: hills. His sprained ankle throbbed as he forced the pedal downward in an effort that was almost beyond him.

And the weather was changing. It rained for two days. Jonas had never seen rain, though he had experienced it often in the memories. He had liked those rains, enjoyed the new feeling of it, but this was different. He and Gabriel became cold and wet, and it was hard to get dry, even when sunshine occasionally followed.

Gabriel had not cried during the long frightening journey. Now he did. He cried because he was hungry and cold and terribly weak. Jonas cried, too, for the same reasons, and another reason as well. He wept because he was afraid now that he could not save Gabriel. He no longer cared about himself.

长难句解析

Now he was hungry. If he had stayed in the community, he would not be. It was as simple as that. Once he had yearned for choice. Then, when he had had a choice, he had made the wrong one: the choice to leave. And now he was starving.

现在他觉得很饿，如果他还是待在那个集体里就不会是现在这个样子。但这其实也不难理解，他曾经很想能自己做出选择，之后他确实有了做选择的机会，但却做了错误的选择：离开了大家。而现在他就面临着错误选择的后果——挨饿。

if条件状语从句表示的是对过去情况的虚拟；as...as 和……一样；once 一旦；when引导时间状语从句。

It became a struggle to ride the bicycle as Jonas weakened from lack of food, and realized at the same time that he was encountering something he had for a long time yearned to see: hills.

由于缺乏食物，乔纳斯日渐虚弱，以至于骑自行车都很困难，同时乔纳斯也知道到他马上就可以看到他心念已久的山了。

it 引导的形式主语中，其后的不定式才是真正的主语。lack of，缺乏；at the same time，同时；that引导的是宾语从句。

Gabriel had not cried during the long frightening journey. Now he did.

加百利在长时间让人害怕的行程中从未哭过，但他现在落泪了。

He did = He cried

Jonas cried, too, for the same reasons, and another reason as well. He wept because he was afraid now that he could not save Gabriel.

因为同一个原因，乔纳斯也哭了，但他哭泣还有另一个原因：他怕自己救不了加百利。

as well 也、又、还；that引导宾语从句。

---

036 Sister Carrie 嘉莉妹妹

今日关键语导读 Today's Key Points

《嘉莉妹妹》是德莱塞嘉莉妹妹创作的第一部小说，也是美国文学史上最著名的作品之一，是美国伟大的自然主义作家德莱塞的处女作，讲述的是农村少女嘉莉来到大城市芝加哥寻找幸福，为摆脱贫困出卖自己的贞操，先后与推销员和酒店经理同居，后又凭美貌与歌喉成为演员的故事。该作品以真切的现实主义色彩为鲜明的特征，比较真实地揭露20世纪初人们狂热的追求美国梦的悲剧事实，揭示了驱使人们享乐却最终幻灭的本能主题，说明了在以金钱为中心的美国资本主义社会里不可能有真正的幸福。

障碍词先听为快 Words and Expressions

wholesale ['həulseil] adj. 批发的，大规模的

mechanically [mi'kænikəli] adv. 呆板地；机械地

contemplate ['kɔntempleit] v. 沉思，凝视

imposing [im'pəuziŋ] adj. 壮观的；印象深刻的

courage ['kʌridʒ] n. 勇气；胆量

brass [brɑːs] n. 黄铜；黄铜制品

pedestrian [pe'destriən] n. 行人；步行者

realisation [ˌriəlai'zeiʃən] n. 实现，完成

lightsome ['laitsəm] adj. 轻盈的；畅快的

metropolis [mi'trɔpəlis] n. 大都市，首府

好英文娓娓动听 Beautiful stories

"Why, how are all the folks at home?" she began; "how is father, and mother?"

Carrie answered, but was looking away. Down the aisle, toward the gate leading into the waiting-room and the street, stood Drouet. He was looking back. When he saw that she saw him and was safe with her sister he turned to go, sending back the shadow of a smile. Only Carrie saw it. She felt something lost to her when he moved away. When he disappeared she felt his absence thoroughly. With her sister she was much alone, a lone figure in a tossing, thoughtless sea.

Once across the river and into the wholesale district, she glanced about her for some likely door at which to apply. As she contemplated the wide windows and imposing signs, she became conscious of being gazed upon and understood for what she was—a wage-seeker. She had never done this thing before, and lacked courage. To avoid a certain indefinable shame she felt at being caught spying about for a position, she quickened her steps and assumed an air of indifference supposedly common to one upon an errand. In this way she passed many manufacturing and wholesale houses without once glancing in. At last, after several blocks of walking, she felt that this would not do, and began to look about again, though without relaxing her pace. A little way on she saw a great door which, for some reason, attracted her attention. It was ornamented by a small brass sign, and seemed to be the entrance to a vast hive of six or seven floors. "Perhaps," she thought, "they may want some one," and crossed over to enter. When she came within a score of feet of the desired goal, she saw through the window a young man in a grey checked suit. That he had anything to do with the concern, she could not tell, but because he happened to be looking in her direction her weakening heart misgave her and she hurried by, too overcome with shame to enter. Over the way stood a great sixstory structure, labelled Storm and King, which she viewed with rising hope. It was a wholesale dry goods concern and employed women. She could see them moving about now and then upon the upper floors. This place she decided to enter, no matter what. She crossed over and walked directly toward the entrance. As she did so, two men came out and paused in the door. A telegraph messenger in blue dashed past her and up the few steps that led to the entrance and disappeared. Several pedestrians out of the hurrying throng which filled the sidewalks passed about her as she paused, hesitating. She looked helplessly around, and then, seeing herself observed, retreated. It was too difficult a task. She could not go past them.

So severe a defeat told sadly upon her nerves. Her feet carried her mechanically forward, every foot of her progress being a satisfactory portion of a flight which she gladly made. Block after block passed by. Upon streetlamps at the various corners she read names such as Madison, Monroe, La Salle, Clark, Dearborn, State, and still she went, her feet beginning to tire upon the broad stone flagging. She was pleased in part that the streets were bright and clean. The morning sun, shining down with steadily increasing warmth, made the shady side of the streets pleasantly cool. She looked at the blue sky overhead with more realisation of its charm than had ever come to her before.

He left her revived by the possibilities, sure that she had found something at last. Instantly the blood crept warmly over her body. Her nervous tension relaxed. She walked out into the busy street and discovered a new atmosphere. Behold, the throng was moving with a lightsome step. She noticed that men and women were smiling. Scraps of conversation and notes of laughter floated to her. The air was light. People were already pouring out of the buildings, their labour ended for the day. She noticed that they were pleased, and thoughts of her sister's home and the meal that would be awaiting her quickened her steps. She hurried on, tired perhaps, but no longer weary of foot. What would not Minnie say! Ah, the long winter in Chicago--the lights, the crowd, the amusement! This was a great, pleasing metropolis after all. Her new firm was a goodly institution. Its windows were of huge plate glass. She could probably do well there. Thoughts of Drouet returned—of the things he had told her. She now felt that life was better, that it was livelier, sprightlier. She boarded a car in the best of spirits, feeling her blood still flowing pleasantly. She would live in Chicago, her mind kept saying to itself. She would have a better time than she had ever had before--she would be happy.

长难句解析

When he saw that she saw him and was safe with her sister he turned to go, sending back the shadow of a smile.

当他发现她看到了他，并且跟她妹妹都很安全，他转身走了，留下一个微笑的背影。

when作为从属连词，引导状语从句。V+ing，可以作非谓语动词，常表示动作正在进行或同步进行的状态，有延续性。

As she contemplated the wide windows and imposing signs, she became conscious of being gazed upon and understood for what she was—a wage-seeker.

当她正打量着那些宽大的玻璃窗和气派的招牌时，她感觉有人在看她，也意识到人家知道她是干什么的——一个求职者。

being gazed upon“被直愣愣地盯着”；what 引导宾语从句。

When she came within a score of feet of the desired goal, she saw through the window a young man in a grey checked suit. That he had anything to do with the concern, she could not tell, but because he happened to be looking in her direction her weakening heart misgave her and she hurried by, too overcome with shame to enter.

当她距离目标还有二十英尺时，透过窗子她看见一个穿灰格子西装的年轻人。她并不知道这个人与那家商店是否有关系，但是这人正巧朝她的方向看，她充满羞愧，立刻心虚地打退堂鼓，急急忙忙地走开了。

when 引导时间状语从句；happened to be，“碰巧”。had anything to do，“有任何关系”。concern有“公司、企业”的意思。

So severe a defeat told sadly upon her nerves. Her feet carried her mechanically forward, every foot of her progress being a satisfactory portion of a flight which she gladly made.

这么严重的失败使她非常垂头丧气。她的脚带着她机械地往前移动，每前进一步都因为逃离远了一点而心里轻松一点。

which引导定语从句；nerves“神经”。

She noticed that they were pleased, and thoughts of her sister's home and the meal that would be awaiting her quickened her steps. She hurried on, tired perhaps, but no longer weary of foot. What would not Minnie say! Ah, the long winter in Chicago-the lights, the crowd, the amusement!

她看得出他们心情愉快。想到姐姐家，想到等着她的晚餐，她不由加快了脚步。她急急忙忙地走着，虽然疲倦，脚步却不再沉甸甸的了。敏妮知道了，一定会兴奋得滔滔不绝。啊，长长的一整个冬天都留在芝加哥——灯光，人群和种种娱乐！

“She noticed that they were pleased”的that 引导宾语从句；no longer不再。

读书笔记

037 Jane Eyre 简·爱

今日关键语导读 Today's Key Points

《简·爱》是十九世纪英国著名的女作家夏洛蒂·勃朗特的代表作，人们普遍认为《简·爱》是夏洛蒂·勃朗特“诗意的生平写照”，是一部具有自传色彩的作品。讲述一位从小变成孤儿的英国女子在各种磨难中不断追求自由与尊严，坚持自我，最终获得幸福的故事。小说引人入胜地展示了男女主人公曲折起伏的爱情经历，歌颂摆脱一切旧习俗和偏见的勇气，成功塑造了一个敢于反抗，敢于争取自由和平等地位的女性形象。

障碍词先听为快 Words and Expressions

ameliorate [ə'miːljəreit] vt. 改善；减轻（痛苦等）；改良 vi. 变得更好

wretch [retʃ] n. 可怜的人，不幸的人；卑鄙的人

lameness ['leimnis] n. 跛；残废；僵而疼痛的

subside [səb'said] vi. 平息；减弱；沉淀；坐下

auricula [ə'rikjulə] n. [植] 耳状报春花；[解剖] 耳廓

prospect ['prɔspekt] n. 前途；预期；景色 vi. 勘探，找矿 vt. 勘探，勘察

turbid ['təːbid] adj. 浑浊的；混乱的；雾重的

skeleton ['skelitən] n. 骨架，骨骼；纲要；骨瘦如柴的人 adj. 骨骼的；骨瘦如柴的；概略的

verge [vəːdʒ] vi. 濒临，接近；处在边缘 n. 边缘

typhus ['taifəs] n. [内科] 斑疹伤寒症

But the privations, or rather the hardships, of Lowood lessened. Spring drew on: she was indeed already come; the frosts of winter had ceased; its snows were melted, its cutting winds ameliorated. My wretched feet, flayed and swollen to lameness by the sharp air of January, began to heal and subside under the gentler breathings of April; the nights and mornings no longer by their Canadian temperature froze the very blood in our veins; we could now endure the play-hour passed in the garden: sometimes on a sunny day it began even to be pleasant and genial, and a greenness grew over those brown beds, which, freshening daily, suggested the thought that Hope traversed them at night, and left each morning brighter traces of her steps.

Flowers peeped out amongst the leaves; snowdrops, crocuses, purple auriculas, and golden-eyed pansies. On Thursday afternoons (half-holidays) we now took walks, and found still sweeter flowers opening by the wayside, under the hedges.

I discovered, too, that a great pleasure, an enjoyment which the horizon only bounded, lay all outside the high and spike-guarded walls of our garden: this pleasure consisted in prospect of noble summits girdling a great hill-hollow, rich in verdure and shadow; in a bright beck, full of dark stones and sparkling eddies. How different had this scene looked when I viewed it laid out beneath the iron sky of winter, stiffened in frost, shrouded with snow!— when mists as chill as death wandered to the impulse of east winds along those purple peaks, and rolled down 'ing' and holm till they blended with the frozen fog of the beck! That beck itself was then a torrent, turbid and curbless: it tore asunder the wood, and sent a raving sound through the air, often thickened with wild rain or whirling sleet; and for the forest on its banks, that showed only ranks of skeletons.

April advanced to May: a bright, serene May it was; days of blue sky, placid sunshine, and soft western or southern gales filled up its duration. And now vegetation matured with vigour; Lowood shook loose its tresses; it became all green, all flowery; its great elm, ash, and oak skeletons were restored to majestic life; woodland plants sprang up profusely in its recesses; unnumbered varieties of moss filled its hollows, and it made a strange ground-sunshine out of the wealth of its wild primrose plants: I have seen their pale gold gleam in overshadowed spots like scatterings of the sweetest lustre. All this I enjoyed often and fully, free, unwatched, and almost alone: for this unwonted liberty and pleasure there was a cause, to which it now becomes my task to advert.

Have I not described a pleasant site for a dwelling, when I speak of it as bosomed in hill and wood, and rising from the verge of a stream? Assuredly, pleasant enough: but whether healthy or not is another question.

That forest-dell, where Lowood lay, was the cradle of fog and fog-bred pestilence; which, quickening with the quickening spring, crept into the Orphan Asylum, breathed typhus through its crowded schoolroom and dormitory, and, ere May arrived, transformed the seminary into an hospital.

长难句解析

But the privations, or rather the hardships, of Lowood lessened.

然而，罗沃德的贫困，或者不如说艰辛，有所好转了。

or rather 表示选择。

April advanced to May: a bright, serene May it was; days of blue sky, placid sunshine, and soft western or southern gales filled up its duration.

四月已逝，五月来临。这是一个明媚宁静的五月，每天都是蔚蓝的天空，和煦的阳光，来自西部或南部的风一阵阵地刮了起来。

advance 具有前进之意，此处表示到达的意思。

I discovered, too, that a great pleasure, an enjoyment which the horizon only bounded, lay all outside the high and spike-guarded walls of our garden: this pleasure consisted in prospect of noble summits girdling a great hill-hollow, rich in verdure and shadow; in a bright beck, full of dark stones and sparkling eddies

我还发现，就在被尖铁防卫着的花园高墙之外，有一种莫大的愉悦感，它广阔无垠，直达天际，那种愉悦来自被宏伟山峰环抱的和被葱茏绿荫覆盖的大山谷；也来自满是黑色石子和闪光漩涡的明净溪流。

that 引导的宾语从句中有一个由which 引导的定语从句；full of充满。

How different had this scene looked when I viewed it laid out beneath the iron sky of winter, stiffened in frost, shrouded with snow!

这景色与我在冬日铁灰色的苍穹下，冰霜封冻和积雪覆盖时所看到的情景多么不同呀！

how 引导感叹句；when 引导时间状语从句；stiffened in frost，shrouded with snow，都是过去分词做状语。

That forest-dell, where Lowood lay, was the cradle of fog and fog-bred pestilence; which, quickening with the quickening spring, crept into the Orphan Asylum, breathed typhus through its crowded schoolroom and dormitory, and, ere May arrived, transformed the seminary into an hospital.

罗沃德所在的林间山谷，是大雾的摇篮，是雾气诱发的病疫的滋生地。时疫随着春天急速的步伐，加速潜入孤儿院，把斑疹伤寒传进了它拥挤的教室和寝室，五月还没到，就已把整所学校变成了医院。

where 引导地点状语从句；后面which 引导的定语从句修饰the cradle。

038 Autobiography by Thomas Jefferson 杰斐逊自传

今日关键语导读 Today's Key Points

《杰斐逊自传》是杰斐逊在77岁高龄时撰写的，该书详细介绍了杰斐逊思想的精髓，《独立宣言》的起草背景和过程，虽然书中有些背景知识介绍得不够详细，但瑕不掩瑜，该书仍是一部伟大的作品。

障碍词先听为快 Words and Expressions

punctuality [ˌpʌŋktju'æliti] n. 严守时间；正确，规矩

eminence ['eminəns] n. 显赫，卓越

pleasantry ['plezəntri] n. 幽默；开玩笑

portion ['pɔːʃən] n. 一部分

orator ['ɔrətə] n. 演说者，演讲家

dissolve [di'zɔlv] vt. 使溶解

tavern ['tævə(ː)n] n. 小旅馆，客栈

merchandise ['məːtʃəndaiz] n. 商品

voluntary ['vɔləntəri] adj. 自愿的

import [im'pɔːt] vt. 输入

proceeding [prə'siːdiŋ] n. 诉讼，事项，行径，事件，进程（proceeding的名词复数），行动

On the 1st of January, 1772, I was married to Martha Skelton widow of Bathurst Skelton, daughter of John Way les, then 23 years old. Mr. Wayles was a lawyer of much practice, to which he was introduced more by his great industry, punctuality and practical readiness, than by eminence in the science of his profession. He was a most agreeable companion, full of pleasantry and good humor, and welcomed in every society. He acquired a handsome fortune, died in May, 1773, leaving three daughters, and the portion which came on that event to Mrs. Jefferson, after the debts should be paid, which were very considerable, was about equal to my own patrimony, and consequently doubled the ease of our circumstances.

When the famous Resolutions of 1765, against the Stamp-act, were proposed, I was yet a student of law in Williamsburg. I attended the debate, however, at the door of the lobby of the House of Burgesses, and heard the splendid display of Mr. Henry's talents as a popular orator. They were great indeed; such as I have never heard from any other man. He appeared to me, to speak as Homer wrote. Mr. Johnson, a lawyer and member from the Northern Neck, seconded the resolutions, and by him the learning and the logic of the case were chiefly maintained. My recollections of these transactions may be seen page 60 of the "Life of Patrick Henry", by Wirt, to whom I furnished them.

In May, 1769, a meeting of the General Assembly was called by the hovernor, Lord Botetort. I had then become a member; and to that meeting became known the joint resolutions and address of the Lords and Commons of 1768 — 9, on the proceedings in Massachusetts.

Counter-resolutions, and an address to the King, by the House of Burgesses, were agreed to with little opposition, and a spirit manifestly displayed itself of considering the cause of Massachusetts as a common one. The Governor dissolved us: but we met the next day in the Apollo of the Raleigh tavern, formed ourselves into a voluntary convention, drew up articles of association against the use of any merchandise imported from Great Britain, signed and recommended them to the people, repaired to our several counties, and were re—elected without any other exception than of the very few who had declined assent to our proceedings.

长难句解析

Mr. Wayles was a lawyer of much practice, to which he was introduced more by his great industry, punctuality and practical readiness, than by eminence in the science of his profession.

小河先生是一名身经百战的律师，我们给予他这样的评价，多半是因为他勤奋守时及实际的准备，而不是因为他在业界的权威声誉。

be of much practice=practical，“有经验的”；which引导定语从句；more than“比……更多”。

They were great indeed; such as I have never heard from any other man.

他们真的很优秀，我从来没有听说过比他们更厉害的人。

such as例如，后接举例事项；hear from收到……的来信，从…听到，注意与hear of 区分。

He was a most agreeable companion, full of pleasantry and good humor, and welcomed in every society.

他是一个最称心如意的伙伴，为人客气并富有幽默感，在每个社团都受到欢迎。

agreeable“愉悦的、讨人喜欢的”，full of“充满”。

I had then become a member; and to that meeting became known the joint resolutions and address of the Lords and Commons of 1768 — 9, on the proceedings in Massachusetts.

当我成为其中一员的时候，就参加了那个来自1768-1769上议院和下议院联合决议——而后来这项决议变得路人皆知，这件事的地点就在马萨诸塞州。

Massachusetts为马萨诸塞州（美国）。

---

039 Treasure Island 金银岛

今日关键语导读 Today's Key Points

《金银岛》是著名的文学作家罗伯特·路易斯·斯蒂文森一生最畅销的小说之一。描述了十八世纪中期英国少年吉姆从垂危水手彭斯手中得到传说中的藏宝岛信息，在当地乡绅支援下组织探险队前往金银岛。海盗头子约翰西尔弗应征了船上厨师，一群手下也上船充当水手。到达金银岛时，吉姆遇到在荒岛上独居三年的水手班恩，而西尔弗则发动叛变占据帆船。吉姆被掳上帆船，危急时西尔弗出手相救，因而跟其他海盗发生矛盾。最后李福西医生与班恩合作对付海盗，并成功取得宝藏的故事。

障碍词先听为快 Words and Expressions

retire [ri'taiə] vi. 退休；撤退；退却

breeze [bri:z] n. 微风；轻而易举的事；煤屑；焦炭渣；小风波

glow [gləu] vi. 发热；洋溢；绚丽夺目

stoop [stu:p] vi. 弯腰；屈服；堕落

incongruous [in'kɔŋgruəs] adj. 不协调的；不一致的；不和谐的

huddle ['hʌdl] vi. 蜷缩；挤作一团

comical ['kɔmik(ə)l] adj. 滑稽的，好笑的

manoeuvres [mə'nu:və] n. 调遣，换防，对抗演习，操纵；技术动作；策略，巧计；花招，伎俩 vt. 调遣；操纵，控制；诱使，策划

The council of the buccaneers had lasted some time, when one of them re-entered the house, and with a repetition of the same salute, which had in my eyes an ironical air, begged for a moment's loan of the torch. Silver briefly agreed; and this emissary retired again, leaving us together in the dark.

"There's a breeze coming, Jim," said Silver, who had, by this time, adopted quite a friendly and familiar tone.

I turned to the loophole nearest me and looked out. The embers of the great fire had so far burned themselves out, and now glowed so low and duskily, that I understood why these conspirators desired a torch. About half way down the slope to the stockade, they were collected in a group; one held the light; another was on his knees in their midst, and I saw the blade of an open knife shine in his hand with varying colours, in the moon and torchlight. The rest were all somewhat stooping, as though watching the manoeuvres of this last. I could just make out that he had a book as well as a knife in his hand; and was still wondering how anything so incongruous had come in their possession, when the kneeling figure rose once more to his feet, and the whole party began to move together towards the house.

"Here they come," said I; and I returned to my former position, for it seemed beneath my dignity that they should find me watching them.

"Well, let 'em come, lad - let 'em come," said Silver, cheerily. "I've still a shot in my locker."

The door opened, and the five men, standing huddled together just inside, pushed one of their number forward. In any other circumstances it would have been comical to see his slow advance, hesitating as he set down each foot, but holding his closed right hand in front of him.

"Step up, lad," cried Silver. "I won't eat you. Hand it over, lubber. I know the rules, I do; I won't hurt a depytation."

Thus encouraged, the buccaneer stepped forth more briskly, and having passed something to Silver, from hand to hand, slipped yet more smartly back again to hi companions.

长难句解析

When one of them re-entered the house, and with a repetition of the same salute, which had in my eyes an ironical air, begged for a moment's loan of the torch.

其中一个才回到木屋来，再次向西尔弗敬了个礼（在我看来，略带点讽刺意味），想借火把暂用一下。

这是一个when引导的时间状语从句，其中又含有一个with引导的伴随状语修饰one of them，后面的是which 引导的非限定性状语，修饰with引导的名词性短语。

One held the light; another was on his knees in their midst.

一个拿着火把，另一个跪在他们中间。

此句运用句型one...，another...一个人在……，另一个在……。

The door opened, and the five men, standing huddled together just inside.

门开了，五个人站在屋门口挤做一堆。

standing huddled together just inside，是动词的ing 形式做伴随状语，修饰the five men。

I know the rules, I do; I won't hurt a depytation.

我懂得规矩，我不会难为一个使者。

句中的 I do是一个简单的强调句，强调I know the rules.

I could just make out that he had a book as well as a knife in his hand.

我只能看到他手里还拿着一本书，就像一把刀。

that 引导宾语成句；as... as...和……一样，连接两个对等成分。

040 The Old Man and the Sea 老人与海

今日关键语导读 Today's Key Points

本书讲述了一个渔夫的故事。古巴老渔夫圣地亚哥在连续八十四天没捕到鱼的情况下，终于独自钓上了一条大马林鱼，但这鱼实在太大，把他的小船在海上拖了三天才筋疲力尽，被他杀死了绑在小船的一边。在归程中，他再遭到一条鲨鱼的袭击，最后回港时只剩鱼头鱼尾和一条脊骨。而在老圣地亚哥出海的日子里，他的忘年好友一直在海边忠诚地等待，满怀信心地迎接着他的归来。

障碍词先听为快 Words and Expressions

occurrence [ə'kʌrəns] *n.* 发生；出现
companionship [kəm'pænjənʃip] *n.* 友谊；陪伴
beyond [bi'jɔnd] *prep.* 超过；越过
respect [ris'pekt] *v.* 尊敬；遵守
confidence ['kɔnfidəns] *n.* 信心；秘密
spur [spəː] *vt.* 激动；加速

好英文娓娓动听 Beautiful stories

He no longer dreamed of storms, nor of women, nor of great occurrences, nor of great fish, nor fights, nor contests of strength, nor of his wife. He only dreamed of places now and of the lions on the beaChapter. They played like young cats in the dusk and he loved them as he loved the boy.

Why did they make birds so delicate and fine as those sea swallows when the ocean can be so cruel? She is kind and very beautiful. But she can be so cruel and it comes so suddenly and such birds that fly, dipping and hunting, with their small sad voices are made too delicately for the sea.

But the old man always thought of her as feminine and as something that gave or withheld great favors, and if she did wild or wicked things it was because she could not help them. The moon affects her as it does a woman, he thought.

Now is the time to think of only one thing. That which I was born for.

I wish I had the boy.

Santiago longs for the companionship of the boy Manolin, his loyal friend.

He is wonderful and strange and who knows how old he is, he thought. Never have I had such a strong fish nor one who acted so strangely... He cannot know that it is only one man against him, nor that it is an old man. But what a great fish he is and what will he bring in the market if the flesh is good.

My choice was to go there and find him beyond all people. Beyond all people in the world. Now we are joined together and have been since noon. And no one to help either of us.

Fish, I love you and respect you very much. But I will kill you dead before this day ends.

The clouds were building up now for the trade wind and he looked ahead and saw a flight of wild ducks etching themselves against the sky over the water, then blurring, then etching again and he knew no man was ever alone on the sea.

If I were him I would put in everything now and go until something broke. But, thank God, they are not as intelligent as we who kill them; although they are more noble and more able.

But I must have the confidence and I must be worthy of the great DiMaggio who does all things perfectly even with the pain of the bone spur in his heel.

"The fish is my friend too," he said aloud. "I have never seen or heard of such a fish. But I must kill him. I'm glad we do not have to kill the stars.

It is good that we do not have to try to kill the sun or the moon or the stars. It is enough to live on the sea and kill our true brothers.

A man is never lost at sea.

长难句解析

Never have I had such a strong fish nor one who acted so strangely... He cannot know that it is only one man against him, nor that it is an old man.

我从来没有遇过如此强大、不可思议的鱼。它不会知道只有一个人可以对付它，而且是一个老人。

never have I + 过去分词，是现在完成时，never have I是

倒装句式；who在定语从句中，用作限定关系代词；nor区别于neither，当并列分句有两个以上时，只能用nor、当主语是同一个人或物时,只能用nor不能用neither。

The moon affects her as it does a woman, he thought.

他认为，月亮对于海洋的影响，正如月亮对于妇人的影响。

it作为代词，代指月亮对妇人的影响。

But the old man always thought of her as feminine and as something that gave or withheld great favors, and if she did wild or wicked things it was because she could not help them.

可是，老人总是认为海洋是女性，有时带来恩惠，有时带来噩运，而当海洋变得蛮横狂暴或是邪恶时，那是因为她没有办法控制。

that引导宾语从句；because引导原因状语从句，在句中作从属连词；help是帮助，协助的意思，在此指“控制”。

But she can be so cruel and it comes so suddenly and such birds that fly, dipping and hunting, with their small sad voices are made too delicately for the sea.

然而它却同时可以那么残酷，转变的那么突然：那些飞着的鸟，不时还得潜入水中捕食，它们弱小的哀鸣声，在这浩瀚的海洋里实在是太渺小。

that引导定语从句；dipping, hunting，在句中作非谓语，表示主动；delicately表示微妙地；精致地；优美地，在此指“渺小，纤弱”。

读书笔记

041 The Notebook 恋恋笔记本

今日关键语导读 Today's Key Points

《恋恋笔记本》是美国著名作家尼古拉斯·斯帕克思的创作。故事发生在一家风光迤逦的私人疗养院。一位神秘的老男人每天都会准时拜访一位患有老年痴呆症的老女人。他总是在腿上摊开一本褪色的笔记本，轻轻地为女人讲述其中记载的故事，每当女人听到日记中的字句，脸上就会迸发出异样的神采，仿佛再次回到那段激情燃烧的岁月……

障碍词先听为快 Words and Expressions

thermostat ['θəːməstæt] n. 恒温（调节）器

groan [grəun] v. 呻吟；抱怨；发嘎吱声；受重压

spew [spjuː] v. 喷出；涌出；呕吐；吐出

shiver ['ʃivə] v. 颤动；发抖

burrow ['bʌrəu] vt. & vi. 挖掘（洞穴），挖洞

gopher ['gəufə] n. 囊地鼠（产自北美的一种地鼠）

resemble [ri'zembl] vt. 与……相像，类似于

squinted [skwɪnt] adj. 斜视的；斜的

shuffle ['ʃʌfl] v. 拖曳；搅乱；推诿；洗牌；移来移去

muffled ['mʌfld] adj. （指声音）听不清的；低沉的

gnarled [naːld] adj. 树木多瘤节的；粗糙的

prevail [pri'veil] vi. 盛行；获胜；劝说

The sun has come up and I am sitting by a window that is foggy with the breath of a life gone by. I'm a sight this morning: two shirts, heavy pants, a scarf wrapped twice around my neck and tucked into a thick sweater knitted by my daughter thirty birthdays ago. The thermostat in my room is set as high as it will go, and a smaller space heater sits directly behind me. It clicks and groans and spews hot air like a fairy-tale dragon, and still my body shivers with a cold that will never go away, a cold that has been eighty years in the making. Eighty years, I think sometimes, and despite my own acceptance of my age, it still amazes me that I haven't been warm since George Bush was president. I wonder if this is how it is for everyone my age.

My life? It isn't easy to explain. It has not been the rip-roaring spectacular I fancied it would be, but neither have I burrowed around with the gophers. I suppose it has most resembled a blue-chip stock: fairly stable, more ups than downs, and gradually trending upward over time. A good buy, a lucky buy, and I've learned that not everyone can say this about his life. But do not be misled. I am nothing special; of this I am sure. I am a common man with common thoughts, and I've led a common life. There are no monuments dedicated to me and my name will soon be forgotten, but I've loved another with all my heart and soul, and to me, this has always been enough.

The romantics would call this a love story, the cynics would call it a tragedy. In my mind it's a little bit of both, and no matter how you choose to view it in the end, it does not change the fact that it involves a great deal of my life and the path I've chosen to follow. I have no complaints about my path and the places it has taken me; enough complaints to fill a circus tent about other things, maybe, but the path I've chosen has always been the right one, and I wouldn't have had it any other way.

Time, unfortunately, doesn't make it easy to stay on course. The path is straight as ever, but now it is strewn with the rocks and gravel that accumulate over a lifetime. Until three years ago it would have been easy to ignore, but it's impossible now. There is a sickness rolling through my body; I'm neither strong nor healthy, and my days are spent like an old party balloon: listless, spongy, and growing softer over time. I cough, and through squinted eyes I check my watch. I realize it is time to go. I stand from my seat by the window and shuffle across the room, stopping at the desk to pick up the notebook I have read a hundred times. I do not glance through it. Instead I slip it beneath my arm and continue on my way to the place I must go. I walk on tiled floors, white in color and speckled with gray. Like my hair and the hair of most people here, though I'm the only one in the hallway this morning. They are in their rooms, alone except for television, but they, like me, are used to it.

A person can get used to anything, if given enough time. I hear the muffled sounds of crying in the distance and know exactly who is making those sounds. Then the nurses see me and we smile at each other and exchange greetings.

They are my friends and we talk often, but I am sure they

wonder about me and the things that I go through every day. I listen as they begin to whisper among themselves as I pass. "There he goes again," I hear, "I hope it turns out well." But they say nothing directly to me about it. I'm sure they think it would hurt me to talk about it so early in the morning, and knowing myself as I do, I think they're probably right. A minute later, I reach the room. The door has been propped open for me, as it usually is. There are two others in the room, and they too smile at me as I enter. "Good morning," they say with cheery voices, and I take a moment to ask about the kids and the schools and upcoming vacations. We talk above the crying for a minute or so. They do not seem to notice; they have become numb to it, but then again, so have I.

Afterward I sit in the chair that has come to be shaped like me. They are finishing up now; her clothes are on, but still she is crying. It will become quieter after they leave, I know. The excitement of the morning always upsets her, and today is no exception. Finally the shade is opened and the nurses walk out. Both of them touch me and smile as they walk by. I wonder what this means. I sit for just a second and stare at her, but she doesn't return the look. I understand, for she doesn't know who I am. I'm a stranger to her. Then, turning away, I bow my head and pray silently for the strength I know I will need. I have always been a firm believer in God and the power of prayer, though to be honest, my faith has made for a list of questions I definitely want answered after I'm gone. Ready now. On go the glasses, out of my pocket comes a magnifier. I put it on the table for a moment while I open the notebook. It takes two licks on my gnarled finger to get the well-worn cover open to the first page.

Then I put the magnifier in place. There is always a moment right before I begin to read the story when my mind churns, and I wonder, will it happen today? I don't know, for I never know beforehand, and deep down it really doesn't matter. It's the possibility that keeps me going, not the guarantee, a sort of wager on my part. And though you may call me a dreamer or fool or any other thing, I believe that anything is possible.

I realize the odds, and science, are against me. But science is not the total answer. This I know, this I have learned in my lifetime. And that leaves me with the belief that miracles, no matter how inexplicable or unbelievable, are real and can occur without regard to the natural order of things. So once again, just as I do everyday, I begin to read the notebook aloud, so that she can hear it, in the hope that the miracle that has come to dominate my life will once again prevail. And maybe, just maybe, it will.

长难句解析

My life? It isn't easy to explain. It has not been the rip-roaring spectacular I fancied it would be, but neither have I burrowed around with the gophers. I suppose it has most resembled a blue-chip stock: fairly stable, more ups than downs, and gradually trending upward over time.

我的生活？那可很难说清楚。不如我希望的那般热烈，但也不像囊地鼠一般过着洞中沉寂生活。我觉得更像一支绩优股：十分平稳，高潮总比低谷多，并且总体趋势都是向上的。

neither 具有否定含义，在句首构成倒装结构，加强语气。

The romantics would call this a love story, the cynics would call it a tragedy. In my mind it's a little bit of both, and no matter how you choose to view it in the end, it does not change the fact that it involves a great deal of my life and the path I've chosen to follow.

浪漫的人会认为这是一个爱情小说：而悲观的人则会觉得是一个悲剧。在我看来，二者或多或少都有一些，而无论你要如何看待，都不能改变它曾对我的生活带来很大影响的事实且无法改变我所选择坚持的路。

a little bit of 一点，少许；no matter how引导让步状语从句；in the end 结尾，最后；fact后接同位语从句；a great deal of 大量、许多。

Until three years ago it would have been easy to ignore, but it's impossible now. There is a sickness rolling through my body; I'm neither strong nor healthy, and my days are spent like an old party balloon: listless, spongy, and growing softer over time.

直到三年前我还可以轻松地视而不见，但现在是不可能了。现在的我疼痛缠身，强壮与健康都不复存在，我的日子就像老的宴会气球一样：无精打采，软趴趴的而且日渐疲软。

neither...nor“既不...也不...”。

I realize it is time to go. I stand from my seat by the window and shuffle across the room, stopping at the desk to pick up the notebook I have read a hundred times. I do not glance through it. Instead I slip it beneath my arm and continue on my way to the place I must go.

我觉得是时候离开了。我从窗边的凳子上起来，蹒跚的走过房间，在桌子前停下拿起那本读了有一百遍的笔记本，把它塞进胳膊下面，继续前行去往那个我必须去的地方。

stopping非谓语动词作伴随状语，pick up拾起、拿起。

I don't know, for I never know beforehand, and deep down it really doesn't matter. It's the possibility that keeps me going, not the guarantee, a sort of wager on my part. And though you may call me a dreamer or fool or any other thing, I believe that anything is possible.

我不知道，因为我不能未卜先知，而实际上这根本不重要。我相信那可能性，这种信念支撑着我前行。不管你叫我幻想家、傻瓜或者别的什么，我都相信一切皆有可能。

for引导原因状语从句，it is... that 强调句型；though位于句首引导让步状语从句；that引导宾语从句。

042 The Great Gatsby 了不起的盖茨比

今日关键语导读 Today's Key Points

《了不起的盖茨比》是美国著名作家弗·斯格特·菲茨杰拉德的作品，被誉为二十世纪最伟大的英文小说之一。小说的主人公盖茨比出身寒微，一次偶然的机会他认识了富家女黛西，两人一见钟情，私订终身，但是黛西背叛了他，嫁给了有钱人汤姆。盖茨比为了赢得爱情，不择手段聚积金钱，但是他的理想最终还是破灭了，最后盖茨比带着残破的梦死去。

障碍词先听为快 Words and Expressions

raft [rɑːft] n. 筏；救生艇；（美）大量 vt. 筏运；制成筏 vi. 乘筏

foam [fəum] n. 泡沫；水沫；灭火泡沫 v. 起泡沫；吐白沫；起着泡沫流动

omnibus ['ɔmnibəs] n. 公共汽车；精选集；文集 adj. 综合性的；总括的

wagon ['wægən] n. 货车，四轮马车 v. 用运货马车运输货物

brisk [brisk] adj. 敏锐的，活泼的，轻快的；凛冽的 v. 活跃起来；变得轻快

corps [kɔː] n. 军团；兵种；兵队；（德国大学的）学生联合会

canvas ['kænvəs] n. 帆布 v. 用帆布覆盖，用帆布装备 adj. 帆布制的

glistening ['gliːsniŋ] adj. 闪亮的；闪耀的；白花花的

pastry ['peistri] n. 油酥点心；面粉糕饼

innuendo [ˌinju'endəu] n. 暗讽，讽刺；影射 v. 暗示，旁敲侧击地表达

好英文娓娓动听 Beautiful stories

There was music from my neighbor's house through the summer nights. In his blue gardens men and girls came and went like moths among the whisperings and the champagne and the stars. At high tide in the afternoon I watched his guests diving from the tower of his raft or taking the sun on the hot sand of his beach while his two motor-boats slit the waters of the Sound, drawing aquaplanes over cataracts of foam. On week-ends his Rolls-Royce became an omnibus, bearing parties to and from the city, between nine in the morning and long past midnight, while his station wagon scampered like a brisk yellow bug to meet all trains. And on Mondays eight servants including an extra gardener toiled all day with mops and scrubbing-brushes and hammers and garden-shears, repairing the ravages of the night before.

Every Friday five crates of oranges and lemons arrived from a fruiterer in New York—every Monday these same oranges and lemons left his back door in a pyramid of pulpless halves. There was a machine in the kitchen which could extract the juice of two hundred oranges in half an hour, if a little button was pressed two hundred times by a butler's thumb.

At least once a fortnight a corps of caterers came down with several hundred feet of canvas and enough colored lights to make a Christmas tree of Gatsby's enormous garden. On buffet tables, garnished with glistening hors-d'oeuvre, spiced baked hams crowded against salads of harlequin designs and pastry pigs and turkeys bewitched to a dark gold.

In the main hall a bar with a real brass rail was set up, and stocked with gins and liquors and with cordials so long forgotten that most of his female guests were too young to know one from another.

By seven o'clock the orchestra has arrived—no thin five-piece affair but a whole pitful of oboes and trombones and saxophones and viols and cornets and piccolos and low and high drums. The last swimmers have come in from the beach now and are dressing upstairs; the cars from New York are parked five deep in the drive, and already the halls and salons and verandas are gaudy with primary colors and hair shorn in strange new ways and shawls beyond the dreams of Castile. The bar is in full swing and floating rounds of cocktails permeate the garden outside until the air is alive with chatter and laughter and casual innuendo and introductions forgotten on the spot and enthusiastic meetings between women who never knew each other's names.

The lights grow brighter as the earth lurches away from the sun and now the orchestra is playing yellow cocktail music and the opera of voices pitches a key higher. Laughter is easier, minute by minute, spilled with prodigality, tipped out at a cheerful word. The groups change more swiftly, swell with new arrivals, dissolve and form in the same breath--already there are wanderers, confident girls who weave here and there among the stouter and more stable, become for a sharp, joyous moment the center of a group and then excited with triumph glide on through the sea-change of faces and voices and color under the constantly changing light.

Suddenly one of these gypsies in trembling opal, seizes a cocktail out of the air, dumps it down for courage and moving her hands like Frisco dances out alone on the canvas platform. A momentary hush; the orchestra leader varies his rhythm obligingly for her and there is a burst of chatter as the erroneous news goes around that she is Gilda Gray's understudy from the "Follies". The party has begun.

长难句解析

There was music from my neighbor's house through the summer nights.

夏日的夜晚邻居家传来阵阵歌声。

from my neighbor's house 做music 的定语，through 引导状语从句。

There was a machine in the kitchen which could extract the juice of two hundred oranges in half an hour, if a little button was pressed two hundred times by a butler's thumb.

厨房里面有一个机器能够在半小时内榨出两百个橙子的汁，如果有人能够一直不断地按开关两百次的话。

extract 榨取，摘录；句中which 引导的定语从句修饰a machine，if引导条件状语从句。

The last swimmers have come in from the beach now and are dressing upstairs.

最后一批游泳者上岸后回到了房间现在正在楼上穿衣服。

the last swimmers 表示最后一批游泳者，the last... 最后一批……

Laughter is easier, minute by minute, spilled with prodigality, tipped out at a cheerful word.

大多数时候欢笑更容易毫无保留地被表现出来，最终成为了一句开心的话语。

prodigality 表示慷慨、丰富；minute by minute 每分每秒。

读书笔记

043 The Wind in the Willows 柳林风声

今日关键语导读 Today's Key Points

《柳林风声》是英国作家肯尼期·格雷厄姆所著的童话故事。主要描写了生活在柳林中的一群小动物的故事，生动地刻画了柳林中萦绕的友谊与温情。

障碍词先听为快 Words and Expressions

immure [i'mjuə] vt. 禁闭，监禁

noisome ['nɔisəm] adj. <文>有害的；有毒的；恶臭的；讨厌的

abandon [ə'bændən] vt/n. 放弃，抛弃；离弃，丢弃；使屈从

hospitable ['hɔspitəbl] adj. 好客的；热情友好的；（气候，环境）宜人的

intelligent [in'telidʒənt] adj. 聪明的；理解力强的；有智力的；[计]智能的

annoyance [ə'nɔiəns] n. 恼怒，烦恼；使人烦恼的事，令人讨厌的人或事

chivalry ['ʃivəlri] n.（中世纪的）骑士制度；骑士气概，骑士品质

scrape [skreip] vt. 擦，刮；擦去；擦伤；挖空

好英文娓娓动听 Beautiful stories

When Toad found himself immured in a dank and noisome

dungeon, and knew that all the grim darkness of a medieval fortress lay between him and the outer world of sunshine and well-metalled high roads where he had lately been so happy, disporting himself as if he had bought up every road in England, he flung himself at full length on the floor, and shed bitter tears, and abandoned himself to dark despair. "This is the end of everything" (he said), "at least it is the end of the career of Toad, which is the same thing; the popular and handsome Toad, the rich and hospitable Toad, the Toad so free and careless and debonair! How can I hope to be ever set at large again" (he said), "who have been imprisoned so justly for stealing so handsome a motor-car in such an audacious manner, and for such lurid and imaginative cheek, bestowed upon such a number of fat, red-faced policemen!" (Here his sobs choked him.) "Stupid animal that I was" (he said), "now I must languish in this dungeon, till people who were proud to say they knew me, have forgotten the very name of Toad! O wise old Badger!" (he said), "O clever, intelligent Rat and sensible Mole! What sound judgments, what knowledge of men and matters you possess! O unhappy and forsaken Toad!" With lamentations such as these he passed his days and nights for several weeks, refusing his meals or intermediate light refreshments, though the grim and ancient gaoler, knowing that Toad's pockets were well lined, frequently pointed out that many comforts, and indeed luxuries, could by arrangement be sent in—at a price—from outside.

Now the gaoler had a daughter, a pleasant wench and good-hearted, who assisted her father in the lighter duties of his post. She was particularly fond of animals, and, besides her canary, whose cage hung on a nail in the massive wall of the keep by day, to the great annoyance of prisoners who relished an after-dinner nap, and was shrouded in an antimacassar on the parlour table at night, she kept several piebald mice and a restless revolving squirrel. This kind-hearted girl, pitying the misery of Toad, said to her father one day, "Father! I can't bear to see that poor beast so unhappy, and getting so thin! You let me have the managing of him. You know how fond of animals I am. I'll make him eat from my hand, and sit up, and do all sorts of things."

Her father replied that she could do what she liked with him. He was tired of Toad, and his sulks and his airs and his meanness. So that day she went on her errand of mercy, and knocked at the door of Toad's cell.

"Now, cheer up, Toad," she said, coaxingly, on entering, "and sit up and dry your eyes and be a sensible animal. And do try and eat a bit of dinner. See, I've brought you some of mine, hot from the oven!"

It was bubble-and-squeak, between two plates, and its fragrance filled the narrow cell. The penetrating smell of cabbage reached the nose of Toad as he lay prostrate in his misery on the floor, and gave him the idea for a moment that perhaps life was not such a blank and desperate thing as he had imagined. But still he wailed, and kicked with his legs, and refused to be comforted. So the wise girl retired for the time, but, of course, a good deal of the smell of hot cabbage remained behind, as it will do, and Toad, between his sobs, sniffed and reflected, and gradually began to think new and inspiring thoughts: of chivalry, and poetry, and deeds still to be done; of broad meadows, and cattle browsing in them, raked by sun and wind; of kitchen-gardens, and straight herb-borders, and warm snap-dragon beset by bees; and of the comforting clink of dishes set down on the table at Toad Hall, and the scrape of chair-legs on the floor as everyone pulled himself close up to his work.

长难句解析

When Toad found himself immured in a dank and noisome dungeon, and knew that all the grim darkness of a medieval fortress lay between him and the outer world of sunshine and well-metalled high roads where he had lately been so happy, disporting himself as if he had bought up every road in England

蟾蜍被关进了一座阴森森臭哄哄的地牢，他知道，一座暗无天日的中世纪城堡，把他和外面的世界隔绝开来了。外面那个世界，阳光灿烂，碎石子道路纵横交错，前不久，他还在那儿尽情玩乐，好不快活，就像全英国的道路都被他买下了似的。

when引导时间状语从句；that引导宾语从句；where引导地点状语从句；as if 仿佛、好像。

"How can I hope to be ever set at large again" (he said), "who have been imprisoned so justly for stealing so handsome a motor-car in such an audacious manner, and for such lurid and imaginative cheek, bestowed upon such a number of fat, red-faced policemen!" (Here his sobs choked him.)

我胆大妄为，偷了人家一辆漂亮汽车，又厚着脸皮，粗暴无礼，对一大帮红脸膛的胖警察胡说八道，坐牢是我罪有应得，哪还有获释的希望！

how引导了一个感叹句；此处have been done 是现在完成时；a number of 许多、大量。

Now the gaoler had a daughter, a pleasant wench and good-hearted, who assisted her father in the lighter duties of his post.

这狱卒有个女儿，她是位心肠慈善的可爱姑娘。在监狱里帮着父亲干点轻便杂活。

who引导定语从句；assist sb in（doing）sth 帮助某人做某事。

So that day she went on her errand of mercy, and knocked at the door of Toad's cell.

于是有一天，她去做善事，敲开了蟾蜍囚室的门。

errand此处做“使命、差事”理解；knock at the door of 意为敲……的门。

"Now, cheer up, Toad," she said, coaxingly, on entering, "and sit up and dry your eyes and be a sensible animal."

"好啦。蟾蜍，打起精神来，"她一进门就说："坐起来，擦干眼泪，做个懂事的动物。

cheer up 多意为打起精神，振作精神；sit up固定搭配，做起来。

The penetrating smell of cabbage reached the nose of Toad as he lay prostrate in his misery on the floor, and gave him the idea for a moment that perhaps life was not such a blank and desperate thing as he had imagined.

蟾蜍正惨兮兮地伸开四肢躺在地上，卷心菜那股浓烈的香味钻进了他的鼻孔，一时间使他感到，生活也许还不像他想象的那样空虚绝望。

as表示当……的时候，引导时间状语从句；that引导同位语从句，解释idea的内容。

读书笔记

044 Robinson Crusoe 鲁宾逊漂流记

今日关键语导读 Today's Key Points

《鲁宾逊漂流记》是18世纪英国作家达尼尔·笛福的代表作品，也是一部具有广泛世界性影响的作品。小说讲述了1704年一名苏格兰水手亚历山大·薛里基洛克航海遇险，漂流在一个荒岛上，并且单独留居了四年才被救回。小说的主人公鲁宾逊是一名青年，性喜冒险。他不顾父亲的劝阻，决心要进行航海。开始几次的航海颇为顺利，但有一次为土耳其海盗所俘，幸而不久后逃脱至巴西经营蔗糖厂。四年后，他因获暴利又前往非洲贩卖黑奴，却在大海中遇险，船上全部船员葬身鱼腹，仅鲁宾逊一人脱难，漂流至一荒岛上。从此，他孤独一人在岛上生活，直到二十八年后一艘英国船航经荒岛，他才有机会搭船回国。

障碍词先听为快 Words and Expressions

vicissitude [vi'sisitjuːd] n. 变迁

extravagance [ik'strævəgəns] n. 挥霍，奢侈品，夸大其词，奢华

handmaid ['hændmeid] n. 女仆，起辅助作用的人或事

harass ['hærəs] vt. 不断骚扰，烦扰，恐吓

enrage [in'reidʒ] vt. 激怒

precipitate [pri'sipiteit] vt. 引发，加速，抛下，抛出，沉淀

venture ['ventʃə] n. 企业，探索，冒险旅行

hereafter [hiər'ɑːftə] n. 死后的生活 adv. 此后

He bade me observe it, and I should always find that the calamities of life were shared among the upper and lower part of mankind, but that the middle station had the fewest disasters, and was not exposed to so many vicissitudes as the higher or lower part of mankind; nay, they were not subjected to so many distempers and uneasinesses, either of body or mind, as those were who, by vicious living, luxury, and extravagances on the one hand, or by hard labour, want of necessaries, and mean or insufficient diet on the other hand, bring distemper upon themselves by the natural consequences of their way of living; that the middle station of life was calculated for all kind of virtue and all kind of enjoyments; that peace and plenty were the handmaids of a middle fortune; that temperance, moderation, quietness, health, society, all agreeable diversions, and all desirable pleasures, were the blessings attending the middle station of life; that this way men went silently and smoothly through the world, and comfortably out of it, not embarrassed with the labours of the hands or of the head, not sold to a life of slavery for daily bread, nor harassed with perplexed circumstances, which rob the soul of peace and the body of rest, nor enraged with the passion of envy, or the secret burning lust of ambition for great things; but, in easy circumstances, sliding gently through the world, and sensibly tasting the sweets of living, without the bitter; feeling that they are happy, and learning by every day's experience to know it more sensibly.

After this he pressed me earnestly, and in the most

affectionate manner, not to play the young man, nor to precipitate myself into miseries which nature, and the station of life I was born in, seemed to have provided against; that I was under no necessity of seeking my bread; that he would do well for me, and endeavour to enter me fairly into the station of life which he had just been recommending to me; and that if I was not very easy and happy in the world, it must be my mere fate or fault that must hinder it; and that he should have nothing to answer for, having thus discharged his duty in warning me against measures which he knew would be to my hurt; in a word, that as he would do very kind things for me if I would stay and settle at home as he directed, so he would not have so much hand in my misfortunes as to give me any encouragement to go away; and to close all, he told me I had my elder brother for an example, to whom he had used the same earnest persuasions to keep him from going into the Low County wars, but could not prevail, his young desires prompting him to run into the army, where he was killed; and though he said he would not cease to pray for me, yet he would venture to stay to me, that if I did take this follish step, God would not bless me, and I should have leisure hereafter to reflect upon having neglected his counsel when there might be none to assit in my recovery.

长难句解析

Nay, they were not subjected to so many distempers and uneasinesses, either of body or mind, as those were who, by vicious living, luxury, and extravagances on the one hand, or by hard labour, want of necessaries, and mean or insufficient diet on the other hand, bring distemper upon themselves by the natural consequences of their way of living.

不仅如此，他们并没有遭受到那么多的病痛与不安，无论是身体上还是思想上。因为那些人一方面体验过凶狠的生活方式并且挥霍过奢侈品，生活铺张浪费；另一方面要么通过苦力，得到自己想要的生活必需品，三餐要么刚好满足温饱，要么吃了上顿没有下顿。他们这种生活方式因受到自然的影响而将瘟热病带入了他们的生活。

be subjected to 意为“遭遇、遭受”；either or 意为“要么……要么……”；as后面引导原因状语从句；on the one hand，“一方面”；on the other hand“另一方面”。

That this way men went silently and smoothly through the world, and comfortably out of it, not embarrassed with the labours of the hands or of the head, not sold to a life of slavery for daily bread, nor harassed with perplexed circumstances, which rod the soul of peace and the body of rest, nor enraged with the passion of envy, or the secret burning lust of ambition for great things.

那么，以这种生活方式的人将默默无闻地并且平淡的度过一生，最后安逸地离开这个世界。因为他们不会因为是从事体力工作或者脑力工作而感到羞耻；不会为了一日三餐而成为生活的奴隶；也不会因为陷入那打破了内心的宁静和身体上的安逸的困境而自扰；更不会因为强烈的嫉妒而生气；也不会因为一些小想法而放弃自己的伟大理想。

not后面接的是省略主语和谓语动词的并列状语从句；which引导非限定性定语从句；be embarrassed with对……感到羞耻。

And that he should have nothing to answer for, having thus discharged his duty in warning me against measures which he knew would be my hurt.

而且他不用对任何事负责，因此也就无需警告我关于那些会对我造成伤害的举措。

that引导主语从句；which引导定语从句。

读书笔记

045 Anne of Green Gables 绿山墙的安妮

今日关键语导读 Today's Key Points

作品讲述了自幼失去父母的主人公小安妮，阴差阳错地被马修兄妹收养后，在美丽僻静的绿山墙农舍生活并成长的感人故事。在绿山墙农舍，天真热情的安妮经受了挑剔的眼光，也因酷爱想象惹来了许多麻烦，但在家人、朋友、老师的关爱下，聪明的安妮不断充实自己，完善自己，并渐渐成为绿山墙真正的主人。

障碍词先听为快 Words and Expressions

bald [bɔːld] a. 光秃的，秃顶的；单调的；无装饰的 vi. 变秃

bald facts 简单的事实

inculcate [in'kʌlkeit] vt. 教育；谆谆教诲

grasp the thistle 挺身应付难局

parlor ['paːlə] n. 客厅；起居室 a. 客厅的；只会空谈而无实际行动的

scrawny ['skrɔːni] a. 骨瘦如柴的

scrawny records 出版者

scrub [skrʌb] n. 矮小的人 a. 矮小的；临时凑合的；次等的

wit [wit] n. 智慧

at one's wits' end 智穷技尽

sawmill ['sɔːmil] n. 锯木厂，锯木机

"No, I don't want any of your imaginings. Just you stick to bald facts. Begin at the beginning. Where were you born and how old are you?"

"I was eleven last March," said Anne, resigning herself to bald facts with a little sigh. "And I was born in Bolingbroke, Nova Scotia. My father's name was Walter Shirley, and he was a teacher in the Bolingbroke High School. My mother's name was Bertha Shirley. Aren't Walter and Bertha lovely names? I'm so glad my parents had nice names. It would be a real disgrace to have a father named—well, say Jedediah, wouldn't it?"

"I guess it doesn't matter what a person's name is as long as he behaves himself," said Marilla, feeling herself called upon to inculcate a good and useful moral.

"Well, I don't know." Anne looked thoughtful. "I read in a book once that a rose by any other name would smell as sweet, but I've never been able to believe it. I don't believe a rose would be as nice if it was called a thistle or a skunk cabbage. I suppose my father could have been a good man even if he had been called Jedediah; but I'm sure it would have been a cross. Well, my mother was a teacher in the High school, too, but when she married father she gave up teaching, of course. A husband was enough responsibility. Mrs. Thomas said that they were a pair of babies and as poor as church mice. They went to live in a weeny-teeny little yellow house in Bolingbroke. I've never seen that house, but I've imagined it thousands of times. I think it must have had honeysuckle over the parlor window and lilacs in the front yard and lilies of the valley just inside the gate. Yes, and muslin curtains in all the windows. Muslin curtains give a house such an air. I was born in that house. Mrs. Thomas said I was the homeliest baby she ever saw, I was so scrawny and tiny and nothing but eyes, but that mother thought I was perfectly beautiful. I should think a mother would be a better judge than a poor woman who came in to scrub, wouldn't you? I'm glad she was satisfied with me anyhow, I would feel so sad if I thought I was a disappointment to her—because she didn't live very long after that, you see. She died of fever when I was just three months old. I do wish she'd lived long enough for me to remember calling her mother. I think it would be so sweet to say `mother, don't you? And father died four days afterwards from fever too. That left me an orphan and folks were at their wits' end, so Mrs. Thomas said, what to do with me. You see, nobody wanted me even then. It seems to be my fate. Father and mother had both come from places far away and it was well known they hadn't any relatives living. Finally Mrs. Thomas said she'd take me, though she was poor and had a drunken husband. She brought me up by hand. Do you know if there is anything in being brought up by hand that ought to make people who are brought up that way better than other people? Because whenever I was naughty Mrs. Thomas would ask me how I could be such a bad girl when she had brought me up by hand— reproachful-like.

"Mr. and Mrs. Thomas moved away from Bolingbroke to Marysville, and I lived with them until I was eight years old. I helped look after the Thomas children—there were four of them younger than me—and I can tell you they took a lot of looking after. Then Mr. Thomas was killed falling under a train and his mother offered to take Mrs. Thomas and the children, but she didn't want me. Mrs. Thomas was at HER wits' end, so she said, what to do with me. Then Mrs. Hammond from up the river came down and said she'd take me, seeing I was handy with children, and I went up the river to live with her in a little clearing among the stumps. It was a very lonesome place. I'm sure I could never have lived there if I hadn't had an imagination. Mr. Hammond worked a little sawmill up there, and Mrs. Hammond had eight children. She had twins three times. I like babies in moderation, but twins three times in succession is too much. I told Mrs. Hammond so firmly, when the last pair came. I used to get so dreadfully tired carrying them about.

长难句解析

"I was eleven last March," said Anne, resigning herself to bald facts with a little sigh.

安妮说，我三月份刚满十一岁，她轻轻地叹了一口气，接受了这个简单的事实。

resign 有"屈从于"的意思，resign oneself to 表示顺从。

"I guess it doesn't matter what a person's name is as long as he behaves himself," said Marilla, feeling herself called upon to inculcate a good and useful moral.

马瑞拉说：“我认为一个人只要能够做好自己，那么他的名字是什么并不那么重要。”她感觉自己被委任去培育一个善良有用的灵魂。

as long as 表示只要……；call upon 指召唤；feeling 一句做伴随状语。

A husband was enough responsibility. Mrs. Thomas said that they were a pair of babies and as poor as church mice.

作为一个丈夫他已经足够负责了。托马斯夫人说这是一对双胞胎，家里一贫如洗。

that引导宾语从句；a pair of 一双、一对；as poor as church mouse 一贫如洗。

Mrs. Thomas said I was the homeliest baby she ever saw, I was so scrawny and tiny and nothing but eyes, but that mother thought I was perfectly beautiful.

托马斯夫人说我是她遇见过的最简朴的孩子，还说我瘦到只剩下眼睛，但是妈妈认为我特别漂亮。

nothing but 只有，只不过；本句said 后跟两个宾语从句，that 省略。

I'm glad she was satisfied with me anyhow, I would feel so sad if I thought I was a disappointment to her—because she didn't live very long after that, you see.

我很高兴她对我如此满意，如果我曾令她沮丧的话我会感到无比的悲伤，因为，如你所知，她在那不久就去世了。

be satisfied with...，“对……感到满意”；if引导条件状语从句；be a disappointment to sb 令某人感到沮丧。

读书笔记

046 The Wonderful Wizard of Oz 绿野仙踪

今日关键语导读 Today's Key Points

《绿野仙踪》讲的是善良的小姑娘多萝茜被一阵龙卷风刮到了一个陌生而神奇的国度——奥慈国，并迷失了回家的路。在那里，她陆续结识了没有脑子的稻草人、没有心脏的铁皮人和十分胆小的狮子，他们为了实现各自的愿望，互相帮助，携手协作，历经艰险，遇到许多稀奇古怪的事情。最终，他们凭借自己非凡的智能和顽强的毅力，都如愿以偿地完成了自己的心愿。

障碍词先听为快 Words and Expressions

dew [djuː] n. 珠，露水；清新 vt.（露水等）弄湿

chop [tʃɔp] n. 砍，排骨；商标，削球 vt. 剁碎

roast [rəust] n. 烤肉，烘烤 adj. 烘烤的 vt. 烤

peculiar [pi'kjuːljə] n. 特权，特有财产 adj. 特殊的，独特的

awkward ['ɔːkwəd] adj. 尴尬的，笨拙的，棘手的，不合适的

clumsy ['klʌmzi] adj. 笨拙的，不得当的

straw [strɔː] n. 稻草，吸管，一文不值的东西

snug [snʌg] adj. 舒适的，温暖的 n. 雅室

好英文娓娓动听 Beautiful stories

They were obliged to camp out that night under a large tree

in the forest, for there were no houses near. The tree made a good, thick covering to protect them from the dew, and the Tin Woodman chopped a great pile of wood with his axe and Dorothy built a splendid fire that warmed her and made her feel less lonely. She and Toto ate the last of their bread, and now she did not know what they would do for breakfast.

"If you wish," said the Lion, "I will go into the forest and kill a deer for you. You can roast it by the fire, since your tastes are so peculiar that you prefer cooked food, and then you will have a very good breakfast."

"Don't! Please don't," begged the Tin Woodman. "I should certainly weep if you killed a poor deer, and then my jaws would rust again."

But the Lion went away into the forest and found his own supper, and no one ever knew what it was, for he didn't mention it. And the Scarecrow found a tree full of nuts and filled Dorothy's basket with them, so that she would not be hungry for a long time. She thought this was very kind and thoughtful of the Scarecrow, but she laughed heartily at the awkward way in which the poor creature picked up the nuts. His padded hands were so clumsy and the nuts were so small that he dropped almost as many as he put in the basket. But the Scarecrow did not mind how long it took him to fill the basket, for it enabled him to keep away from the fire, as he feared a spark might get into his straw and burn him up. So he kept a good distance away from the flames, and only came near to cover Dorothy with dry leaves when she lay down to sleep. These kept her very snug and warm, and she slept soundly until morning.

When it was daylight, the girl bathed her face in a little rippling brook, and soon after they all started toward the Emerald City.

长难句解析

They were obliged to camp out that night under a large tree in the forest, for there were no houses near.

那天夜里，他们不得不露宿在森林中的一棵大树底下，因为附近没有一间屋子。

be obliged to“感谢，被迫做，不得不做”；be not obliged to do“不是一定要做某事”。camp out野营，露营，到野外露营；for在这里引导原因状语从句。

And the Scarecrow found a tree full of nuts and filled Dorothy's basket with them, so that she would not be hungry for a long time.

稻草人寻到一棵长满了坚果的树。他就摘下坚果，装满了多萝茜的篮子，这样她在一段时间内就不会觉得饥饿了。

full of 充满、富有、充盈，其后的句子作后置定语修饰a tree；so that 在这引导目的状语从句。

His padded hands were so clumsy and the nuts were so small that he dropped almost as many as he put in the basket.

他那填塞着稻草的手很不灵巧，坚果又这么小，使他落掉了的坚果和放进篮子里的一样多。

so...that...，如此……以致于……；as...as... 像……一样。

These kept her very snug and warm, and she slept soundly until morning.

这些树叶子，使她觉得十分舒适和温暖，一直酣睡到早晨。

these在这里指代上文提到的leaves；sleep soundly= sound sleep“酣睡”。

When it was daylight, the girl bathed her face in a little rippling brook, and soon after they all started toward the Emerald City.

天亮了，小女孩醒来起身，在一条水声潺潺的小河里洗过脸后，立刻和大家一块儿动身，向翡翠城进发。

when引导时间状语从句；bath沐浴、洗澡，bath face=wash face“洗脸”，如：Blacken easily with cold bath face? 用冷水洗脸容易变黑吗?

047 Macbeth 麦克白

今日关键语导读 Today's Key Points

苏格兰国王邓肯的表弟麦克白将军，为国王平叛和抵御入侵立功归来，路上遇到三个女巫。女巫对他说了一些预言和隐语，说他将进爵为王，但他并无子嗣能继承王位，反而是同僚班柯将军的后代要做王。麦克白是有野心的英雄，他在夫人的怂恿下谋杀邓肯，做了国王。为掩人耳目和防止他人夺位，他一步步害死了邓肯的侍卫，害死了班柯，害死了贵族麦克德夫的妻子和小孩。恐惧和猜疑使麦克白越来越冷酷。麦克白夫人因神经失常而自杀，对他也是一大刺激。在众叛亲离的情况下，麦克白面对邓肯之子和他请来的英格兰援军的围攻，落得枭首的下场。

障碍词先听为快 Words and Expressions

volume ['vɔljuːm] n. 量；体积；卷；音量；大量；册 adj. 大量的

trifle ['traifl] n. 琐事；蛋糕；少量 vi. 开玩笑；闲混；嘲弄

predominance [pri'dɔminəns] n. 优势；卓越

entomb [in'tuːm] vt. 埋葬；成为……的坟墓

beauteous ['bjuːtjəs] adj. 美丽的；美妙的

stall [stɔːl] n. 货摊；畜栏；托辞 vi. 停止，停转；拖延

sovereignty ['sɔvrinti] n. 主权；主权国家；君主；独立国

obedience [ə'biːdjəns,ə'biːdiəns] n. 顺从；服从；遵守

benison ['benizn] n. 祝福

dreadful ['dredful] adj. 可怕的；糟透的，令人不快的

好英文娓娓动听 Beautiful stories

Old Man: Threescore and ten I can remember well: within the volume of which time I have seen hours dreadful and things strange; but this sore night hath trifled former knowings.

ROSS: Ah, good father, thou seest, the heavens, as troubled with man's act, threaten his bloody stage: by the clock, 'tis day, and yet dark night strangles the travelling lamp: Isn't night's predominance, or the day's shame, that darkness does the face of earth entomb, when living light should kiss it ?

Old Man: 'Tis unnatural, even like the deed that's done. On Tuesday last, A falcon, towering in her pride of place, was by a mousing owl hawk'd at and kill'd.

ROSS: And Duncan's horses-a thing most strange and certain-beauteous and swift, the minions of their race, turn'd wild in nature, broke their stalls, flung out, contending 'gainst obedience, as they would make, war with mankind.

Old Man: 'Tis said they eat each other.

ROSS: They did so, to the amazement of mine eyes, that look'd upon't. here comes the good Macduff.

[Enter MACDUFF]

How goes the world, sir, now?

MACDUFF: Why, see you not?

ROSS: It's know who did this more than bloody deed?

MACDUFF: Those that Macbeth hath slain.

ROSS: Alas, the day! What good could they pretend?

MACDUFF: They were suborn'd: Malcolm and Donalbain, the king's two sons, are stol'n away and fled; which puts upon them suspicion of the deed.

ROSS: 'Gainst nature still! Thriftless ambition, that wilt ravin up thine own life's means! Then'tis most like the sovereignty will fall upon Macbeth.

MACDUFF: He is already named, and gone to Scone to be invested

ROSS: Where is Duncan's body?

MACDUFF: Carried to Colmekill, the sacred storehouse of his predecessors, and guardian of their bones.

ROSS: Will you to Scone ?

MACDUFF: No, cousin, I'll to Fife.

ROSS: Well, I will thither.

MACDUFF: Well, may you see things well done there: adieu! lest our old robes sit easier than our new!

ROSS: Farewell, father.

Old Man: God's benison go with you; and with those that would make good of bad, and friends of foes !

长难句解析

Threescore and ten I can remember well: within the volume of which time I have seen hours dreadful and things strange; but this sore night hath trifled former knowings.

七十年岁月历历如在眼前，风风雨雨，什么糟心的事儿、千奇百怪事儿没见过；可今夜的惨事还是头一遭见。

which引导定语从句

Ah, good father, thou seest, the heavens, as troubled with man's act, threaten his bloody stage: by the clock,'t is day, and yet dark night strangles the travelling lamp: Is't night's predominance, or the day's shame, that darkness does the face of earth entomb, when living light should kiss it.

啊，好老爹，你看啊，老天爷对人类的行为厌烦了，向着这血淋淋的舞台发出了威胁。按钟点算，此时该是白天了，然而沉沉黑夜却将那天空中运行的明灯遮了个严严实实。难道是夜统治了一切，或是白昼感到了羞愧，以至于本该火辣辣的阳光亲吻大地时，黑漆漆的夜却笼罩了一切？

when引导时间状语从句。

Tis unnatural, even like the deed that's done. On Tuesday last, A falcon, towering in her pride of place, was by a mousing owl hawk'd at and kill'd.

这是反常的，就像那桩谋杀案一样。上星期二，一只隼高高翱翔在空中，却被一只吃耗子的猫头鹰扑过来，啄死了。

towering作伴随状语。

They were suborn'd: Malcolm and Donalbain, the king's two sons, are stol'n away and fled; which puts upon them suspicion of the deed.

他们是受人指使：国王的两个儿子马尔康和道纳本偷偷摸摸地逃跑了，这就使他们受到了怀疑。

which引导定语从句，代指前面整句话。

God's benison go with you; and with those that would make good of bad, and friends of foes !

上帝保佑您，也保佑那些化恶为善、化敌为友的人！

make good of充分利用；that引导定语从句

读书笔记

048 The Catcher in the Rye 麦田里的守望者

今日关键语导读 Today's Key Points

《麦田里的守望者》是美国作家杰罗姆·大卫·塞林格的唯一一本长篇小说。故事的主人公是16岁的中学生霍尔顿·考尔菲德，霍尔顿出身于纽约一个富裕的中产阶级家庭，学校里的老师和自己的家长强迫他好好读书，为的是出人头地，而他看不惯周围的一切，根本没心思用功读书，因而老是挨罚。当他第四次被开除时，他不敢回家？便只身在美国最繁华的纽约城游荡了一天两夜。本书反映了现代美国社会中各种微妙的人际关系，描述了主人公在心灵上的压抑与生活中的孤独。

障碍词先听为快 Words and Expressions

dough [dəu] n. [俚语]钱，金钱，货币，现钞

terrific [tə'rifik] adj. 极好的；极其的，非常的；可怕的

slap [slæp] v. 掴；拍击

phony ['fəuni] n. [美国口语] 骗子；假冒者；伪造者

rye [rai] n. 黑麦

cliff [klif] n. 悬崖；绝壁

belch [beltʃ] v. 打嗝；喷出

catcher ['kætʃ] n. 捕手；接球员；捕捉者；捕捉器

"Lawyers are all right, I guess—but it doesn't appeal to me," I said. "I mean they're all right if they go around saving innocent guys' lives all the time, and like that, but you don't do that kind of stuff if you're a lawyer. All you do is make a lot of dough and play golf and play bridge and buy cars and drink Martinis and look like a hot-shot. And besides. Even if you did go around saving guys' lives and all, how would you know if you did it because you really wanted to save guys' lives, or because you did it because what you really wanted to do was be a terrific lawyer, with everybody slapping you on the back and congratulating you in court when the goddam trial was over, the reporters and everybody, the way it is in the dirty movies? How would you know you weren't being a phony? The trouble is, you wouldn't."

I'm not too sure old Phoebe knew what the hell I was talking about. I mean she's only a little child and all. But she was listening, at least. If somebody at least listens, it's not too bad.

"Daddy's going to kill you. He's going to kill you," she said.

I wasn't listening, though. I was thinking about something else—something crazy. "You know what I'd like to be?" I said. "You know what I'd like to be? I mean if I had my goddam choice?"

"What? Stop swearing."

"You know that song 'If a body catch a body comin' through the rye'? I'd like—"

"It's 'If a body meet a body coming through the rye'!" old Phoebe said. "It's a poem. By Robert Burns."

"I know it's a poem by Robert Burns."

She was right, though. It is "If a body meet a body coming through the rye." I didn't know it then, though.

"I thought it was 'If a body catch a body,'" I said. "Anyway, I keep picturing all these little kids playing some game in this big field of rye and all. Thousands of little kids, and nobody's around—nobody big, I mean—except me. And I'm standing on the edge of some crazy cliff. What I have to do, I have to catch everybody if they start to go over the cliff—I mean if they're running and they don't look where they're going I have to come out from somewhere and catch them. That's all I'd do all day. I'd just be the catcher in the rye and all. I know it's crazy, but that's the only thing I'd really like to be. I know it's crazy."

Old Phoebe didn't say anything for a long time. Then, when she said something, all she said was, "Daddy's going to kill you."

"I don't give a damn if he does," I said. I got up from the bed then, because what I wanted to do, I wanted to phone up this guy that was my English teacher at Elkton Hills, Mr. Antolini. He lived in New York now. He quit Elkton Hills. He took this job teaching English at N.Y.U. "I have to make a phone call," I told Phoebe. "I'll be right back. Don't go to sleep." I didn't want her to go to sleep while I was in the living room. I knew she wouldn't but I said it anyway, just to make sure.

While I was walking toward the door, old Phoebe said, "Holden!" and I turned around.

She was sitting way up in bed. She looked so pretty. "I'm taking belching lessons from this girl, Phyllis Margulies," she said. "Listen."

I listened, and I heard something, but it wasn't much. "Good," I said. Then I went out in the living room and called up this teacher I had, Mr. Antolini.

长难句解析

"I thought it was 'If a body catch a body,'" I said. "Anyway, I keep picturing all these little kids playing some game in this big field of rye and all. Thousands of little kids, and nobody's around—nobody big, I mean—except me. And I'm standing on the edge of some crazy cliff. What I have to do, I have to catch everybody if they start to go over the cliff—I mean if they're running and they don't look where they're going I have to come out from somewhere and catch them. That's all I'd do all day. I'd just be the catcher in the rye and all. I know it's crazy, but that's the only thing I'd really like to be. I know it's crazy."

"我还以为是'你要是在麦田里捉住我'呢，"我说，"不管怎样，我老是在想象，有那么一群小孩子在一大块麦田里做游戏。几千几万个小孩子，附近没有一个人——没有一个大人，我是说——除了我。我呢，就站在那混账的悬崖边。我的职务是在那儿守望，要是有哪个孩子往悬崖边奔来，我就把他捉住——我是说孩子们都在狂奔，也不知道自己是在往哪儿跑，我得从什么地方出来，把他们捉住。我整天就干这样的事。我只想当个麦田的守望者。我知道这有点异想天开，可我真正喜欢干的就是这个。我知道这有些疯狂。"

多次出现以if引导的条件状语从句，表假设虚拟。

Old Phoebe didn't say anything for a long time. Then, when she said something, all she said was, "Daddy's going to kill you.

老菲比有好一会儿没有说话。后来她开口了，可她说了句："你爸爸会要了你的命。"

for 后接时间段表示持续的时间；be going to do sth将要做某事。

While I was walking toward the door, old Phoebe said, "Holden!" and I turned around.

我正朝着门边走去，忽然听见老菲比喊了声"霍尔顿！"我马上转过身去。

while引导的时间状语从句，表示正在进行的动作；turn around 转身。

读书笔记

049 The Opal Deception 猫眼的诡计

今日关键语导读 Today's Key Points

《猫眼的诡计》是作家欧因·科弗所著的阿特米斯奇幻历险系列的第四部。讲述了主人公阿特米斯失去了对仙人国的回忆，又回到了他原来的生活轨迹，却准备从德国银行拿到一幅著名的印象派油画，却还不知道自己的宿敌奥珀尔从监狱里逃出来了，并开始向那些使她入狱的人复仇，当然，其中也包括阿特米斯。

障碍词先听为快 Words and Expressions

utterly ['ʌtəli] adv. 完全地，绝对地，全然地，彻底地，十足地

congested [kən'dʒestid] adj. 堵塞的，拥挤的； v. 挤满，超负荷（congest的过去分词）

privacy ['praivəsi] n. 隐私，秘密，隐居，隐居处

acquisition [ˌækwi'ziʃən] n. 获得物，获得

prosthetic [prɔs'θetik] adj. 假体的

physiotherapy [ˌfiziəu'θerəpi] n. 物理疗法

subterfuge ['sʌbtəfjuːdʒ] n. 托词，借口，诡计

justifiable ['dʒʌstifaiəbl] adj. 可辩解的，有道理的，可证明为正当的

surveillance [səː'veiləns] n. 监督，监视

gossamer ['gɔsəmə] n. 蛛丝；薄纱；小蜘蛛网 adj. 轻飘飘的；薄弱的

Munich during working hours was like any other major city in the world: utterly congested. In spite of the U-bahn, an efficient and comfortable rail system, the general population preferred the privacy and comfort of their own cars, with the result that Artemis and Butler were stuck on the airport road in a rush-hour traffic jam that stretched all the way from the International Bank to the Kronski Hotel.

Master Artemis did not like delays. But today he was too focused on his latest acquisition, The Fairy Thief, still sealed in its Perspex tube. Artemis itched to open it, but the previous owners, Sparrow and Crane, could have somehow booby-trapped the container.

"He is wonderful, gushed Angeline."I am surprised how well he is. That prosthetic leg of his is marvelous, and so is his outlook. He never complains. I honestly think that he's got a better attitude toward life now than he did before he lost his leg. He's under the care of a remarkable therapist, who says the mental is far more important than the physical. In fact, we leave for the private spa in Westmeath this evening. They use this marvelous seaweed treatment, which should do wonders for your father's muscles."

"Is he doing his physiotherapy exercises twice a day?"

Angeline laughed again, and suddenly Artemis wished he were home.

Artemis didn't know how to reply. Half of him wanted to point out that there really would be no family business if it weren't for him secretly safeguarding it. The other half of him wanted to get on a plane home and wander the grounds with his family.

"Whatever you like. I know bugs are uncomfortable, but it's better than a dose of food poisoning. You could have been laid low for weeks. Drink plenty of water, and try to sleep."

The first task was to deflect any inquiries from the school as to his activities. He would need at least two days to authenticate the painting, as some of the tests would need to be contracted out.

It was a harmless lie. Butler would escort him home, and his education would not suffer through a few days' absence. As for stealing The Fairy Thief, theft from thieves was not real crime. It was almost justifiable.

He did so, carefully slitting the seal with a craft knife. Artemis put on a set of surgical gloves and teased the painting from the cylinder. It plopped onto the table in a tight roll, but sprung loose almost immediately. It hadn't been in the tube long enough to retain the shape. Artemis spread the canvas wide, weighing the corners with smooth gel sacs. He knew immediately that this was no fake. His eye for art took in the primary colors and layered brushwork. Herve's figures seemed to be composed of light. So beautifully were they painted that the picture seemed to sparkle. It was exquisite. In the picture a swaddled baby slept in its sun-drenched cot near an open window. A fairy with green skin and gossamer wings had alighted on the windowsill and was preparing to snatch the baby from its cradle. Both of the creature's feet were on the outside of the sill.

长难句解析

He's under the care of a remarkable therapist, who says the mental is far more important than the physical. In fact, we leave for the private spa in Westmeath this evening.

他受一个了不起的、认为精神比物质更重要的治疗师的照顾。事实上，我们今晚要动身去Westmeath的一个私人温泉。

under the care of 在……的照顾下；who引导定语从句，修饰therapist；more...than 比……更多；in fact，事实上、实际上。

Half of him wanted to point out that there really would be no family business if it weren't for him secretly safeguarding it. The other half of him wanted to get on a plane home and wander the grounds with his family.

他一边想说如果没有他的暗中保护就绝不会有家族企业，一边又希望能坐飞机回家和家人一起漫步。

if it weren't for him 为对现在的假设，但表示假设时，be动词只能用were，否定直接在be动词后加not 。

You could have been laid low for weeks. Drink plenty of water, and try to sleep.

你本可以休息几周的。多喝水，试着睡一觉。

could have done意为“本可以做某事”；第二句动词开头，为祈使句。

He would need at least two days to authenticate the painting, as some of the tests would need to be contracted out.

他至少需要两天鉴定那幅画，比如有些测试需要进行。

“would”表推测；“need to be done”意为“需要被做……”。

So beautifully were they painted that the picture seemed to sparkle. It was exquisite. In the picture a swaddled baby slept in its sun-drenched cot near an open window.

他们画得如此漂亮，那幅画看起来似乎在闪闪发光。它很精致。画中阳光普照，一个襁褓中的宝宝正睡在靠近一扇开着的窗户的床上。

“so...that...”意为“如此……以至于……”；exquisite 精致的，精妙，玲珑。

050 The Secret Garden 秘密花园

今日关键语导读 Today's Key Points

《秘密花园》是美国作家弗朗西丝·霍奇森·伯内特最成功的一部小说。小说主人公玛丽·伦诺克斯是一个自私而且被宠坏了的小孩子。经历变故之后的玛丽被送去与舅舅同住，讨厌这一切的玛丽意外地在知更鸟的帮助下找到了秘密花园的大门和钥匙，并且，她还听到了一个神秘的哭声，吸引着她去探索庄园之谜。最终，玛丽在迪肯的帮助下，使荒芜的花园重现生机。

障碍词先听为快 Words and Expressions

coax [kəuks] *v.* 哄，用好话劝诱，哄骗，轻轻地弄好

robin ['rɔbin] *n.* 知更鸟

perennial [pə'renjəl] *n.* 多年生的，四季不断的

shrub [ʃrʌb] *n.* 灌木丛

freshly ['freʃli] *adv.* 刚刚地，新近地

mole [məul] *n.* 鼹鼠

rust [rʌst] *adj.* 生锈的

brass [brɑːs] *n.* 黄铜

frightened ['frait(ə)nd] *v.* 害怕；使吃惊 *adj.* 害怕的；受惊的

whisper ['(h)wispə] *n.* 私语；谣传；飒飒的声音 *vi.* 耳语；密谈

She chirped, and talked, and coaxed and he hopped and flirted his tail and twittered. It was as if he were talking. His red waistcoat was like satin and he puffed his tiny breast out and was so fine and so grand and so pretty that it was really as if he were showing her how important and like a human person a robin could be. Mistress Mary forgot that she had ever been contrary in her life when he allowed her to draw closer and closer to him, and bend down and talk and try to make something like robin sounds.

Oh! To think that he should actually let her come as near to him as that! He knew nothing in the world would make her put out her hand toward him or startle him in the least tiniest way. He knew it because he was a real person—only nicer than any other person in the world. She was so happy that she scarcely dared to breathe.

The flower-bed was not quite bare. It was bare of flowers because the perennial plants had been cut down for their winter rest, but there were tall shrubs and low ones which grew together at the back of the bed, and as the robin hopped about under them she saw him hop over a small pile of freshly turned up earth. He stopped on it to look for a worm. The earth had been turned up because a dog had been trying to dig up a mole and he had scratched quite a deep hole.

Mary looked at it, not really knowing why the hole was there, and as she looked she saw something almost buried in the newly-turned soil. It was something like a ring of rusty iron or brass and when the robin flew up into a tree nearby she put out her hand and picked the ring up. It was more than a ring, however; it was an old key which looked as if it had been buried a long time.

Mistress Mary stood up and looked at it with an almost frightened face as it hung from her finger.

"Perhaps it has been buried for ten years," she said in a whisper. "Perhaps it is the key to the garden!"

长难句解析

The flower-bed was not quite bare. It was bare of flowers because the perennial plants had been cut down for their winter rest, but there were tall shrubs and low ones which grew together at the back of the bed, and as the robin hopped about under them she saw him hop over a small pile of freshly turned up earth.

花坛并不完全寸草不生。之所以没有花，是因为到了冬天，花坛内的植物花草变得干枯凋零，都被锄掉了，但在花坛的后面还生长着高高低低的灌木丛。知更鸟蹿进了灌木丛里，紧接着，玛丽看到它跃过一小堆刚刚翻新过的土堆。

在but引导的并列句中，有which引导的定语从句，其后又是由as引导的时间状语从句。句子偏长但结构不是很复杂，需要先细心找出主干以及并列句，然后再翻译过程中注意调整句式逻辑顺序和结构。earth 在此处不能理解为“地球”而是“泥土”。

It was something like a ring of rusty iron or brass and when the robin flew up into a tree nearby she put out her hand and picked the ring up.

它像是一个生了锈的铁环或铜环。当知更鸟飞向身旁的那棵树时，她伸出手把圆环捡了起来。

when引导时间状语从句。

It was more than a ring, however; it was an old key which looked as if it had been buried a long time.

然而，它不仅仅是一个圆环，而是把旧钥匙，看起来好像是被埋藏了很久。

which引导定语从句；as if 是仿佛的意思。

"Perhaps it has been buried for ten years," she said in a whisper. "Perhaps it is the key to the garden!"

“也许它被埋藏了十年，”她小声说。“也许这是去花园的钥匙！”

it has been done现在完成时的被动语态，in a whisper，“耳语、低声说”，the key to，……的关键、……的钥匙。

051 Vanity Fair 名利场

今日关键语导读 Today's Key Points

《名利场》是英国伟大现实主义作家和幽默大师萨克雷的代表作。穷画家的女儿蓓姬·夏普，自幼失去父母，但绝顶聪明。她以半工半读的方式从寄宿学校毕业后，由一名家庭小教师起步，牢牢抓住每一个机会，削尖了脑袋钻进维多利亚时代的上流社会，成为一颗光芒四射的交际明星。作品辛辣地讽刺了买卖良心和荣誉的“名利场”中的各种丑恶现象，作者善于运用深刻的心理描写和生动的细节勾勒来刻画人物，是一部现实主义的杰作。

障碍词先听为快 Words and Expressions

churchyard ['tʃəːtʃjaːd] n. 境内；教堂院落，多做墓地

disconsolate [dis'kɔnsəlit] adj. 郁郁不乐的；忧郁的；孤独的

academy [ə'kædəmi] n. 学院；研究院；学会；专科院校

pompous ['pɔmpəs] adj. 自大的；浮夸的；华而不实的；爱炫耀的

mahogany [mə'hɔgəni] n. 桃花心木，红木；红褐色

grandchildren [g'ræntʃɪldrən] n. 孙子；孙（女），外孙（女）（grandchild的名词复数）

tumbler ['tʌmblə] n. 不倒翁（玩具）；杂技演员；翻筋斗者；一杯的容量；滚筒；平底玻璃

canvas ['kænvəs] n. 帆布 adj. 帆布制的 vt. 用帆布覆盖，用帆布装备

As the manager of the Performance sits before the curtain on the boards and looks into the Fair, a feeling of profound melancholy comes over him in his survey of the bustling place. There isa great quantity of eating and drinking, making love and jilting, laughing and the contrary, smoking, cheating, fighting, dancing and fiddling; there are bullies pushing about, bucks ogling the women, knaves picking pockets, policemen on the look-out, quacks (other quacks, plague take them!) bawling in front of their booths, and yokels looking up at the tinselled dancers and poor old rouged tumblers, while the light-fingered folk are operating upon their pockets behind. Yes, this is VANITY FAIR; not a moral place certainly; nor a merry one, though very noisy. Look at the faces of the actors and buffoons when they come off from their business; and Tom Fool washing the paint off his cheeks before he sits down to dinner with his wife and the little Jack Puddings behind the canvas.

Although schoolmistresses' letters are to be trusted no more nor less than churchyard epitaphs; yet, as it sometimes happens that a person departs this life who is really deserving of all the praises the stone cutter carves over his bones; Who is a good Christian, a good present, a good child,a good wife or a good husband, who actually does leave a disconsolate family to mourn his loss.; so in academies of the male and female sex it occurs every now and then that the pupil is fully worthy of the praises bestowed by the disinterested instructor. Now, Miss Amelia Sedley was a young lady of this singular species; and deserved not only all that

Miss Pinkerton said in her praise, but had many charming qualities which that pompous old Minerva of a woman could not see, from the differences of rank and age between her pupil and herself.

……

Mr sedley was neutral. "Let Jos marry whom he likes," he said, "it's no affair of mine. This girl has no fortune; no more had Mrs Sedley. She seems good-humoured and clever, and will keeps him in order, perhaps. Better she, my dear, than a black Mrs Sedley and a dozen of mahogany grandchildren."

……

In honour of the young bride's arrival, her mother thought it necessary to prepare I don't know what festive entertainment, and after the first ebullition of talk, took leave of Mrs. George Osborne for a while,and divid down to the lower regions of the house to a sort of kitchen-parlour, there to take measures for the preparing of a grandchildren omamented tea.

"Fast and loose!" Howled out old Osbome. "Fast and loose! Why, hang me, those are the very words my gentleman used himself when he gave himself airs, last Thursday was a fortonight, and talked about the British army to his father who made him, what, it's you who have been a setting of him up—is it? And my service to you, Captain. It's you who want to introduce beggars into my family. Thank you for nothing, Captain. Marry her indeed—he, he! Why should he? I warrant you she'd go to him fast enough without."

长难句解析

Who is a good Christian, a good present, a good child,a good wife or a good husband, who actually does have a disconsolate family to mourn his loss.

真的是虔诚的教徒，慈爱的父母，孝顺的儿女，贤良的妻子，尽职的丈夫，他们家里的人也的确哀思绵绵地追悼他们。

good 一词根据语境可译为虔诚、慈爱、孝顺、贤良、尽职。

Mr sedley was neutral. "Let Jos marry whom he likes,"he said, "it's no affair of mine. This girl has no fortune; no more had Mrs Sedley. She seems good-humoured and clever, and will keeps him in order, perhaps. Better she my dear, than a black Mrs Sedley and a dozen of mahogany grandchildren."

赛特笠先生是无所谓。他说:"乔斯爱娶谁就娶谁，反正不关我的事。那女孩子没有钱，可是当年赛特笠太太也一样穷。她看上去性情温顺，也很聪明，也许会把乔斯管得好好的。亲爱的，还是她吧，总比娶个黑不溜秋的媳妇回来，养出十来个黄黑脸皮的孙子孙女儿好些。"

be no affair of sb 不关某人的事。

In honour of the young bride's arrival, her mother thought it necessary to prepare I don't know what festive entertainment, and after the first ebullition of talk, took leave of Mrs. George Osborne for a while,and divid down to the lower regions of the house to a sort of kitchen-parlour, there to take measures for the preparing of a magnificent omamented tea.

她的母亲要给刚回门的新娘做面子，不知该怎么招待她才好。她和女儿好好地谈了一会儿，暂时离开乔治·奥斯本夫人钻到屋子底层的一间厨房，打算要做一桌吃起来丰盛、看起来花哨的茶点。

a magnificent omamented tea 根据语境译为一桌吃起来丰盛、看起来花哨的茶点。

"Fast and loose!" Howled out old Osbome. "Fast and loose! Why, hang me, those are the very words my gentleman used himself when he gave himself airs, last Thursday was a fortonight, and talked about the British army to his father who made him, what, it's you who have been a setting of him up—is it? And my service to you, Captain. It's you who want to introduce beggars into my family. Thank you for nothing, Captain. Marry her indeed-he, he! Why should he? I warrant you she'd go to him fast enough without."

老奥斯本大喝一声："反复无常！反复无常！我们家的少爷跟我吵架，说的正是这话。那天是星期四，到今天两个多星期了。他支起好大的架子，说什么我侮辱了英国军队的军官了。他还不是我做父亲的一手栽培起来的？多谢你，上尉。原来是你要把叫花子请到我们家里来。不劳费心，上尉。娶她！哼哼，何必呢？保管不必明媒正娶，她也肯来。"

fast and loose反复无常；when引导时间状语从句。

052 Ella Enchanted 魔法灰姑娘

今日关键语导读 Today's Key Points

魔法灰姑娘是美国作家盖尔·卡森·乐文的作品，该书讲述了出生在一个色彩斑斓的奇幻世界中的主人公爱拉被仙女施予了必须无条件地服从任何人的任何要求的魔咒，哪怕是极其苛刻与无理的要求都要马上照办。否则，就会引起身体上的种种不舒服，比如头晕目眩、呕吐等等。主人公用不屈服命运的倔强品格最终为爱打破了咒语。

障碍词先听为快 Words and Expressions

pursuit [pə'sjuːt] n. 追赶，追求；职业，工作

conceal [kən'siːl] vt. 隐藏；隐瞒

solitary ['sɔlitəri] adj. 孤独的；独居的

wary ['wɛəri] adj. 谨慎的；机警的；惟恐的；考虑周到的

twilight ['twailait] n. 黎明，黄昏；薄暮；衰退期；朦胧状态

doom [duːm] vt. 注定；判决；使失败

daze [deiz] vt. 使茫然；使眼花缭乱；使晕眩

lacy ['leisi] adj. 花边的；丝带的

motion ['məuʃən] n. 动作；移动；手势；请求；意向

trunk [trʌŋk] n. 树干；躯干；象鼻；汽车车尾的行李箱

Beyond Jenn, I left the road, following it, but too far away to be seen from it. I didn't fear pursuit by Madame Edith, who would probably conceal my disappearance for as long as possible in hopes I might return. The baker's worries about ogres and bandits I thought exaggerated, since a solitary traveler would hardly be worthwhile prey. However, I was wary of strangers. With my curse, I had to be.

I wondered if I would meet Char on his way to the Fens. I liked thinking he might be near, but whether he was ahead of me or behind, or whether he had taken this route at all, I had no idea, and I wished my magic book had told me more.

The road was little trafficked, and I was too happy about my escape to feel much fear. I was free of orders. If I wanted to eat my breakfast under a maple tree and watch the day grow between its leaves, I could — and did. If I wanted to skip or hop or run and slide on dew-wet leaves, I could — and did. And when the mood took me, I whistled or recited poems that I made up on the spot.

I spent two glorious days this way, the best since before Mother had died. I saw deer and hares, and once, at twilight, I swear I saw a phoenix rise, trailing smoke.

On the third day, I began to despair about reaching the giants in time. I hadn't even come to the elves' Forest. If I had any chance of getting to the wedding, I should have passed the Forest on the second day, unless the baker had been mistaken about the distance from the Forest to the giants. Perhaps they were much closer to each other than he thought.

On the fourth day, I finished my last bit of traveler's bread. The land changed to sandy fields and low scrub, and I began to despair about reaching the giants before the newlyweds celebrated their first anniversary.

On the fifth day, I knew I was doomed to wander in endless barrens till I died.

On the sixth day, there were more trees, but I was too dazed by hunger to realize their significance. I was searching the ground for the lacy flowers of the wild carrot when I caught a shift in the shadows ahead of me, a flash of motion among the tree trunks. A deer? A walking bush? There, I saw it again. An elf!

长难句解析

With my curse, I had to be.

因为我所背负的咒语，我必须这样做。

with为介词，表原因。

I liked thinking he might be near, but whether he was ahead of me or behind, or whether he had taken this route at all, I had no idea, and I wished my magic book had told me more.

我一直在想也许他就在附近，但是不论他在我前方或是在我后方，又或者他已经走过这条路了，我对此一无所知，我希望我的魔法书能告诉我更多。

thinking 表示一直在持续的动作；wish引导虚拟语气，表明魔法书其实不能再告诉我更多。

If I wanted to skip or hop or run and slide on dew-wet leaves, I could — and did.

如果我想跳，想跑或者想躺在湿润的叶子上，我都可以做到并且我也这样做了。

if引导虚拟语气。

If I had any chance of getting to the wedding, I should have passed the Forest on the second day, unless the baker had been mistaken about the distance from the Forest to the giants.

如果我有机会去婚礼，我就应该在第二天的时候穿越丛林，除非面包工人弄错了从森林到巨人族的距离。

if引导的虚拟语气，表示与过去事实相反，从句用过去完成时；主句用shuold (would)+v.原形。

On the fifth day, I knew I was doomed to wander in endless barrens till I died.

第五天，我知道我注定要死在这片一望无垠的荒地了。

be doomed to do sth. 注定做某事。

053 Magic world 魔法世界

今日关键语导读 Today's Key Points

伊迪丝・内斯比特（已婚名伊迪丝・布兰德）是英国作家和诗人，其写给孩子们的作品多以E.内斯比特的中性名字发表。她的很多作品已被改编为电影和电视。她开创了从日常的设置所产生的神奇冒险的新流派，并已被许多作家模仿。

障碍词先听为快 Words and Expressions

dip [dip] vi. 浸；下降，下沉；倾斜；舀，掏
dazzlingly ['dæzliŋli] adv. 耀眼地；灿烂地
shuffling ['ʃʌflɪŋ] adj. 支吾的，曳步的 v. 拖着脚走；搪塞
glorious ['glɔːriəs] adj. 光荣的；辉煌的；极好的
splendor ['splendə] n. 光彩；壮丽；显赫
mast [maːst] n. 桅杆；柱；橡树果实
intense [in'tens] adj. 强烈的；紧张的；非常的；热情的
wholly ['həuli] adv. 完全地；全部；统统
mantle ['mæntl] n. 地幔；斗篷；覆盖物 vi. 覆盖；脸红
tunic ['tjuːnik] n. 束腰外衣

好英文娓娓动听 Beautiful stories

He had learned that expression in a school in Salisbury, a long time ago as it seemed. The stone on which he lay dipped and rose to a rhythm which he knew well enough. He had felt it when he and his mother went in a little boat from Key haven to Alum Bay in the Isle of Wight. There was no doubt in his mind. He was on a ship. But how, but why? Who could have carried him all that way without waking him? Was it magic? Accidental magic? The St. John's wort perhaps? And the stone—it was not the same. It was new, clean cut, and, where the wind displaced a corner of the curtain, dazzlingly white in the sunlight.

There was the pat of bare feet on the deck, a dull sort of shuffling as though people were arranging themselves. And then people outside the awning began to sing. It was a strange song, not at all like any music you or I have ever heard. It had no tune, no more tune than a drum has, or a trumpet, but it had a sort of wild rough glorious exciting splendor about it, and gave you the sort of intense all-alive feeling that drums and trumpets give.

Quentin lifted a corner of the purple curtain and looked out.

Instantly the song stopped, drowned in the deepest silence Quentin had ever imagined. It was only broken by the flip-flapping of the sheets against the masts of the ship. For it was a ship, Quentin saw that as the bulwark dipped to show him an unending waste of sea, broken by bigger waves than he had ever dreamed of. He saw also a crowd of men, dressed in white and blue and purple and gold. Their right arms were raised towards the sun, half of whose face showed across the sea—but they seemed to be, as my old nurse used to say, "struck so," for their eyes were not fixed on the sun, but on Quentin. And not in anger, he noticed curiously, but with surprise and... could it be that they were afraid of him?

Quentin was shivering with the surprise and newness of it all. He had read about magic, but he had not wholly believed in it, and yet, now, if this was not magic, what was it? You go to sleep on an old stone in a ru- in. You wake on the same stone, quite new, on a ship. Magic, magic, if ever there was magic in this wonderful, mysterious world!

The silence became awkward. Some one had to say something. “Good-morning,” said Quentin, feeling that he ought perhaps to be the one. Instantly every one in sight fell on his face on the deck. Only one, a tall man with a black beard and a blue mantle, stood up and looked Quentin in the eyes. “Who are you?” he said. “Answer, I adjure you by the Sacred Tau!” Now this was very odd, and Quentin could never understand it, but when this man spoke Quentin understood him perfectly, and yet at the same time he knew that the man was speaking a foreign language. So that his thought was not, “Hullo, you speak English!” but ‘Hullo, I can understand your language.” “I am Quentin De Ward,” he said. “A name from other stars! How came you here?” asked the blue- mantled man. “I don’t know,” said Quentin. “He does not know. He did not sail with us. It is by magic that he is here,” said Blue Mantle. “Rise, all, and greet the Chosen of the Gods.” They rose from the deck, and Quentin saw that they were all bearded men, with bright, earnest eyes, dressed in strange dress of something like jersey and tunic and heavy golden ornaments.

长难句解析

It was a strange song, not at all like any music you or I have ever heard. It had no tune, no more tune than a drum has, or a trumpet, but it had a sort of wild rough glorious exciting splendour about it, and gave you the sort of intense all-alive feeling that drums and trumpets give.

这是一首奇怪的歌，一点儿也不像我们曾经听到的音乐。它没有调子，不是鼓的调子，也不是喇叭的调子，但是它里面有一种粗犷的非常激动人心，壮丽的东西，它可以给你一种鼓和喇叭所给予你的强烈的身临其境的感觉。

not at all一点也不；a sort of 一种，一类；that引导定语从句。

Their right arms were raised towards the sun, half of whose face showed across the sea—but they seemed to be, as my old nurse used to say, "struck so," for their eyes were not fixed on the sun, but on Quentin.

他们中一半的人面朝大海，在太阳下举起了右手。但他们好像我曾经的护士说的一样，因为他们的眼睛是盯着昆廷的，而不是盯着太阳。

for 引导原因状语从句；seem to be好像是；be fixed on 集中于。

For it was a ship, Quentin saw that as the bulwark dipped to show him an unending waste of sea, broken by bigger waves than he had ever dreamed of.

因为是一艘船，昆廷看到，当那些堡垒掉到海里，向他展示大海的无尽浪费时，那些堡垒被更大的海浪摧毁了，而这些海浪是他做梦都没见过的。

for引导原因状语从句；that 引导宾语从句；dream of 梦想。

He had read about magic, but he had not wholly believed in it, and yet, now, if this was not magic, what was it?

他已经读过了魔法，但是他并不完全相信，现在，如果这不是魔法，那这是什么?

believe in sth. 相信某事；if引导条件状语从句。

They rose from the deck, and Quentin saw that they were all bearded men, with bright, earnest eyes, dressed in strange dress of something like jersey and tunic and heavy golden ornaments.

他们从甲板上升起，昆廷看见他们全部都是有胡子的男人，眼睛明亮，眼里满是诚挚，他们穿着奇怪的衣服如运动衫和无袖式的束腰外衣以及很重的黄金装饰物。

rise from 从……升起，that引导定语从句。

---

054 The Adventures of Pinocchio 木偶奇遇记

今日关键语导读 Today's Key Points

《木偶奇遇记》是科洛迪的代表作，它叙述老人泽皮德把一块能哭会笑的木头雕成木偶，并把获得生命的小木偶当成儿子。而小木偶匹诺曹一开始并不懂事，经历了很多挫折，但最后他的善良天真、正义勇敢换来了幸福的生活，最终成为了真正的人类孩子。

障碍词先听为快 Words and Expressions

carpenter ['kaːpintə] n. 木工，木匠

puppet ['pʌpit] n. 木偶，玩偶；傀儡

jail [dʒeil] n. 监狱；监牢；拘留所 vt. 监禁；下狱

naughty ['nɔːti] adj. 顽皮的；淘气的

ax [æks] n. 斧子

stuck [stʌk] v. 刺（stick 的过去式及过去分词） adj. 动不了的；被卡住的

tongue [tʌŋ] n. 舌头，语言，口条，语言，说话方式 v. 舔，闲谈，斥责；吹乐器

neck [nek] n. 脖子，颈

catch [kætʃ] vt. 捕捉；赶上（车）；染上（病） n. 捕获物

The carpenter gave the strange piece of wood to Geppetto. The old man took the wood home. He sat down at his table and began to make the new puppet. "I will call this new puppet Pinocchio," he thought. First, he cut out the puppet's head. Suddenly, the puppet's head began to laugh. "Why are you laughing?" said Geppetto.

"Stop it right now!" The puppet stopped laughing, but it stuck out its tongue.

"Such a naughty puppet," said Geppetto. "Behave yourself, or I will not make your legs or your feet!"

The puppet was quiet. Geppetto made the neck, the arms, the chest, and finally, the legs. Now, the puppet was finished. Geppetto wanted Pinocchio to walk. He put him on the floor. He showed him how to move his legs. The puppet learned fast. He started walking faster and faster. Then, he was running around the room. "Ha! This is fun!" cried Pinocchio. He ran to the door and out of the house.

"Stop!" cried Geppetto, but Pinocchio wouldn't listen. He ran down the street. Geppetto followed him, but he was too slow. He couldn't catch the little puppet. Pinocchio hid behind a wall. A policeman saw the puppet and picked him up.

"Who are you?" asked the policeman. "I've never seen a running puppet before."

Just then, Geppetto arrived. He took Pinocchio in his hands, and shook him. "You are a naughty boy!" he yelled. "You must listen to big people! We are going home and I'm going to punish you!"

The policeman heard Geppetto, and took his arm. "You shouldn't hurt young boys," he said. "I'm going to take you to jail." Then, he put Pinocchio on the ground and took Geppetto away.

长难句解析

"Stop it right now!" The puppet stopped laughing, but it stuck out its tongue.

"Such a naughty puppet," said Geppetto. "Behave yourself, or I will not make your legs or your feet!"

"现在不准笑！"木偶不再笑了，但是它却吐舌头。

"真是个顽皮的小木偶，"格培多说。"规矩点，要不然我就不刻你的腿和脚！"

behave yourself 请检点一点，行为规矩些；stick out one's tongue 伸出舌头。

"Stop!" cried Geppetto, but Pinocchio wouldn't listen. He ran down the street. Geppetto followed him, but he was too slow. He couldn't catch the little puppet. Pinocchio hid behind a wall. A policeman saw the puppet and picked him up.

"停下来！"格培多叫道，但是匹诺曹不听。他沿街跑下去，格培多追着他跑，但是他动作太慢了，抓不到这个小木偶。匹诺曹躲在一面墙后面，一位警察看到了这个木偶，就把他抓了起来。

pick sb. up 把某人抓起来了；hid 隐藏。

Geppetto wanted Pinocchio to walk. He put him on the floor. He showed him how to move his legs. The puppet learned fast. He started walking faster and faster.

格培多要匹诺曹走动一下，他把他放在地板上，教他如何移动双腿，小木偶学得很快，他开始走得越来越快了。

show sb.（how）to do sth.，示范某人如何做某事；“比较级 and 比较级”，表示越来越……。

读书笔记

055 The Alchemist 牧羊少年奇幻之旅

今日关键语导读 Today's Key Points

《牧羊少年奇幻之旅》是巴西著名作家保罗·柯艾略的一部寓言式小说。故事讲述了牧羊少年圣地亚哥连续两次做了同一个梦，梦见埃及金字塔附近藏有一批宝藏，在撒冷之王的引导下卖掉羊群前往埃及寻找宝藏的经历。

障碍词先听为快 Words and Expressions

crystal ['kristl] adj. 水晶的；透明的，清澈的

merchant ['məːtʃənt] n. 商人，批发商；店主

entire [in'ta] adj. 全部的，整个的；全体的

mumble ['mʌmbl] vi. 含糊地说话

commission [kə'miʃən] n. 委员会；佣金；犯；委任；委任状

calculate ['kælkjuleit] vt. 计算；预测；认为；打算

bottom ['bɔtəm] n. 底部；末端

shepherd ['ʃepəd] n. 牧羊人；牧师；指导者

attraction [ə'trækʃən] n. 吸引，吸引力；引力；吸引人的事物

好英文娓娓动听 Beautiful stories

The boy had been working for the crystal merchant for almost a month, and he could see that it wasn't exactly the kind of job that would make him happy. The merchant spent the entire day mumbling behind the counter, telling the boy to be careful with the pieces and not to break anything.

But he stayed with the job because the merchant, although he was an old grouch, treated him fairly; the boy received a good commission for each piece he sold, and had already been able to put some money aside. That morning he had done some calculating: if he continued to work every day as he had been, he would need a whole year to be able to buy some sheep.

"I'd like to build a display case for the crystal," the boy said to the merchant. "We could place it outside, and attract those people who pass at the bottom of the hill."

"I've never had one before," the merchant answered. "People will pass by and bump into it, and pieces will be broken."

"Well, when I took my sheep through the fields some of them might have died if we had come upon a snake. But that's the way life is with sheep and with shepherds."

The merchant turned to a customer who wanted three crystal glasses. He was selling better than ever... as if time had turned back to the old days when the street had been one of Tangier's major attractions.

"Business has really improved," he said to the boy, after the customer had left. "I'm doing much better, and soon you'll be able to return to your sheep. Why ask more out of life?"

"Because we have to respond to omens," the boy said, almost without meaning to; then he regretted what he had said, because the merchant had never met the king.

"It's called the principle of favorability, beginner's luck. Because life wants you to achieve your destiny," the old king had said.

长难句解析

The boy had been working for the crystal merchant for almost a month, and he could see that it wasn't exactly the kind of job that would make him happy.

这个男孩已经为水晶商人工作近一个月了，他知道这不是那种可以使他开心的工作。

had been doing过去完成进行时，表示动作从过去开始并持续；and连接并列分句，第一个that引导宾语从句，后面一个that引导定语从句；the kind of表种类。

The merchant spent the entire day mumbling behind the counter, telling the boy to be careful with the pieces and not to break anything.

商人花了一整天在柜台后面喃喃自语，告诉男孩要小心，不要破坏任何东西。

telling 现在分词作伴随状语；spend time in doing sth. 花费时间做某事。

That morning he had done some calculating: if he continued to work every day as he had been, he would need a whole year to be able to buy some sheep.

那天早上他做了一些计算：如果他继续每天为他工作，他需要一整年才能够买一些羊。

had done 表示过去完成时；if后连接一个条件状语从句。

We could place it outside, and attract those people who pass at the bottom of the hill.

我们可以把它放在外面，去吸引那些通过山底部的人。

could是can的过去式，后接动词原形；who引导定语从句修饰people；place意为放置。

As if time had turned back to the old days when the street had been one of Tangier's major attractions.

仿佛时间已经回到过去，当时街道已经成为丹吉尔的主要景点之一。

as if 虚拟语气用法，表示好像，仿佛；when引导一个时间状语从句。

056 The Chronicles of Narnia 纳尼亚传奇

今日关键语导读 Today's Key Points

《纳尼亚传奇》是英国作家C.S.刘易斯在19世纪50年代所著的奇幻儿童故事，讲述了几个小孩偶然进入了一个叫做纳尼亚的异世界，并在那里经历了一连串不可思议的冒险。

障碍词先听为快 Words and Expressions

wardrobe ['wɔːdrəub] n. 衣柜，行头；全部戏装

alarming [ə'lɑːmiŋ] adj. 令人担忧的，令人慌恐的 v. 使恐慌

interrupt [ˌintə'rʌpt] n. 打断 v. 中断；打断；插嘴；妨碍

bundle ['bʌndl] n. 束；捆 vt. 捆 vi. 匆忙离开

好英文娓娓动听 Beautiful stories

After this things were a good deal better for Lucy. Peter saw to it that Edmund stopped jeering at her, and neither she nor anyone else felt inclined to talk about the wardrobe at all. It had become a rather alarming subject. And so for a time it looked as if all the adventures were coming to an end; but that was not to be.

This house of the Professor's - which even he knew so little about - was so old and famous that people from all over England used to come and ask permission to see over it. It was the sort of house that is mentioned in guide books and even in histories; and well it might be, for all manner of stories were told about it, some of them even stranger than the one I am telling you now. And when parties of sightseers arrived and asked to see the house, the Professor always gave them permission, and Mrs Macready, the housekeeper, showed them round, telling them about the pictures and the armour, and the rare books in the library. Mrs Macready was not fond of children, and did not like to be interrupted when she was telling visitors all the things she knew. She had said to Susan and Peter almost on the first morning (along with a good many other instructions), "And please remember you're to keep out of the way whenever I'm taking a party over the house."

"Just as if any of us would want to waste half the morning trailing round with a crowd of strange grown-ups!" said Edmund, and the other three thought the same. That was how the adventures began for the second time.

A few mornings later Peter and Edmund were looking at the suit of armour and wondering if they could take it to bits when the two girls rushed into the room and said, "Look out! Here comes the Macready and a whole gang with her."

"Sharp's the word," said Peter, and all four made off through the door at the far end of the room. But when they had got out into the Green Room and beyond it, into the Library, they suddenly heard voices ahead of them, and realized that Mrs Macready must be bringing her party of sightseers up the back stairs - instead of up the front stairs as they had expected. And after that - whether it was that they lost their heads, or that Mrs Macready was trying to catch them, or that some magic in the house had come to life and was chasing them into Narnia they seemed to find themselves being followed everywhere, until at last Susan said, "Oh bother those trippers! Here - let's get into the Wardrobe Room till they've passed. No one will follow us in there." But the moment they were inside they heard the voices in the passage - and then someone fumbling at the door - and then they saw the handle turning.

"Quick!" said Peter, "there's nowhere else," and flung open the wardrobe. All four of them bundled inside it and sat there, panting, in the dark. Peter held the door closed but did not shut it; for, of course, he remembered, as every sensible person does, that you should never never shut yourself up in a wardrobe.

长难句解析

And so for a time it looked as if all the adventures were coming to an end; but that was not to be.

所以，在相当长的一段时间里，一切奇遇似乎都已成了过去，但事实却并不如此。

as if仿佛、好像；come to an end结束、终止。

This house of the Professor's - which even he knew so little about - was so old and famous that people from all over England used to come and ask permission to see over it.

教授的这栋房屋——即使他自己也了解得很少——是这样古老，又是这样闻名，全国各地的人都常常要求来此参观。

used to 过去常常；which 引导的定语从句修饰the house。

A few mornings later Peter and Edmund were looking at the suit of armour and wondering if they could take it to bits when the two girls rushed into the room and said, "Look out! Here comes the Macready and a whole gang with her."

几天以后，彼得和爱德蒙正望着那副盔甲出神，想试试能否把它拆卸下来，两个女孩忽然奔进屋里说："不好啦，玛卡蕾蒂带着一群人来了！"

if 引导条件状语从句；here comes 一句属于倒装现象，表地点的小副词放句首，句子用完全倒装；rush into冲进、闯入。

They suddenly heard voices ahead of them, and realized that Mrs Macready must be bringing her party of sightseers up the back stairs - instead of up the front stairs as they had expected.

这时他们突然听到前面有说话的声音，然后意识到玛卡蕾蒂太太一定是带着观光的人群到后楼去了，而没有像他们预料的那样到前楼来。

instead of 而不是；that引导宾语从句；as像……一样。

057 The Golden Fleece
金羊毛

今日关键语导读 Today's Key Points

《金羊毛》，希腊神话故事。故事中希腊北部国王阿塔玛斯有两个孩子，法瑞克斯和赫勒。当国王离开第一个妻子和一个名叫伊诺的坏女人结婚后，两个孩子受到后母残忍虐待，整个王国也受到毁灭性的瘟疫的侵袭。伊诺在丈夫耳边进谗言，终于使国王相信：他的儿子法瑞克斯是这次灾害的罪魁祸首，并要将他献给宙斯以结束瘟疫。可怜的孩子被推上了祭坛，将要被处死。正在此时，上帝派了一只浑身上下长着金色羊毛的公羊来将两个孩子驮在背上带走了。当他们飞过隔开欧洲和亚洲的海峡时，赫勒由于看到浩瀚的海洋而头晕目眩，最终掉进大海淹死了。这片海洋古时候的名称叫赫勒之海，赫勒拉旁海峡（恰纳卡莱海峡）便由此而来。金色公羊驮着法瑞克斯继续向前飞去，来到了黑海东岸的科尔契斯。在那里，法瑞克斯将公羊献给了宙斯；而将金羊毛送给了埃厄忒斯国王。国王将羊毛钉在一棵圣树上，并派了一条不睡觉的龙负责看护。

障碍词先听为快 Words and Expressions

weep [wiːp] v. 哭泣；流泪

palace ['pælis] n. 宫殿；宅邸；豪华住宅

golden ['gəuld(ə)n] adj. 金色的，黄金般的；珍贵的；金制的

special ['speʃəl] adj. 特别的；专门的，专用的

fleece [fliːs] n. 羊毛，绒头织物

dedicated ['dedikeitid] adj. 专用的；专注的；献身的

afterward ['ɑːftəwəd] adv. 以后，后来

treasure ['treʒə] n. 财富，财产；财宝；珍品

terrible ['terəbl] adj. 可怕的；很糟的；令人讨厌的

sorrowfully ['sɒrəʊfəlɪ] adv. 悲哀地；悔恨地

好英文娓娓动听 Beautiful stories

"To the king and to the people Phrixus told his story, weeping to tell of Helle and her fall. Then King Aeetes brought him into the city, and he gave him a place in the palace, and for the golden ram he had a special fold made.

"Soon after the ram died, and then King Aeetes took its golden fleece and hung it upon an oak tree that was in a place dedicated to Ares, the god of war. Phrixus wed one of the daughters of the king, and men say that afterward he went back to Thebes, his own land.

"And as for the Golden Fleece it became the greatest of King Aeetes's treasures. Well indeed does he guard it, and not with armed men only, but with magic powers. Very strong and very cunning is King Aeetes, and a terrible task awaits those who would take away from him that Fleece of Gold." So Alcimide spoke, sorrowfully telling to the women the story of the Golden Fleece that her son Jason was going in quest of. So she spoke, and the night waned, and the morning of the sailing of the Argo came on.

And when the Argonauts beheld the dawn upon the high

peaks of Pelion they arose and poured out wine in offering to Zeus, the highest of the gods. Then Argo herself gave forth a strange cry, for the beam from Dodona that had been formed into her prow had endued her with life. She uttered a strange cry, and as she did the heroes took their places at the benches, one after the other, as had been arranged by lot, and Tiphys, the helmsman, went to the steering place. To the sound of Orpheus's lyre they smote with oars the rushing sea water, and the surge broke over the oar blades. The sails were let out and the breeze came into them, piping shrilly, and the fishes came darting through the green sea, great and small, and followed them, gamboling along the watery paths. And Chiron, the king-centaur, came down from the Mountain Pelion, and standing with his feet in the foam cried out, "Good speed, O Argonauts, good speed, and a sorrow less return."

长难句解析

Then King Aeetes brought him into the city, and he gave him a place in the palace, and for the golden ram he had a special fold made.

埃厄忒斯国王带他进城并且在宫殿了给了他一个地方，和有一个为金色羊毛的公羊而设的独特的羊栏。

bring...into... 带……到……；give sb. sth. "给某人某物"；and作连词，在此连接并列的两个句子；had a special...made在此是定制……。

Soon after the ram died, and then King Aeetes took its golden fleece and hung it upon an oak tree that was in a place dedicated to Ares, the god of war.

不久之后公羊死去了，埃厄忒斯国王把金羊毛带走并将其挂在一棵橡树上，那是一个献身于阿瑞斯，战争之神的地方。

soon after 稍后，不久以后；hang upon 系在，挂在；that 引导定语从句，修饰tree。

And as for the Golden Fleece it became the greatest of King Aeetes's treasures.

至于金羊毛，那变成了埃厄忒斯国王最大的财富了。

as for至于，关于；the greatest 表示最大的，最棒的，其中the特指一个事物，great的最高级是greatest。

Very strong and very cunning is King Aeetes, and a terrible task awaits those who would take away from him that Fleece of Gold.

埃厄忒斯国王非常强大,非常狡猾,一个可怕的任务等待着那些从他那里带走金羊毛的人。

cunning狡猾；and用来补充语意起强调作用；who引导定语从句，修饰those；take away from表示“从……拿走”。

So Alcimide spoke, sorrowfully telling to the women the story of the Golden Fleece that her son Jason was going in quest of.

阿基米德这样说,悲哀地把那个女人的儿子杰森探寻的金羊毛的故事告诉了她。

sorrowfully 作副词，表示“悲哀地”，修饰telling；that引导定语从句；in quest of表示“探寻，寻求；为了追求……”。

读书笔记

058 The Gadfly 牛虻

今日关键语导读 Today's Key Points

《牛虻》是爱尔兰女作家艾捷尔·丽莲·伏尼契的作品。青年亚瑟因少不更事而泄露组织秘密，挨了心爱的女友琼玛一记耳光，无比懊悔。接着，他又得知自己竟然是所崇拜的神父的私生子，因此陷入迷茫甚至绝望。他制造了投海自尽的假象，从此流亡南美。十三年后回国时，他已成为革命者牛虻，一个为意大利的自由而战的斗士。归来，意味着他此生再无安宁。最后，为了理想，牛虻割舍了爱情和亲情，含笑走向刑场……本书既是慷慨动人的革命书籍，又是高雅纯正的文学名著，深刻描写了人情人性，充满了艺术感染力。

障碍词先听为快 Words and Expressions

arrogance ['ærəgəns] *n.* 傲慢，自大，自负；气焰

torture ['tɔːtʃə] *v.* 使痛苦，使苦恼

carbine ['kaːbain] *n.* （原为骑兵团的）卡宾枪，轻型半自动步枪或步枪

quicksand ['kwiksænd] *n.* 流沙，敏捷，危险而捉摸不定的事

magnolia [mæg'nəuliə] *n.* 木兰花

execute ['eksikjuːt] *v.* 执行，处死，处决，履行完成

squad [skwɔd] *n.* 雏鸟，矮胖子

groan [grəun] *vi.* 呻吟，发牢骚

shiver ['ʃivə] v. 发抖，颤抖，碎步

convulse [kən'vʌls] v. 使抽搐，使剧烈震动

好英文娓娓动听 Beautiful stories

The automatic station is at the specified location, just look at a spectacular sunrise. He again asked to be blindfolded him, his arrogance stern face forced the captain reluctantly agreed. Both of them forget they are tortured in the soldiers.

His smiling face they stood, short barrel carbine in their hands shake.

" I'm ready." He said.

Lieutenant stepped forward, moved to tremble. He had previously ordered executed.

"Ready — shooting gun!"

Gadfly tottered, immediately returned to balance, a bullet missed, and scratched his face, a few drops of blood fell on the white scarf, another bullet hit in the knee upper part. After the smoke cleared, the soldiers saw him still smile, was the only disability hand wiping cheeks on the blood.

" Guys, playing too bad!" he said, his voice clear and loud, those poor soldiers terrified, "again."

This horse Marines give a groan, they shiver. Everyone to go to the side of target, a secret hope that the fatal bullet is fired beside him, instead he shot. Gadfly stood there, smiling at them. They only put a shot into the massacre, this terrible thing will begin again. Suddenly, they were driven to distraction. They lay down short barrel carbine, but listening to officer angry curse and scold be convulsed with fear, stared at had been shot but not killed.

Command takes them face shook his fist, viciously ordered each of them and took place, to end this thing. He and they lose presence o f mind, dare not go to stand down the terrible image. When the Gadfly spoke to him a dig, heard the voice, he was frightened, trembling.

" Colonel, you brought a terrible death squads to have a look! I can put their conditioning. Okay, guys! Put your tools for higher, you left a little. Cheer up, man, you get is not a carbine, frying pan! You all ready? Then to prepare himself —"

"Shoot!" shouted the captain rushed forward to. This guy actually ordered the execution of his death sentence, is really unbearable.

Also a be fusillade. Subsequent formation is scattered, shivering soldiers crowded into a mass, wide-eyed look forward. A soldier without even shot, he dropped his rifle, squat body moan: "I can't — I can't!"

The smoke dispersed slowly, and then rising up, into the dawn. They saw the Gadfly has fallen, they saw that he was not dead. Zero time, soldiers and officers stood there, it turned to stone. They looked at the terrible thing writhing on the ground struggles. Then the doctor and captain ran, screamed, because he supported a knee brace yourself, still face the soldiers, still laughing.

" Missed again! — once again, the boys have a look — if you can't"

He suddenly began to shake, and then to the side down on the grass.

He was still smiling, is the only disability hand wiping the blood on her face

He slowly raised his right hand has been interrupted, open cross, Jesus's face was smeared with blood.

Father, your God — he satisfied?

What I can offer, only one, that is to say, a broken heart.

If I must die, I will marry the darkness be my bride.

......

After a fortnight beside the Lake of Lucerne Arthur and Montanelli returned to Italy by the St. Gothard Pass. They had been fortunate as to weather and had made several very pleasant excursions; but the first charm was gone out of their enjoyment. Montanelli was continually haunted by an uneasy thought of the "more definite talk" for which this holiday was to have been the opportunity. In the Arve valley he had purposely put off all reference to the subject of which they had spoken under the magnolia tree; it would be cruel, he thought, to spoil the first delights of Alpine scenery for a nature so artistic as Arthur's by associating them with a conversation which must necessarily be painful. Ever since the day at Martigny he had said to himself each morning; "I will speak to-day," and each evening: "I will speak to-morrow;" and now the holiday was over, and he still repeated again and again: "To-morrow, to-morrow." A chill, indefinable sense of something not quite the same as it had been, of an invisible veil falling between himself and Arthur, kept him silent, until, on the last evening of their holiday, he realized suddenly that he must speak now if he would speak at all. They were stopping for the night at Lugano, and were to start for Pisa next morning. He would at least find out how far his darling had been drawn into the fatal quicksand of Italian politics.

"The rain has stopped, carino," he said after sunset; "and this is the only chance we shall have to see the lake. Come out; I want to have a talk with you."

They walked along the water's edge to a quiet spot and sat down on a low stone wall. Close beside them grew a rose-bush, covered with scarlet hips; one or two belated clusters of creamy blossom still hung from an upper branch, swaying mournfully and heavy with raindrops. On the green surface of the lake a little boat, with white wings faintly fluttering, rocked in the dewy breeze. It looked as light and frail as a tuft of silvery dandelion seed flung upon the water. High up on Monte Salvatore the window of some shepherd's hut opened a golden eye. The roses hung their heads and dreamed under the still September clouds, and the water plashed and murmured softly among the pebbles of the shore.

"This will be my only chance of a quiet talk with you for a long time," Montanelli began. "You will go back to your college work and friends; and I, too, shall be very busy this winter. I want to understand quite clearly what our position as regards each other is to be; and so, if you—" He stopped for a moment and then continued more slowly: "If you feel that you can still trust me as you used to do, I want you to tell me more definitely than that night in the seminary garden, how far you have gone."

长难句解析

After the smoke cleared, the soldiers saw him still smile, was the only disability hand wiping cheeks on the blood.

当烟雾消散后，士兵们看着他仍然微笑着，并用唯一的残疾了的一只手擦着脸上的血迹。

after引导时间状语从句。

Put your tools for higher, you left a little. Cheer up, man, you get is not a carbine, frying pan! You all ready? Then to prepare himself--"

把你的工具举得更高，你再慢慢地离开。振作起来，伙计，你得到的不是一把卡宾枪！你准备好了吗？然后准备——"

"put" "cheer up"，位于句首，是两个祈使句；cheer up 译为"振作起来"！

They were stopping for the night at Lugano, and were to start for Pisa next morning. He would at least find out how far his darling had been drawn into the fatal quicksand of Italian politics.

他们在卢加诺停留了一夜，并计划第二天早上启程去比萨。至少他要明白他的爱人在意大利政坛致命的流沙中卷入了多深。

be to表示将来时态；how far在这里表示”多远”的意思。fatal译为“致命的，毁灭性的”。

They walked along the water's edge to a quiet spot and sat down on a low stone wall. Close beside them grew a rose-bush, covered with scarlet hips.

他们沿着湖边走到一个安静的地方，坐在一座低矮的石头墙旁边。他们旁边长着一丛玫瑰花，覆盖着鲜红的蔷薇果。

walk along 译为“沿着……走”，covered with...做后置定语。

"If you feel that you can still trust me as you used to do, I want you to tell me more definitely than that night in the seminary garden, how far you have gone."

“如果你觉得你可以像之前一样信任我，我想让你比那晚在神学院花园里更明确地告诉我，你走了多远了。”

if 引导条件状语从句，表假设。as ...as... 译为”和……一样”。

059 Gone with the Wind
飘

今日关键语导读 Today's Key Points

《飘》是美国女作家玛格丽特的成名之作，作品讲述了美国南北战争期间，主人公斯佳丽曲折悲哀的婚姻故事。起初，斯佳丽爱上了艾希礼，但艾希礼却选择了善良的梅勒妮。出于妒恨，斯佳丽嫁给了梅勒妮的弟弟查尔斯。内战爆发后，艾希礼和查尔斯应征入伍。查尔斯不幸去世，斯佳丽成了寡妇。战后，斯佳丽同弗兰克结婚。弗兰克不久去世，斯佳丽再次成为寡妇。后来瑞德向她求婚，她答应了。但瑞德认为斯佳丽依然暗恋着艾希礼，二人感情破裂。经过一系列变故，斯佳丽终于明白了父亲曾经对她说过的一句话："世界上唯有土地与明天同在。"她决定守在她的土地上重新创造新的生活，期盼着美好明天的到来。

障碍词先听为快 Words and Expressions

cruel ['kruəl] adj. 残酷的，残忍的；使人痛苦的，让人受难的

sword [sɔːd] n. 剑，刀；武力，战争；兵权，权力

imagine [i'mædʒin] v. 想，设想；想象；料想，猜想；误认为

exist [ig'zist] v. 存在；生存；生活；继续存在

miserable ['mizərəbl] adj. 悲惨的；令人痛苦的；少的可怜的；卑鄙的

misty ['misti] adj. 多雾的，被雾笼罩的；模糊的

struggle ['strʌgl] vi. 搏斗；奋斗；努力；争取

cotton ['kɔtn] *n.* 棉；棉线；棉织物

porch [pɔːtʃ] *n.* 门廊；游廊，走廊

determination [ditəːmi'neiʃən] *n.* 决心；决定，确定

好英文娓娓动听 Beautiful stories

"Scarlett, it isn't going to be like that. I waited here for you tonight because I have something to tell you. I'm leaving, Scarlett. I can't live here anymore."

"But...why, Rhett?" Scarlett said.

"Scarlett, I always loved you, and I thought you knew it. You're so cruel to the people who love you, Scarlett. You take their love and use it, like a sword. I saw you do this with Charles Hamilton, with Frank, and then with me. When Bonnie was born, I imagined that she was just like you as a little girl. I thought I could win your love somehow, by treating Bonnie so well. But when Bonnie died...she took everything."

"I'm tired, Scarlett. You have taken all the love out of me. So I'm leaving now. I'm going to find a quiet place somewhere where the old South still exists, where I can rest."

"Rhett...I'm sorry, I'm so sorry! Please don't leave me, I love you so. I'm so sorry! Please don't leave me, I love you so. I understand things now. We can have a new life together!" cried Scarlett.

Rhett smiled gently. "Oh, Scarlett, you can't say 'I'm sorry' and take all the past away. It's too late, my dear. I am leaving now, this minute."

"But Rhett, don't you understand what I'm saying?" cried Scarlett. She was miserable. How could this be happening?

Rhett looked at her gently and kissed her on the cheek. Scarlett was too shocked to say anything. She watched him walk out of the dining room, out the door and disappear into the cold, misty night.

She closed the door and sat down on the steps. "Oh, what am I going to do? How can I make Rhett understand that I love him?" she cried out to herself. She had never felt unhappier in her life--not even when she found out Ellen was dead.

"Oh, I can't think about it now," Scarlett said out loud. "I'll go crazy if I think about it all now! I'll think about it tomorrow...at Tara!"

The wonderful of her youth called out to her. No matter what else Scarlett lost in her life, she still had Tara. She had struggled and fought for it. Scarlett wanted to see the green cotton fields and the peaceful sunset. She wanted to sit on the porch and remember the old days. She needed to think about Rhett, and about the future.

Scarlett stood up. The old determination was in her eyes. "I'll go home--home to Tara!" she said. "At Tara, I'll think about a way to get Rhett back...tomorrow! After all, tomorrow is another day!"

长难句解析

"Scarlett, it isn't going to be like that. I waited here for you tonight because I have something to tell you. I'm leaving, Scarlett. I can't live here anymore."

"斯佳丽，事情不会像你想的那样了。今晚我在这里等你是因为我有事要对你说。我要走了，斯佳丽，我在这里待不下去了。"

because 引导原因状语从句；not...anymore 不再……。

"I'm tired, Scarlett. You have taken all the love out of me. So I'm leaving now. I'm going to find a quiet place somewhere where the old South still exists, where I can rest."

"我累了，斯佳丽，你夺走了我全部的爱。所以，现在我要走了。我要去寻找一个安静的地方，一个昔日南部还存在于世的地方，一个可以让我休息的地方。"

where引导地点状语从句，两个where均指代前面的"somewhere"。

Rhett looked at her gently and kissed her on the cheek. Scarlett was too shocked to say anything.

瑞德温文尔雅地看着她，在她的脸上吻了吻，斯佳丽吃惊得一句话也说不出来。

look at 注视；too...to"太……而不能"。

"Oh, I can't think about it now," Scarlett said out loud. "I'll go crazy if I think about it all now! I'll think about it tomorrow...at Tara!"

"噢，现在我不能再想了，"斯佳丽大声说，"再想下去我要发疯了！我要明天再想……去塔拉！"

if 引导真实条件句，是主将从现原则。

The wonderful of her youth called out to her. No matter what else Scarlett lost in her life, she still had Tara. She had struggled and fought for it.

她年轻时的那个美妙家园在召唤她。不管斯佳丽在生活中失去了什么，她毕竟还拥有塔拉。她曾经为它拼搏过，奋斗过。

call out 唤起；召集；叫喊；调来；no matter what= whatever，位于句首引导让步状语从句。

读书笔记

060 Slumdog Millionaire 贫民窟的百万富翁

今日关键语导读 Today's Key Points

《贫民窟的百万富翁》是维卡斯·斯瓦卢的长篇处女小说，该小说讲述了十八岁的酒吧服务员罗摩，生活在孟买的贫民窟里。从未上过学甚至不读报的他凭借在生活中接触到的人和事，在一个名为“谁将赢得十个亿”的电视知识问答竞赛中，奇迹般地连续答对了十二道问题，一举赢得最高累积奖金——十亿卢比的故事，同时也揭示了印度各个层面的人物与生活。

障碍词先听为快 Words and Expressions

retrospect ['retrəuspekt] *n.* 回顾，追溯

innocence ['inəsns] *n.* 清白，无罪；天真无邪

galvanize ['gælvənaiz] *vt.* 镀锌；通电；刺激

bleary ['bliəri] *adj.* 朦胧的；眼睛模糊的

trite [trait] *adj.* 陈腐的；平庸的；老一套的

doddery ['dɔdəri] *adj.* 蹒跚的；衰老的（等于doddered；doddering）

bartender ['bɑːtendə(r)] *n.* 酒保，酒吧间销售酒精饮料的人；酒吧侍者

grouchy ['grautʃi] *adj.* 不高兴的，不满的；不平的

bastard ['bæstəd] *n.* 私生子

rabid ['ræbid] *adj.* 激烈的；狂暴的；偏激的；患狂犬病的

In retrospect, perhaps I should have kicked and screamed. Protested my innocence, raised a stink, galvanized the neighbours. Not that it would have helped. Even if I had succeeded in waking some of the residents, they would not have raised a finger to defend me. With bleary eyes they would have watched the spectacle, made some trite remark like 'There goes another one,' yawned, and promptly gone back to sleep. My departure from Asia's biggest slum would make no difference to their lives. There would be the same queue for water in the morning, the same daily struggle to make it to the seven-thirty local in time.

They wouldn't even bother to find out the reason for my arrest. Come to think of it, when the two constables barged into my hut, even I didn't. When your whole existence is 'illegal', when you live on the brink of penury (poverty) in an urban wasteland where you jostle for every inch of space and have to queue even for a shit, arrest has a certain inevitability about it. You are conditioned to believe that one day there will be a warrant with your name on it, that eventually a jeep with a flashing red light will come for you.

There are those who will say that I brought this upon myself. By dabbling in that quiz show, they will wag a finger at me and remind me of what the elders in Dharavi say about never crossing the dividing line that separates the rich from the poor. After all, what business did a penniless waiter have to be participating in a brain quiz? The brain is not an organ we are authorized to use. We are supposed to use only our hands and legs.

If only they could see me answer those questions. After my performance they would have looked upon me with new respect. It's a pity the show has yet to be telecast. But word seeped out that I had won something. Like a lottery. When the other waiters heard the news, they decided to have a big party for me in the restaurant. We sang and danced and drank late into the night. For the first time we did not eat Ramzi's stale food for dinner. We ordered chicken biryani and seekh kebabs from the five-star hotel in Marine Drive. The doddery (mentally or physically infirm due to old age) bartender offered me his daughter in marriage. Even the grouchy manager smiled indulgently at me and finally gave me my back wages. He didn't call me a worthless bastard that night. Or a rabid dog.

Now Godbole calls me that, and worse. I sit cross-legged in a ten-by-six-foot cell with a rusty metal door and a small square window with a grille, through which a shaft of dusty sunlight streams into the room. The lock-up is hot and humid. Flies buzz around the mushy remains of an over-ripe mango lying squished on the stone floor. A sad-looking cockroach lumbers up to my leg. I am beginning to feel hungry. My stomach growls.

长难句解析

With bleary eyes they would have watched the spectacle, made some trite remark like 'There goes another one,' yawned, and promptly gone back to sleep.

他们只会用朦胧的双眼静观其变，作出诸如“又是一个”的评论，然后打着哈欠继续回去睡觉。

with 引导的让步状语从句。

When your whole existence is 'illegal', when you live on the brink of penury (poverty) in an urban wasteland where you jostle for every inch of space and have to queue even for a shit, arrest has a certain inevitability about it.

当你的存在完全是“不合法”的，当你生活在西边城市贫穷的边缘，为了一英寸的地方而推挤甚至为了连大便都得排队时，被逮捕就成了一件必然的事。

when引导时间状语从句；where引导地点状语从句；inevitability 表示不可避免性。

You are conditioned to believe that one day there will be a warrant with your name on it, that eventually a jeep with a flashing red light will come for you.

你都已经习惯性地去相信，总有一天会出现一张写有你名字的逮捕令，一辆闪烁着红灯的吉普会朝你开来。

with your name on it 作warrant的补语。

By dabbling in that quiz show, they will wag a finger at me and remind me of what the elders in Dharavi say about never crossing the dividing line that separates the rich from the poor.

涉足竞赛节目，他们会对我指指点点让我想起在达拉维贫民窟里的长老说过，永远不要跨过贫富之间的界限。

what 引导的从句做宾语，that引导的定语从句部分修饰line。

I sit cross-legged in a ten-by-six-foot cell with a rusty metal door and a small square window with a grille, through which a shaft of dusty sunlight streams into the room.

我双腿盘着坐在一个有着破旧铁门大概10×6英尺大小的小隔间里，阳光穿过一个有着栏杆的方形小窗户照进来。

with 引导的成分做cell的补语，which 引导的从句修饰window。

读书笔记

061 The Chocolate War
巧克力战争

今日关键语导读 Today's Key Points

《巧克力战争》是美国作家罗伯特·科米尔的作品。小说主要讲了十四岁的杰里刚到一个名叫“三位一体”的天主教高中就读，却被这个学校的秘密组织“守夜会”首领阿奇看上，利用他来和代理校长利昂修士进行激烈的权力斗争，没想到最后却变成杰里一个人孤身作战。

障碍词先听为快 Words and Expressions

scrape [skreip] *v.* 刮掉；刮出刺耳声

intact [in'tækt] *adj.* 完整的；原封不动的；未受损伤的

novelty ['nɔvəlti] *n.* 新奇；新奇的事物；新颖小巧而廉价的物品

coward ['kauəd] *n.* 懦夫，懦弱的人

bellow ['beləu] *vt.* 大声喊叫；大声发出

contempt [kən'tempt] *n.* 轻视，蔑视；耻辱

spit [spit] *vi.* 吐痰；吐口水

spit on 向……吐唾沫

好英文娓娓动听 Beautiful stories

The coach's voice scraped like sandpaper against his ears. He opened his eyes flutteringly. "I'm all right," he said to nobody in particular, or to his father maybe. Or the coach. He was unwilling to abandon this lovely lassitude but he had to, of course. He was sorry to leave the earth, and he was vaguely curious about how he was going to get up, with both legs smashed and his skull battered in. He was astonished to find himself on his feet, intact, bobbing like one of those toy novelties dangling from car windows, but erect.

"For Christ's sake," the coach bellowed, his voice juicy with contempt. A spurt of saliva hit Jerry's cheek.

Hey, coach, you spit on me, Jerry protested. Stop the spitting, coach. What he said aloud was, "I'm all right, coach," because he was a coward about stuff like that, thinking one thing and saying another, planning one thing and doing another - he had been Peter a thousand times and a thousand cocks had crowed in his lifetime.

"How tall are you, Renault?"

"Five nine," he gasped, still fighting for breath.

"Weight?"

"One forty-five," he said, looking the coach straight in the eye.

"Soaking wet, I'll bet," the coach said sourly. "What the hell you want to play football for? You need more meat on those bones. What the hell you trying to play quarterback for? You'd make a better end. Maybe."

The coach looked like an old gangster: broken nose, a scar on his cheek like a stitched shoestring. He needed a shave, his stubble like slivers of ice. He growled and swore and was merciless. But a helluva coach, they said. The coach stared at him now, the dark eyes probing, pondering. Jerry hung in there, trying not to sway, trying, not to faint.

"All right," the coach said in disgust. "Show up tomorrow. Three o'clock sharp or you're through before you start."

Inhaling the sweet sharp apple air through his nostrils— he was afraid to open his mouth wide, wary of any movement that was not absolutely essential— he walked tentatively toward the sidelines, listening to the coach barking at the other guys. Suddenly, he loved that voice, "Show up tomorrow."

He trudged away from the field, blinking against the afternoon sun, toward the locker room at the gym. His knees were liquid and his body light as air, suddenly.

Know what? he asked himself, a game he played sometimes.

What?

I'm going to make the team.

Dreamer, dreamer.

Not a dream: it's the truth.

As Jerry took another deep breath, a pain appeared, distant, small— a radar signal of distress. Bleep, I'm here. Pain. His feet scuffled through crazy cornflake leaves. A strange happiness invaded him. He knew he'd been massacred by the oncoming players, capsized and dumped humiliatingly on the ground. But he'd survived— he'd gotten to his feet. "You'd made a better end." Was the Coach thinking he might try him at end? Any position, as long as he made the team. The bleep grew larger, localized now, between his ribs on the right side. He thought of his mother and how drugged she was at the end, not recognizing anyone, neither Jerry nor his father. The exhilaration of the moment vanished and he sought it in vain, like seeking ecstasy's memory an instant after jacking off and encountering only shame and guilt.

长难句解析

The coach's voice scraped like sandpaper against his ears. He opened his eyes flutteringly. "I'm all right," he said to nobody in particular, or to his father maybe. Or the coach.

教练的声音像对着他耳朵刮砂纸一样刺耳，他颤抖地睁开眼睛："我没事。"他没有特意对谁说，对他的父亲，又或是对教练。

in particular 特别，尤其。

He was sorry to leave the earth, and he was vaguely curious about how he was going to get up, with both legs smashed and his skull battered in. He was astonished to find himself on his feet, intact, bobbing like one of those toy novelties dangling from car windows, but erect.

他很遗憾将要离开地球，很好奇他在双腿残废和头盖骨被重创的情况下该怎样站起来。然而他惊讶地发现他的腿完好无缺，摆动的样子就像一个玩具小礼品从车窗里晃来晃去，但是特别笔直。

be sorry to，对……感到抱歉；be curious about...对……感到好奇。

What he said aloud was, "I'm all right, coach," because he was a coward about stuff like that, thinking one thing and saying another, planning one thing and doing another.

他大声说出来的却是："我没事，教练"。因为他是像这样的一个懦夫，总是想是一回事儿说又是另一回事儿，计划是一回事儿做又是另一回事儿。

what在这里引导名词性从句，在此处作said 的宾语。

读书笔记

062 Persuasion 劝导

今日关键语导读 Today's Key Points

《劝导》描写了一个曲折多磨的爱情故事。贵族小姐安妮·埃利奥特同青年军官温特沃思倾心相爱，订下了婚约。可是，她的父亲沃尔特爵士和教母拉塞尔夫人嫌温特沃思出身卑贱，没有财产，极力反对这门婚事。安妮出于"谨慎"，接受了教母的劝导，忍痛同心上人解除了婚约。八年后，在战争中升了官、发了财的温特沃思上校休役回乡，随姐姐、姐夫当上了沃尔特爵士的房客。他虽说对安妮怨忿未消，但两人不忘旧情，终于历经曲折，排除干扰，结成良缘。

障碍词先听为快 Words and Expressions

engage [in'geidʒ] v. 使参加、引起、吸引、雇佣

tidings ['taidiŋz] npl. 消息

inferior [in'fiəriə] adj. 较差的

resent [ri'zent] vt. 对……感到愤恨

shew [ʃəu] v. 展出、炫耀

acquaintance [ə'kweintəns] n. 相识的人、结识、了解

cease [siːs] v. & n. 停止

awkward ['ɔːkwəd] adj. 使用不便的、局促不安的、笨拙的

interval ['intəvəl] n. 间隔、中场休息

heir [ɛə] n. 继承人

He was at that time a very young man, just engaged in the study of the law; and Elizabeth found him extremely agreeable, and every plan in his favour was confirmed. He was invited to Kellynch Hall; he was talked of and expected all the rest of the year; but he never came. The following spring he was seen again in town, found equally agreeable, again encouraged, invited and expected, and again he did not come; and the next tidings were that he was married. Instead of pushing his fortune in the line marked out for the heir of the house of Elliot, he had purchased independence by uniting himself to a rich woman of inferior birth.

Sir Walter has resented it. As the head of the house, he felt that he ought to have been consulted, especially after taking the young man so publicly by the hand: "For they must have been seen together," he observed, "Once at Tattersal's, and twice in the lobby of the House of Commons." His disapprobation was expressed, but apparently very little regarded. Mr Elliot had attempted do apology, and shewn himself as unsolicitous of being longer noticed by the family, as Sir Walter considered him unworthy of it: All acquaintance between them had ceased.

This very awkward history of Mr Elliot was still, after an interval of several years, felt with anger by Elizabeth, who had liked the man for himself, and still more for being her father's heir, and whose strong family pride could see only in him a proper match for Sir Walter Elliot's eldest daughter. There was not a baronet from A to Z whom her feelings could have so willingly acknowledged as an equal. Yet so miserably had he conducted himself, that though she was at this present time (the summer of 1814) wearing black ribbons for his wife, she could not admit him to be worth thinking of again. The disgrace of his first marriage might, perhaps, as there was no reason to suppose it perpetuated by offspring, have been got over, had he not done worse; but he had, as by the accustomary intervention of kind friends, they had been informed, spoken most disrespectfully of them all, most slightingly and contemptuously of the very blood he belonged to, and the honours which were hereafter to be his own. This could not be pardoned.

But now, another occupation and solicitude of mind was beginning to be added to these. Her father was growing distressed for money. She knew, that when he now took up the Baronetage, it was to drive the heavy bills of his trades people, and the unwelcome hints of Mr Shepherd, his agent, from his thoughts. The Kellynch property was good, but not equal to Sir Walter's apprehension of the state required in its possessor. While Lady Elliot lived, there had been method, moderation, and economy, which had just kept him within his income; but with her had died all such right-mindedness, and from that period he had been constantly exceeding it. It had not been possible for him to spend less; he had done nothing but what Sir Walter Elliot was imperiously called on to do; but blameless as he was, he was not only growing dreadfully in debt, but was hearing of it so often, that it became vain to attempt concealing it longer, even partially, from his daughter. He had given her some hints of it the last spring in town; he had gone so far even as to say, "Can we retrench?

Does it occur to you that there is any one article in which we can retrench?" and Elizabeth, to do her justice, had, in the first ardour of female alarm, set seriously to think what could be done, and had finally proposed these two branches of economy, to cut off some unnecessary charities, and to refrain from new furnishing the drawing-room; to which expedients she afterwards added the happy thought of their taking no present down to Anne, as had been the usual yearly custom. But these measures, however good in themselves, were insufficient for the real extent of the evil, the whole of which Sir Walter found himself obliged to confess to her soon afterwards.

长难句解析

He was at that time a very young man, just engaged in the study of the law.

在那时，他仅仅只是一个沉迷于研究法律的年轻人。

“engaged”过去分词做后置定语。

The following spring he was seen again in town, found equally agreeable, again encouraged, invited, and expected, and again he did not come;

来年春天他又被看见出现在镇上，同样地讨人喜欢，又一次被鼓舞，被邀请，被期待——他还是没有现身。

following 表示接下来的。

There was not a baronet from A to Z whom her feelings could have so willingly acknowledged as an equal.

天下的准男爵中，还没有一个人可以像他那样，使她如此心甘情愿地承认与她正相匹配呢。

“A to Z”这里字面上是A到Z，可以理解为从大到小，有顺序的，有等级之分的；whom 引导定语从句；acknowledge 表示承认，认可。

读书笔记

063 Of Human Bondage 人性的枷锁

今日关键语导读 Today's Key Points

小说主人公菲利普·凯里自幼父母双亡，不幸又先天残疾，在冷漠而陌生的环境中度过了童年，性格因此孤僻而敏感。在寄宿学校度过的岁月让他饱受不合理的学校制度的摧残，而当他走入社会后，又在爱情上经历伤痛。在坎坷的人生道路上，他每跨一步，都要付出艰辛的挣扎，但思想和个性都独立不羁的凯里，一直努力挣脱宗教和小市民意识这两条禁锢自己精神的桎梏，力图在混沌纷扰的生活漩涡中，寻求人生的真谛。

障碍词先听为快 Words and Expressions

subtle ['sʌtl] *adj.* 微妙的；敏感的；狡猾的；巧妙的

sympathy ['simpəθi] *n.* 意气相投，同感；同情

inmost ['inməust] *adj.* 最内的；最深的；纯粹私人的；最秘密的

exhilaration [ig,zilə'reiʃən] *n.* 愉快的心情，高兴；豪兴

vehemence ['viːiməns] *n.* 热烈；强烈；猛烈；愤怒

breathe [briːð] *vi.* 呼吸；活着

engaged [in'geidʒd] *adj.* 已订婚的；（指电话）占线的；忙碌的

violent ['vaiələnt] *adj.* 暴力引起的；剧烈的

punish ['pʌniʃ] *v.* 处罚，惩罚

glow with 伴随

He was surprised at himself because he ceased to believe so easily, and, not knowing that he felt as he did on account of the subtle workings of his inmost nature, he ascribed the certainty he had reached to his own cleverness. He was unduly pleased with himself. With youth's lack of sympathy for an attitude other than its own he despised not a little Weeks and Hayward because they were content with the vague emotion which they called God and would not take the further step which to himself seemed so obvious. One day he went alone up a certain hill so that he might see a view which, he knew not why, filled him always with wild exhilaration. It was autumn now, but often the days were cloudless still, and then the sky seemed to glow with a more splendid light: it was as though nature consciously sought to put a fuller vehemence into the remaining days of fair weather. He looked down upon the plain, a-quiver with the sun, stretching vastly before him: in the distance were the roofs of Mannheim and ever so far away the dimness of Worms. Here and there a more piercing glitter was the Rhine. The tremendous spaciousness of it was glowing with rich gold. Philip, as he stood there, his heart beating with sheer joy, thought how the tempter had stood with Jesus on a high mountain and shown him the kingdoms of the earth. To Philip, intoxicated with the beauty of the scene, it seemed that it was the whole world which was spread before him, and he was eager to step down and enjoy it. He was free from degrading fears and free from prejudice. He could go his way without the intolerable dread of hell-fire. Suddenly he realized that he had lost also that burden of responsibility which made every action of his life a matter of urgent consequence. He could breathe more freely in a lighter air. He was responsible only to himself for the things he did. Freedom! He was his own master at last. From old habit, unconsciously he thanked God that he no longer believed in Him.

Drunk with pride in his intelligence and in his fearlessness, Philip entered deliberately upon a new life. But his loss of faith made less difference in his behavior than he expected. Though he had thrown on one side the Christian dogmas it never occurred to him to criticize the Christian ethics; he accepted the Christian virtues, and indeed thought it fine to practice them for their own sake, without a thought of reward or punishment. There was small occasion for heroism in the Frau Professor's house, but he was a little more exactly truthful than he had been, and he forced himself to be more than commonly attentive to the dull, elderly ladies who sometimes engaged him in conversation. The gentle oath and the violent adjective which are typical of our language and which he had cultivated before as a sign of manliness, he now elaborately eschewed.

Having settled the whole matter to his satisfaction he sought to put it out of his mind, but that was more easily said than done; and he could not prevent the regrets nor stifle the misgivings which sometimes tormented him. He was so young and had so few friends that immortality had no particular attractions for him, and he was able without trouble to give up belief in it; but there was one thing which made him wretched; he told himself that he was unreasonable, he tried to laugh himself out of such pathos; but the tears really came to his eyes when he thought that he would never see again the beautiful mother whose love for him had grown more precious as the years since her death passed on. And sometimes, as though the influence of innumerable ancestors, God fearing and devout, were working in him unconsciously, there seized him a panic fear that perhaps after all it was all true, and there was, up there behind the blue sky, a jealous God who would punish in everlasting flames the atheist. At these times his reason could offer him no help, he imagined the anguish of a physical torment which would last endlessly, he felt quite sick with fear and burst into a violent sweat. At last he would say to himself desperately:

"After all, it's not my fault. I can't force myself to believe. If there is a God after all and he punishes me because I honestly don't believe in Him I can't help it."

长难句解析

He was surprised at himself because he ceased to believe so easily, and, not knowing that he felt as he did on account of the subtle workings of his inmost nature, he ascribed the certainty he had reached to his own cleverness.

他对自己感到吃惊，竟如此轻而易举地抛弃了信仰。他进入了心明神清的不惑之境，将此归因于自己的小聪明，殊不知他之所以会有这样的感受，乃是由于内在性格的微妙作用。

be surprised at sth. 对……感到惊讶；because引导原因状语从句；that引导宾语从句；on account of因为、由于。

One day he went alone up a certain hill so that he might see a view which, he knew not why, filled him always with wild exhilaration.

一天，他为了登高远望，独自来到某座山岗。他自己也不明白，为什么野外景色总能使他心旷神怡。

so that 引导目的状语从句。

He accepted the Christian virtues, and indeed thought it fine to practice them for their own sake, without a thought of reward or punishment.

他接受了基督教倡导的各种美德，并且进而认为，要是能因其本身的价值而身体力行，并不顾及报偿或惩罚，那倒也不失为好事。

for one's sake 站在某人的角度。

He could not prevent the regrets nor stifle the misgivings which sometimes tormented him.

他无法排除那些后悔的念头，也不能抑制那此时折磨着自己的疑虑情绪。

stifle在此处意思是抑制的意思。

"After all, it's not my fault. I can't force myself to believe. If there is a God after all and he punishes me because I honestly don't believe in Him I can't help it."

"这毕竟不是我的过错。我不能强迫自己去相信。若是果真有个上帝，而且就因为我老实表示不相信他而一定要惩罚我，那我也只得随他去了。"

if 引导的条件状语从句；after all毕竟。

读书笔记

064 Tarzan of the Apes 人猿泰山

今日关键语导读 Today's Key Points

约翰·格雷斯托克勋爵带着新婚妻子去英国在非洲的殖民地任职。不料途中，轮船上的水手叛乱，勋爵及其夫人死里逃生，并定居非洲原始丛林。不过，由于丛林环境恶劣，在生下“小泰山”后，夫妻俩双双罹难。“小泰山”被丧子的母猿卡拉抚养长大，10年的丛林生活，使泰山练就了超强的生存技能，却丧失了人类的基本情感，直到珍妮出现后，改变了他，但珍妮的同伴为了利益要毁灭丛林，泰山带领猿族奋起反击，利用自己的丛林技能和智慧，保卫了他的家园和他所爱的人。

障碍词先听为快 Words and Expressions

vessel ['vesl] n. 船，舰

anchor ['æŋkə] n. 锚 v. 抛锚

dozen ['dʌzən] n. 十二个，一打

wreckage ['rekidʒ] n. 残骸；失事

barkentine ['bɑːkəntiːn] n. 三桅船

coastwise [kəustwaiz] adj. 沿岸的；近海的

motley ['mɔtli] adj. 杂色的；混杂的

enact [i'nækt] vt. 颁布，制定法律

ludicrous ['luːdikrəs] adj. 滑稽的；荒唐的

We know only that on a bright May morning in 1888, John, Lord Greystoke, and Lady Alice sailed from Dover on their way to Africa.

A month later they arrived at Freetown where they chartered a small sailing vessel, the Fuwalda, which was to bear them to their final destination.

And here John, Lord Greystoke, and Lady Alice, his wife, vanished from the eyes and from the knowledge of men.

Two months after they weighed anchor and cleared from the port of Freetown a half dozen British war vessels were scouring the south Atlantic for trace of them or their little vessel, and it was almost immediately that the wreckage was found upon the shores of St. Helena which convinced the world that the Fuwalda had gone down with all on board, and hence the search was stopped ere it had scarce begun; though hope lingered in longing hearts for many years.

The Fuwalda, a barkentine of about one hundred tons, was a vessel of the type often seen in coastwise trade in the far southern Atlantic, their crews composed of the offscourings of the sea—unhanged murderers and cutthroats of every race and every nation.

The Fuwalda was no exception to the rule. Her officers were swarthy bullies, hating and hated by their crew. The captain, while a competent seaman, was a brute in his treatment of his men. He knew, or at least he used, but two arguments in his dealings with them—a belaying pin and a revolver—nor is it likely that the motley aggregation he signed would have understood aught else.

So it was that from the second day out from Freetown John Clayton and his young wife witnessed scenes upon the deck of the Fuwalda such as they had believed were never enacted outside the covers of printed stories of the sea.

It was on the morning of the second day that the first line was forged in what was destined to form a chain of circumstances ending in a life for one then unborn such as has never been paralleled in the history of man.

Two sailors were washing down the decks of the Fuwalda, the first mate was on duty, and the captain had stopped to speak with John Clayton and Lady Alice.

The men were working backwards toward the little party who were facing away from the sailors. Closer and closer they came, until one of them was directly behind the captain. In another moment he would have passed by and this strange narrative would never have been recorded.

But just that instant the officer turned to leave Lord and Lady Greystoke, and, as he did so, tripped against the sailor and sprawled headlong upon the deck, overturning the water-pail so that he was drenched in its dirty contents.

For an instant the scene was ludicrous; but only for an instant. With a volley of awful oaths, his face suffused with the scarlet of mortification and rage, the captain regained his feet, and with a terrific blow felled the sailor to the deck.

The man was small and rather old, so that the brutality of the act was thus accentuated. The other seaman, however, was neither old nor small—a huge bear of a man, with fierce black mustachios, and a great bull neck set between massive shoulders.

As he saw his mate go down he crouched, and, with a low snarl, sprang upon the captain crushing him to his knees with a single mighty blow.

长难句解析

We know only that on a bright May morning in 1888, John, Lord Greystoke, and Lady Alice sailed from Dover on their way to Africa.

我们只知道，在1888年五月一个明亮的早晨，约翰，格雷斯托克勋爵和夫人爱丽丝从多佛起航前往非洲。

句中that 引导宾语从句，on the bright May morning表示在一个明亮的早晨，sail from表示起航前往……

It was almost immediately that the wreckage was found upon the shores of St. Helena which convinced the world that the Fuwalda had gone down with all on board, and hence the search was stopped ere it had scarce begun; though hope lingered in longing hearts for many years.

这残骸立刻在圣海伦娜海滩被发现了，向全世界宣告了Fuwalda已经全面沉没。搜寻工作刚开始就结束了，虽然多年后人们心中还怀有希望。

句中it was...that...引导强调句，which引导定语从句，

that引导宾语从句；on board在船上；linger in 徘徊在。

Two sailors were washing down the decks of the Fuwalda, the first mate was on duty, and the captain had stopped to speak with John Clayton and Lady Alice.

两个水手正在清洗Fuwalda里的甲板，其中一人在值班，船长也已经停止与约翰·克来顿和爱丽丝小姐的交谈。

句中were washing 为过去进行时；on duty 当值；stop to do 停止去做某事；the deck of...，在……的甲板上。

For an instant the scene was ludicrous; but only for an instant.

一瞬间这场景是可笑的，但只是一瞬间。

for an instant，一瞬间；ludicrous 可笑的，荒唐的。

As he saw his mate go down he crouched, and, with a low snarl, sprang upon the captain crushing him to his knees with a single mighty blow.

当他看到同伴走下来，他蹲了下来，低声咆哮着给船长的膝盖重重一击。

句中as引导状语从句，with引导伴随状语。

065 The Cat Who Went to Heaven 上了天堂的猫

今日关键语导读 Today's Key Points

《上了天堂的猫》获得了1931年美国纽贝瑞文学奖。故事发生在日本，讲述了笃信佛教的穷画家收养了一只流浪猫，这只猫儿给他带来了奇妙的好运气……其中贯穿了悉达多成佛的经历，以及对各种动物的描写。这是一个关于无私与爱的故事，充满了东方的哲学色彩。

障碍词先听为快 Words and Expressions

Buddha ['budə] n. 佛；佛像

coax [kəuks] v. 哄；诱骗；灵巧慢慢地做

quiver ['kwivə] v. 颤抖；振动

whisker ['hwiskə] n. 腮须胡须

glisten [glisn] v. 闪光；闪耀

murmur ['məːmə] v. 低语；发出连续轻柔的声音；低声抱怨 n. 低语；连续轻柔的声音；低声的抱怨

bib [bib] n. 围嘴；围裙上部 v. 喝酒

scarlet ['skaːlit] n. 猩红；绯红色；红衣 adj. 绯红色的；猩红的

contemplation [ˌkɔntem'pleiʃən] n. 注视；沉思；打算

humble ['hʌmbl] adj. 谦逊的；粗陋的；卑下的；微末的 vt. 使……卑下；贬低

In the following days the artist painted the various gods of the earth and sky and the disciples who came to say farewell to the Buddha. Sometimes the painting came easy, sometimes it came hard; sometimes the artist was pleased with what he had done, sometimes he was disgusted. He would have grown very thin, if the old woman hadn't coaxed him early and late, now with a little bowl of soup, now with a hot dumpling. Good fortune went softly about the house, quivering with excitement. She, too, had plenty to eat these days. Her coat shone like silk. Her little whiskers glistened. Whenever the housekeeper's back was turned, she darted in to watch the artist and his mysterious paints and brushes.

"It worries me, sir," said the old housekeeper, when she found the cat tucked behind the artist's sleeve for the twentieth time that day. "She doesn't seem like a cat. She doesn't try to play with the brushes, that I could understand. At night all the things come back to me that you said when I brought her home in the bamboo basket. If she should turn out to be bad and hurt your picture, I should not wish to live."

The artist shook his head. A new idea had come to him and he was too busy to talk.

"Good Fortune will do no harm," he murmured before he forgot about them all, the old woman, the little cat, and even his own hand that held the brushes.

"I hope so, indeed," said the housekeeper anxiously. She picked up Good Fortune, who now wore about her neck a flowered bib on a scarlet silk cord, and looked like a cat of importance. It was at least half an hour before Good Fortune was able to get out of the kitchen. And her master still lost in contemplation, and sat behind him like a light spot in his shadow. The artist, having finished gods and men, was about to draw the animals who had come to bid farewell to the Buddha before he died. He was considering which animal ought to come first --perhaps the great white elephant which is the largest of beasts, and a symbol of the Buddha; perhaps the horse that served him; or the lion, since his followers sometimes called him the lion of his race. Then the artist thought of how the Buddha loved humble things and he remembered a story.

长难句解析

At night all the things come back to me that you said when I brought her home in the bamboo basket. If she should turn out to be bad and hurt your picture, I should not wish to live.

晚上我把她装在竹筐中带回家的时候，你对我说的所有事情都涌上心头。如果她表现不好，弄坏了你的画，我也不想活了。

that引导定语从句，提示前面的说话内容，when引导时间状语从句；if引导条件状语从句，主句应用虚拟语气（should + v.原形），表示假设情况。

The artist shook his head. A new idea had come to him and he was too busy to talk.

艺术家摇摇头。一个新的想法涌上心头，他忙得说不上话。

shake one's head 摇摇头，为固定搭配。too...to“太……而不能”，为否定含义。

It was at least half an hour before Good Fortune was able to get out of the kitchen.

招财进宝离开厨房至少有半小时了。

it 做形式主语；at least 至少；be able to 能够；get out of 脱离、逃跑。

And her master still lost in contemplation, and sat behind him like a light spot in his shadow.

她的主人仍然陷入在深深的沉思中，坐在他身后，就像他影子中的一盏灯一样。

lost in contemplation“陷入深思”；spot“斑点、地点”，也有“灯光”的意思。

---

066 The Cricket in Times Square 时代广场的蟋蟀

今日关键语导读 Today's Key Points

这是一个有关蟋蟀、老鼠和猫之间的友谊的故事，一个有关各种生命之间爱和关怀的故事，一个源自大自然、涤荡心弦的音乐之声的故事。来自康州乡下的蟋蟀柴斯特有着奇妙无比的鸣叫声。无意间，它被地铁送到了纽约，一个地铁站报刊亭的主人收养了它，并和塔克老鼠、亨利猫成为好朋友。柴斯特蟋蟀的歌声吸引了每一个坐地铁的乘客，很快便成了走红的地铁歌唱家，但最令它感到幸福的还是亨利猫和塔克鼠的关怀。秋天来临，柴斯特在亨利猫与塔克老鼠的帮助下离开了纽约，回到家乡，纽约的地铁少了往日优美的歌声，但却多了一份亲切和柔静。

障碍词先听为快 Words and Expressions

stumbling ['stʌmbl] adj. 摇摇晃晃或跌跌撞撞的 v.（不顺畅地）说（stumble的现在分词）；跌跌撞撞地走；绊脚；（说话、演奏等）出错

cricket ['krikit] n. 蟋蟀；板球；矮木凳 vi. 打板球 adj. 公平的；复数：crickets

commuter [kə'mjuːtə] n.（远距离）上下班往返的人；复数：commuters

Connecticut [kə'netikət] n. 康涅狄格州（美国）

arsonist ['ɑːsənist] n. 纵火犯

farewell ['fɛə'wel] n. 告别，欢送；欢送会；告别辞 int. 再见，再会；一路平安 adj. 告别的，送行的；复数：farewells

overwhelming [ˌəuvə'welmiŋ] adj. 势不可挡的，压倒一切的，巨大的；压倒一切的欢乐

financially [fə'nænʃəlɪ] adv. 财政上，金融上，经济上

germs [dʒɜːm] n. 微生物（germ的名词复数）；病菌；起源；发端

square [skwɛə] n. 正方形；广场；平方；方格 adj. 成直角的；平方的；（尤指在生意上）公平的；正方形的 adv. 四四方方地；成直角地；正直地；坚定地 vt. 使成正方形；使成直角；检测……的角度；调整，改正

好英文娓娓动听 Beautiful stories

The story is about a cricket from Connecticut named Chester who gets caught on a commuter train heading for New York. After stumbling on the subway, Chester ends up in Times Square. Mario Bellini, who helps his parents run a financially struggling newsstand, finds Chester and takes him to the newsstand, as he wants to keep the cricket as a pet and for good luck. Mama Bellini is concerned that the cricket will give the family germs, but Papa Bellini is more easy-going about the cricket's presence. At the newsstand, Chester meets Tucker Mouse and Harry Cat, who spend their time scrounging the city for food and other thrown away items. They show him Times Square, which Chester finds overwhelming. During the story, Chester reveals his musical chirping talent. Mario takes Chester to Chinatown (via the 1 train), where he buys Chester a cricket cage from the Chinatown shop owner Sai Fong.

At one point, Chester accidentally eats a two dollar bill from the newsstand cashier. Mama Bellini wants Chester to go, but Tucker gives part of his coin collection that he's collected from scrounging to save Chester and replace the money. Later in the story during a party that Chester, Harry, and Tucker are having, they accidentally set fire to the newsstand. The fire is put out, but Mama Bellini is extremely angry, accuses Chester of being an arsonist, and demands that Mario get rid of Chester, much to the boy's dismay. However, at the right moment, Chester chirps Mama Bellini's favorite song, which she sings along to and which also leads her to change her mind. It soon becomes clear that Chester has a perfect memory for music, as he chirps opera selections, which surprises Papa Bellini.

Later, Chester chirps classical music pieces and hymns for a music teacher, Mr. Smedley, the Bellini's best newsstand customer, who is impressed and writes a letter to the New York Times about it. This is printed in the newspaper, and brings attention to the newsstand when Chester starts playing concerts there. This causes the poor fortune of the newsstand to turn around, and the Bellinis' sales quickly pick up.

Mario senses that Chester has become unhappy, and says out loud that he wishes Chester hadn't come to the newsstand if he wasn't going to be happy. This makes Chester decide that he wants to return to the countryside. He tells Tucker and Harry this, and Tucker tries to convince Chester to stay. However, Harry says that Chester should do what he wants with his life and stop the concerts if he isn't happy.

With the advent of fall, Chester decides to go home to Connecticut. He gives a final concert that causes Times Square and blocks of New York City to fall still, with everyone stopping to listen to the music. Mario plays one last time with Chester at the newsstand after that last concert, and falls asleep after a while. Later that same night, after Chester gives a farewell chirp to Mario, Harry and Tucker take Chester to Grand Central Terminal so that Chester can hop on to a train. At Grand Central, they all say good-bye. Later, when Mario wakes up as his parents have returned, he realizes later that Chester has gone home, but accepts this by saying: "And I'm glad." The story ends with Tucker telling Harry that maybe they'll visit the country one day, "in Connecticut".

长难句解析

The story is about a cricket from Connecticut named Chester who gets caught on a commuter train heading for New York.

这个故事讲述的是一只来自康涅狄格州，名叫切斯特的蟋蟀，在一辆驶往纽约的列车上被抓住。

句中，who引导定语从句，head for 表示通向……

Mario Bellini, who helps his parents run a financially struggling newsstand, finds Chester and takes him to the newsstand, as he wants to keep the cricket as a pet and for good luck.

马里奥贝利尼，他帮助他的父母经营一家陷入经济困境的报摊，他发现了切斯特，并将它带去报摊，他想把蟋蟀作为宠物并认为那会带来好运气。

句中who引导定语从句，take...to...表示带……到……，as...作为……。

Mama Bellini wants Chester to go, but Tucker gives part of his coin collection that he's collected from scrounging to save Chester...

妈妈贝里尼想要切斯特离开，但塔克将收集用来救切斯特的钱给了她一部分……

句中that引导同位语从句修饰collection；part of... ……的一部分。

Later in the story during a party that Chester, Harry, and Tucker are having, they accidentally set fire to the newsstand.

在后来的故事中，切斯特，哈利，塔克，他们意外地点燃了报摊。

句中later in the story表示在后来的故事中；set fire 点燃；newsstand 报摊。

The fire is put out, but Mama Bellini is extremely angry, accuses Chester of being an arsonist, and demands that Mario get rid of Chester, much to the boy's dismay. However, at the right moment, Chester chirps Mama Bellini's favorite song, which she sings along to and which also leads her to change her mind.

火被扑灭了，但妈妈贝利尼极其愤怒，指责切斯特纵火，并要求马里奥摆脱切斯特，让他感到很沮丧。然而，这时，切斯特唱出了妈妈贝里尼最喜欢的歌，这也使她改变主意。

句中be put out 表示被扑灭；get rid of丢弃，遗弃，however 表示转折；at the right moment在这时；which引导非限制性定语从句。

读书笔记

067 A Wrinkle in Time 时间的皱纹

今日关键语导读 Today's Key Points

《时间的皱纹》是美国青少年文学作家马德琳·英格的一本科幻题材小说。15岁的女孩麦格为了寻找失踪的科学家爸爸，踏上了一条非同寻常的道路。尽管旅途中布满了艰辛和危险，但她和她的小伙伴从没有动摇过他们要找到并救出爸爸的决心。爸爸对麦格的亲子之爱，弟弟与麦格的手足之情，加尔文与麦格的朋友之谊……麦格肩负着这些爱，战胜了邪恶，最终重返家园。

障碍词先听为快 Words and Expressions

scud [skʌd] vi. 疾行；顺风行驶

frantically ['fræntɪklɪ] adv. 疯狂似地；狂暴地

toss [tɔs] vi. 辗转；被乱扔；颠簸

scornfully ['skɔːnfəlɪ] adv. 轻蔑地；藐视地

ounce [auns] n. 盎司；少量；雪豹

bruise [bruːz] n. 擦伤；挫伤；青肿

delinquent [di'liŋkwənt] adj. 有过失的；怠忽的；拖欠债务的

grimly [grɪmlɪ] adv. 可怕地；冷酷地；严格地

好英文娓娓动听 Beautiful stories

It was a dark and stormy night.

In her attic bedroom Margaret Murry, wrapped in an old patchwork quilt, sat on the foot of her bed and watched the trees tossing in the frenzied lashing of the wind. Behind the trees clouds scudded frantically across the sky. Every few moments the moon ripped through them, creating wraith—like shadows that raced along the ground.

The house shook.

Wrapped in her quilt, Meg shook.

She wasn't usually afraid of weather. It's not just the weather, she thought. It's the weather on top of everything else. On top of me. On top of Meg Murry doing everything wrong.

School. School was all wrong. She'd been dropped down to the lowest section in her grade. That morning one of her teachers had said crossly, "Really, Meg, I don't understand how a child with parents as brilliant as yours are supposed to be can be such a poor student. If you don't manage to do a little better you'll have to stay back next year."

During lunch she'd rough-housed a little to try to make herself feel better, and one of the girls said scornfully, "After all, Meg, we aren't grammar-school kids any more. Why do you always act like such a baby?

And on the way home from school, walking up the road with her arms full of books, one of the boys had said something about her "dumb baby brother." At this she'd thrown die books on the side of the road and tackled him with every ounce of strength she had, and arrived home with her blouse torn and a big bruise under one eye.

Sandy and Dennys, her ten-year-old twin brothers, who got home from school an hour earlier than she did, were disgusted. "Let us do the fighting when it's necessary," they told her. A delinquent, that's what I am, she thought grimly. That's what they'll be saying next. Not Mother. But Them. Everybody Else. I wish Father?

But it was still not possible to think about her father without the danger of tears. Only her mother could talk about him in a natural way, saying, "When your father gets back?

Gets back from where? And when? Surely her mother must know what people were saying, must be aware of the smugly vicious gossip. Surely it must hurt her as it did Meg. But if it did she gave no outward sign. Nothing ruffled the serenity other expression.

Why can't I hide it, too? Meg thought. Why do I always have to show everything?

The window rattled madly in the wind, and she pulled the quilt dose about her. Curled up on one of her pillows a gray fluff of kitten yawned, showing its pink tongue, tucked its head under again, and went back to sleep.

Everybody was asleep. Everybody except Meg. Even Charles Wallace, the "dumb baby brother," who had an uncanny way of knowing when she was awake and unhappy, and who would come, so many nights, tiptoeing up the attic stairs to her—even Charles Wallace was asleep. How could they sleep? All day on the radio there had been hurricane warnings. How could they leave her up in the attic in the rickety brass bed, knowing that the roof might be blown right off the house, and she tossed out into the wild night sky to land who knows where?

长难句解析

In her attic bedroom Margaret Murry, wrapped in an old patchwork quilt, sat on the foot of her bed and watched the trees tossing in the frenzied lashing of the wind. Behind the trees clouds scudded frantically across the sky.

麦格·莫瑞独自一人待在她的小阁楼里。她裹着打满补丁的旧棉被蜷缩在床脚边，两眼一直望着窗外的树在飓风中狂乱摇摆，树后的云朵急速地掠过天空。

wrap in“把……包在……里”，on the foot of“在……脚边”。

During lunch she'd rough-housed a little to try to make herself feel better, and one of the girls said scornfully, "After all, Meg, we aren't grammar-school kids any more. Why do you always act like such a baby?

午饭时间到了，为了忘掉那些讨厌的话，麦格自娱自乐起来，她觉得这样子会好受些。可是，一个女孩轻蔑地挖苦她：“麦格，你以为我们还是小学生吗？为什么你还跟个孩子似的？”

during 引导时间状语；rough house 本来是“胡闹，大打出手”的意思，在这用作动词，意为做某事自娱自乐；after all“毕竟”。

At this she'd thrown die books on the side of the road and tackled him with every ounce of strength she had, and arrived home with her blouse torn and a big bruise under one eye.

她把手上的书一股脑儿摔在路边，然后用尽全力跟他扭打起来。等她到家时，她的衣服已被扯得破破烂烂，一只眼睛也成了熊猫眼。

on the side of“在……的一边”，tackle with“处理”，every ounce of“竭尽全力”。

读书笔记

068 Hatchet 手斧男孩

今日关键语导读 Today's Key Points

布莱恩13岁了，他要去爸爸那里过暑假，爸爸在加拿大北方的原始森林里从事油田的开采工作。布莱恩如何才能到达自己向往已久的原始森林呢？一天，机会终于来了，有一架飞机要飞回油田，布莱恩便成了这架小飞机上的唯一乘客。然而，谁曾料到巨大的不幸这时却降临了，驾驶员心脏病突发猝死，飞机摔落在杳无人烟的森林深处。还好，布莱恩幸免一死，但密林深处危机重重，生存陷入困境——绝望、恐惧、饥饿、大黑熊、狼、驼鹿……上飞机前，妈妈送了他一把手斧，手握斧头的布莱恩能够生存下来吗？

障碍词先听为快 Words and Expressions

split [split] vt. 分裂，分开 n. 划分，分歧，裂缝，劈叉

court [kɔːt] n. 法院；庭院奉承 v. 献殷勤；追求；招致

sudden ['sʌdn] adj. 突然的，未预见到的，急躁的，仓促的，快的，迅速的

embarrassing [im'bærəsiŋ] adj. 令人为难的；尴尬的

obviously ['ɔbviəsli] adv. 明显地

mechanical [mi'kænikl] adj. 机械的，机械学的，呆板的，体力的，手工操作的

drilling ['driliŋ] n. 演练 v. 钻（孔）（drill的现在分词），打

（眼），操练，训练

emergency [iˈməːdʒnsi] n. 紧急情况，突发事件，非常时刻 adj. 紧急的，应急的

好英文娓娓动听 Beautiful stories

The big split. Brian's father did not understand as Brian did, knew only that Brian's mother wanted to break the marriage apart. The split had come and then the divorce, all so fast, and the court had left him with his mother except for the summers and what the judge called "visitation rights". So formal. Brian hated judges as he hated lawyers. Judges that leaned over the bench and asked Brian if he under- stood where he was to live and why. Judges who did not know what had really happened. Judges with the caring look that meant nothing as lawyers said legal phrases that meant nothing.

In the summer Brian would live with his father. In the school year with his mother. That's what the judge said after looking at papers on his desk and listening to the lawyers talk. Talk. Words. Now the plane lurched slightly to the right and Brian looked at the pilot. He was rubbing his shoulder again and there was the sudden smell of body gas in the plane. Brian turned back to avoid embarrassing the pilot, who was obviously in some discomfort. Must have stomach troubles. So this summer, this first summer when he was allowed to have "visitation rights" with his father, with the divorce only one month old, Brian was heading north. His father was a mechanical engineer who had designed or invented a new drill bit for oil drilling, a self-cleaning, self-sharpening bit. He was working in the oil fields of Canada, up on the tree line where the tundra started and the forests ended.

Brian was riding up from New York with some drilling equipment—it was lashed down in the rear of the plane next to a fabric bag the pilot had called a survival pack, which had emergency supplies in case they had to make an emergency landing—that had to be specially made in the city, riding in a bush plane with the pilot named Jim or Jake or something who had turned out to be an all right guy, letting him fly and all.

Except for the smell. Now there was a constant odor, and Brian took another look at the pilot, found him rubbing the shoulder and down the arm now, die left arm, letting go more gas and wincing. Probably something he ate, Brian thought.

His mother had driven him from the city to meet the plane at Hampton where it came to pick up the drilling equipment. A drive in silence, a long drive in silence. Two and a half hours of sitting in the car, staring out the window just as he was now staring out the window of the plane. Once, after an hour, when they were out of the city she turned to him.

长难句解析

The big split. Brian's father did not understand as Brian did, knew only that Brian's mother wanted to break the marriage apart.

一个大的分歧。布莱恩的父亲像布莱恩一样无法理解，只知道布莱恩的妈妈想结束婚姻。

as“像……一样”；that引导宾语从句；break apart“结束，分离”。

Judges who did not know what had really happened. Judges with the caring look that meant nothing as lawyers said legal phrases that meant nothing.

法官不知道到底发生了什么，法官面带关心的神色不能说明什么，律师说出的法律条款也不能说明什么。

who引导定语从句，what引导宾语从句，that引导定语从句，as引导原因状语从句。

So this summer, this first summer when he was allowed to have "Vis itation rights" with his father, with the divorce only one month old, Brian was heading north.

所以今年夏天，这是第一个他被允许探视他父亲的夏天，距离婚只有一个月时间，布莱恩朝北方驶去。

when引导时间状语从句；be allowed to“被允许做……”；visitation rights“探视权”。

His mother had driven him from the city to meet the plane at Hampton where it came to pick up the drilling equipment.

他母亲从城里驱车带他来到汉普顿看飞机，这里有一些钻井设备。

where引导地点状语从句；pick up 捡起，搭载，（非正式）学到。

读书笔记

069 A Tale of Two Cities 双城记

今日关键语导读 Today's Key Points

《双城记》是英国作家查尔斯·狄更斯所著的一部以法国大革命为背景的长篇历史小说。小说将巴黎、伦敦两个大城市联结起来，围绕着莫奈特一家和以德法奇夫妇为首的圣安东尼区展开，主要描写了贵族的生活如何腐朽，如何欺压百姓，以及人民心中积压的对贵族的仇恨。本书的主要思想是为了爱而自我牺牲。

障碍词先听为快 Words and Expressions

mender ['mendə] n. 修改者，修理者；修缮者
coach [kəutʃ] n. 教练；旅客车厢；长途公车；四轮大马车
murder ['məːdə] vt. 谋杀，凶杀 n. 谋杀，凶杀 vi. 杀人，犯杀人罪
hang [hæŋ] vt. 悬挂，垂下；装饰；绞死；使悬而未决
knitted ['nɪtɪd] adj. [纺] 针织的；编织 v. 编织；使紧密结合
quite [kwait] adv. 很；相当；完全
revenge [ri'vendʒ] n. 报仇 vt. 报复；替……报仇；洗雪 vi. 报仇；雪耻
hurry ['hʌri] v. 使赶紧；使匆忙，使急忙

In Monsieur Defarge's wine—shop in Saint Antoine customers came and went all the time. They came to drink the thin, rough wine, but more often they came to listen and to talk, and to wait for news.

One day there were more customers than usual. Defarge had been away for three days, and when he returned that morning, he brought a stranger with him, a man who repaired roads.

"Madame," Defarge said to his wife, "this man, who is called Jacques, has walked a long way with me." One customer got up and went out. "This mender of roads," continued Defarge, "who is called Jacques, is a good man. Give him something to drink." A second man got up and went out. The man who repaired roads sat down and drank. A third man got up and went out.

"Have you finished, my friend?" said Defarge. "Then come and see the room I promised you."

They went upstairs, to the room where Dr Manette had sat making shoes. The three men who had left the wine—shop were waiting. Defarge spoke to them.

"No names. You are Jacques One, Jacques Two and Jacques Three. I am Jacques Four. This is Jacques Five. He brings us news of our poor friend Gaspard, whose child was killed by the Marquis's coach a year ago."

"I first saw Gaspard," said Jacques Five, "holding on under the Marquis's coach as it drove into our village. He ran away, but that night the Marquis was murdered. Gaspard disappeared and was only caught a few weeks ago. The soldiers brought him into the village and hanged him. And they have left his body hanging in the village square, where the women go to fetch water, and our children play."

When Jacques Five had left them, Jacques One said to his friends, "What do you say? Shall we put their names on the list?"

"Yes, all of them. The castle and all of the family of Evrémonde."

"Is the list safe?" asked Jacques Two.

"Yes, my friend," said Defarge. "My wife remembers everything. But more than that, every name is carefully knitted into her work. Nothing can be forgotten."

A few days later Defarge reported to his wife some news from his friend Jacques' in the police.

"A new spy has been sent to Saint Antoine. His name is Barsad, John Barsad. He's English."

"What does he look like? Do we know?"

"He's about forty years old, quite tall, black hair, thin face," said Defarge.

"Good," said his wife. "I'll put him on the list tomorrow. But you seem tired tonight. And sad."

"Well," said Defarge, "it is a long time."

"It takes time to prepare for change. The crimes against the people of France cannot be revenged in a day."

"But we may not live to see the end."

"Even if that happens," replied Madame Defarge, "we shall help it to come. But I believe that we shall see the day of our revenge against these hated noblemen."

The next day a stranger came into the wine—shop. At once, Madame Defarge picked up a rose from the table and put it in her hair. As soon as they saw this, the customers stopped talking and, one by one, without hurrying, left the wine—shop.

长难句解析

Defarge had been away for three days, and when he returned that morning, he brought a stranger with him, a man who repaired roads.

德法尔热已经出去3天了。当他那天早上回来时，他带回来了一个陌生人，一个修路工。

had been……过去完成时，表示过去某一段时间或某一动作已经发生或完成了并造成了影响。

They went upstairs, to the room where Dr. Manette had sat making shoes. The three men who had left the wine—shop were waiting.

他们上了楼，来到马奈特医生曾坐着做鞋子的房间。那三个刚才离开酒店的男人正在等着他们。

where引导地点状语从句。

"Even if that happens," replied Madame Defarge, "we shall help it to come."

"即使是这样，"德法尔热夫人说，""我们也要尽力让它到来。

even if引导条件状语从句；shall表示"必须"。

"Have you finished, my friend?" said Defarge. "Then come and see the room I promised you."

"喝完了吗，我的朋友？"德法尔热说。"那就过来看看我答应给你的房间吧。"

promise sb. sth. 承诺某人某事。

As soon as they saw this, the customers stopped talking and, one by one, without hurrying, left the wine—shop.

顾客们一看到这个动作便立刻停止了交谈，并一个接着一个从容地离开了酒店。

stop doing sth. 停止做某事；stop to do sth. 停下（手头的事情）去做另外一件事。

070 The Legend of Sleepy Hollow 睡谷的传说

今日关键语导读 Today's Key Points

《睡谷的传说》是美国作家华盛顿·欧文创作的著名短篇小说。传说在美国独立战争时期的一次战役中，一个赫塞骑兵的头被炮弹打飞了。此后，他的阴魂常骑马在夜间飞驰，到战场上去寻找他的头颅。在睡谷有位从康涅狄格州来的教师，名叫伊卡包德·克兰，他对那些离奇的传说笃信不疑。在美丽的山村塔里敦里，乡村教师伊卡博德·克莱恩偶遇“无头骑士”的故事正在上演。

障碍词先听为快 Words and Expressions

denominated [dɪ'nɒmɪneɪt] v. 命名；称……为

prudently ['pruːdntlɪ] adv. 谨慎地；慎重地

adjacent [ə'dʒeisənt] adj. 邻近的；毗连的；接近的

inveterate [in'vetərit] adj. 根深蒂固的；成瘾的

propensity [prə'pensiti] n. 倾向；习性

vouch [vautʃ] v. 担保；保证；证明；确定

exploit [iks'plɔit] n. 功绩；英勇行为 vt. 剥削；利用；开发；开拓

inhabitant [in'hæbitənt] n. 居民

descendant [di'send(ə)nt] n. 后裔；子孙；后代

rustic ['rʌstik] adj. 乡村的；纯朴的；手工粗糙的 n. 乡下人；村夫

pervade [pə(ː)'veid] vt. 弥漫；遍及；蔓延

enchanted [ɪn'tʃɑːntɪd] adj. 被施魔法的；陶醉的；入迷的

In the bosom of one of those spacious coves which indent the eastern shore of the Hudson, at that broad expansion of the river denominated by the ancient Dutch navigators the Tappan Zee, and where they always prudently shortened sail and implored the protection of St. Nicholas when they crossed, there lies a small market town or rural port, which by some is called Greens burgh, but which is more generally and properly known by the name of Tarry Town. This name was given, we are told, in former days, by the good housewives of the adjacent country, from the inveterate propensity of their husbands to linger about the village tavern on market days. Be that as it may, I do not vouch for the fact, but merely advert to it, for the sake of being precise and authentic. Not far from this village, perhaps about two miles, there is a little valley or rather lap of land among high hills, which is one of the quietest places in the whole world. A small brook glides through it, with just murmur enough to lull one to repose; and the occasional whistle of a quail or tapping of a woodpecker is almost the only sound that ever breaks in upon the uniform tranquility. I recollect that, when a stripling, my first exploit in squirrel-shooting was in a grove of tall walnut-trees that shades one side of the valley. I had wandered into it at noontime, when all nature is peculiarly quiet, and was startled by the roar of my own gun, as it broke the Sabbath stillness around and was prolonged and reverberated by the angry echoes. If ever I should wish for a re treat whither I might steal from the world and its distractions, and dream quietly away the remnant of a troubled life, I know of none more promising than this little valley.

From the listless repose of the place, and the peculiar character of its inhabitants, who are descendants from the original Dutch settlers, this sequestered glen has long been known by the name of SLEEPY HOLLOW, and its rustic lads are called the Sleepy Hollow Boys throughout all the neighboring country. A drowsy, dreamy influence seems to hang over the land, and to pervade the very atmosphere. Some say that the place was bewitched by a High German doctor, during the early days of the settlement; others, that an old Indian chief, the prophet or wizard of his tribe, held his powwows there before the country was discovered by Master Hendrick Hudson. Certain it is, the place still continues under the sway of some witching power, that holds a spell over the minds of the good people, causing them to walk in a continual reverie. They are given to all kinds of marvelous beliefs; are subject to trances and visions, and frequently see strange sights, and hear music and voices in the air. The whole neighborhood abounds with local tales, haunted spots, and twilight superstitions; stars shoot and meteors glare oftener across the valley than in any other part of the country, and the nightmare, with her whole nine-fold, seems to make it the favorite scene of her gambols.

The dominant spirit, however, that haunts this enchanted region, and seems to be commander-in-chief of all the powers of the air, is the apparition of a figure on horseback, without ahead. It is said by some to be the ghost of a Hessian trooper, whose head had been carried away by a cannonball, in some nameless battle during the Revolutionary War, and who is ever and-anon seen by the country folk hurrying along in the gloom of night, as if on the wings of the wind. His haunts are not confined to the valley, but extend at times to the adjacent roads, and especially to the vicinity of a church at no great distance. Indeed, certain of the most authentic historians of those parts, who have been careful in collecting and collating the floating facts concerning this specter, allege that the body of the trooper having been buried in the churchyard, the ghost rides forth to the scene of battle in nightly quest of his head, and that the rushing speed with which he sometimes passes along the Hollow, like a midnight blast, is owing to his being belated, and in a hurry to get back to the church yard before daybreak.

长难句解析

Not far from this village, perhaps about two miles, there is a little valley or rather lap of land among high hills, which is one of the quietest places in the whole world. A small brook glides through it, with just murmur enough to lull one to repose; and the occasional whistle of a quail or tapping of a woodpecker is almost the only sound that ever breaks in upon the uniform tranquility.

离这个小镇不远，大约两英里左右的高山中有一个小山谷或是些许高高的山坡地。这里是世界上最寂静的地方之一。一条小溪穿流而过，潺潺的溪流声使人昏昏欲睡，只有小鸟偶尔的鸣叫声才打破了山谷的宁静。

far from 离……距离远；which引导非限定性定语从句。

The dominant spirit, however, that haunts this enchanted region, and seems to be commander-in-chief of all the powers of the air, is the apparition of a figure on horseback, without a head. It is said by some to be the ghost of a Hessian trooper, whose head had been carried away by a cannonball, in some nameless battle during the Revolutionary War, and who is ever and-anon seen by the country folk hurrying along in the gloom of night, as if on the wings of the wind.

在这个地区所提到的幽灵中最神奇的那个好像成了这里一切的统治者。在睡谷的人们看来，那幽灵的外貌像是骑在马上的一个人，一个无头的家伙。据说那是在革命战争中被枪打掉了脑袋的黑森雇佣兵的鬼魂。据说这个无头骑士经常在夜间飞快地游荡，就像乘着风的翅膀。

第一句中的 that 引导定语从句；the powers of，……的能量；whose引导定语从句；最后一句中 as if表虚拟语气。

From the listless repose of the place, and the peculiar character of its inhabitants, who are descendants from the original Dutch settlers, this sequestered glen has long been known by the name of SLEEPY HOLLOW, and its rustic lads are called the Sleepy Hollow Boys throughout all the neighboring country. A drowsy, dreamy influence seems to hang over the land, and to pervade the very atmosphere.

这个山谷的名字因此地的与世隔绝产生，来自那些原始的居住者。这个山谷因此得名“睡谷”，并且这里的农夫被邻村的人叫作“睡谷人”。一个沉睡的、梦魇般的东西似乎无处不在，无时不有。

who引导定语从句；the name of，……的名字；hang over 挂在……之上，悬浮在……之上，威胁，即将降临（发生）。

I recollect that, when a stripling, my first exploit in squirrel-shooting was in a grove of tall walnut-trees that shades one side of the valley. I had wandered into it at noontime, when all nature is peculiarly quiet, and was startled by the roar of my own gun, as it broke the Sabbath stillness around and was prolonged and reverberated by the angry echoes. If ever I should wish for a re treat whither I might steal from the world and its distractions, and dream quietly away the remnant of a troubled life, I know of none more promising than this little valley.

我记得，当时我还是一个小伙子，我第一次的英勇行为是在遮蔽了半个山谷的大胡桃树林中捕获了几只松鼠。那是一个中午，我闲逛进了山谷，当时万籁俱寂，这短暂的宁静被我响亮的枪声打破，在山谷久久地回荡。我若是想逃避尘世的烦恼，与世隔绝，安安静静虚度此生，再也没有比这小山谷更合适的地方了。

第一个that跟在动词recollect后，引导宾语从句；第二个that 引导定语从句修饰walnut-trees（胡桃树）；one side of，……的一边；when引导时间状语从句；be startled by为某事而震惊；the roar of轰鸣声中；if 后的从句用到虚拟语气，表示假设，主句用might(could)+v.原形；none(no) more than只是；至多；只不过；无非。

Certain it is, the place still continues under the sway of some witching power, that holds a spell over the minds of the good people, causing them to walk in a continual reverie. They are given to all kinds of marvelous beliefs; are subject to trances and visions, and frequently see strange sights, and hear music and voices in the air.

可以确定的是，这个地方一直受控于某种巫术的力量，坚持着所谓善类的思想，以至于他们一直活在白日梦里。他们倾心于各种令人惊异的信念，受制于幻象，常常看见奇异之境，听见空中来音。

causing为现在分词做状语，表伴随；are given to有……癖好，倾向于，沉湎；all kinds of各种各类的，五花八门；be subject to受支配，从属于，可以……的，常遭受……。

读书笔记

071 He's Just Not That Into You 他没那么喜欢你

今日关键语导读 Today's Key Points

你真的了解你的男人吗?

也许他满口甜言蜜语，但其实他并不是真心喜欢你!

也许他和你约会，也打电话跟你聊天，但其实他并不是真心喜欢你。

也许他和你肌肤相亲，但其实他并不是真心喜欢你!

在世界各地的都市人中掀起了一股“欲望潮”的都市系列剧《欲望都市》的顾问与编剧不想再看见女人被男人耍得晕头转向，于是，他们以《欲望都市》为起点又编写了《他其实没那么喜欢你》这本书，戳破男人的假面具与谎言，拯救沉浮于无奈与彷徨的女性同胞们早日脱离苦海!书中字字句句都实话实说，没有废话与陈词滥调，数十个赤裸裸的真实案例与针针见血的剖析，绝对会让女性朋友们恍然大悟，洞彻男人的内心。

障碍词先听为快 Words and Expressions

divorce [di'vɔːs] v. 离婚，分开

stuff [stʌf] n. 材料，原料，资料 vt. 塞满，填塞，让吃饱

massive ['mæsiv] adj. 大的，重的，大块的，大量的，魁伟的

thrill [θril] v. 使激动，使陶醉，使颤动 n. [病]震颤，震颤感，兴奋感

despite [dis'pait] prep. 不管，尽管（自己）不愿意，不在乎，虽然 n. 侮辱，憎恨，怨恨，轻蔑的拒绝或不承认

inclination [ˌinkliˈneiʃən] n. 倾向，爱好，斜坡

trick [trik] n. 戏法，把戏，骗局，恶作剧 v. 哄骗，欺骗，打扮 adj. 弄虚作假的，欺诈的

conference [ˈkɔnfərəns] n. 会议，讨论 v. 举行或参加（系列）会议

branch [braːntʃ] n. 树枝，分支，部门，分科，支流 v. 使分支，使分叉

courtesy [ˈkəːtisi,ˈkɔːtisi] n. 礼貌；好意；恩惠

好英文娓娓动听 Beautiful stories

The "Maybe He Wants to Take It Slow" Excuse

Dear Greg,

There's this guy who calls me all the time. He's recently divorced, and in AA. We got back in touch recently, had lots of phone calls, and then hung out twice in one week and it was real cool. No flirting or making out or anything, but fun. Since then, he calls me all the time but doesn't ever suggest we see each other in person again. It's like he got scared or something. I would understand if because of the divorce/alcoholic/starting-a-whole-new-life stuff he wanted to take things slow. But he still calls me all the time to have long heart-to-heart talks. what the hell should I do with this guy?

Jen

FROM THE DESK OF GERG

Dear Pillow Talk

Sadly, not wanting to see you in person is massive as far as dating obstacles go. And as far as the recently divorced/newly sober/starting-a-new-life parts, blah blah blah, I'm getting sleepy, it's hot, I'm going down for a nap. When I wake up from that nap I'll probably thrill to the news that your friend is taking control of his life. You, however, will still not be going on a date, because despite all your excuses for him, he's still not asking you out. Now, if you're a person who enjoys a slightly satisfying phone relationship, talk on! But at this point it seems like he's just not that into you. Be his friend if you're at all interested on that level, but move your romantic inclinations onto a more suitable future husband.

If a guy truly likes you, but for personal reasons he needs to take things slow, he will let you know that immediately. He won't keep you guessing, because he'll want to make you sure you don't get frustrated and go away.

The "But He Gave Me His Number" Excuse

Dear Greg,

I met a really cute guy at a bar this week. He gave me his number and told me to give him a call sometime. I thought that was kind of cool, that he gave me control of the the situation like that. I can call him, right?

Lauren

FROM THE DESK OF GREG

Dear control Freak,

Did he give you control, or did he just get you to do the heavy lifting? what he just did was a magic trick: It seems like he gave you control, but really he now gets to decide if he wants to go out with you—or even return your call. Why don't you take Copperfield's number, roll it in a newspaper, pour milk in it, and make it disappear.

"Give me a call." "E-mail." "Tell Joey we should all hang out sometime." Don't let him trick you into asking him out. When men want you, they do the work. I Know it sounds old school, but when men like women, they ask them out.

The "Maybe He Forgot to Remember Me" Excuse

Dear Greg

Okay, Greg. Listen to this one: I was at a conference for work and met a guy from another branch of my company. We hit it off immediately. He was just about to ask for my number, I swear, when the Big Blackout of 2003 happened. In the mayhem, I didn't get to give him my number. I think the Big Blackout of 2003 is a good enough excuse to call him, don't you think? It's only common courtesy for me to check up on him, right? If I don't call, he's probably going to be all sad thinking that I'm just not that into him.

Judy

FROM THE DESK OF GREG

Dear Judy Blackout,

The city balcked out. He didn't. You said you work for different branches of the same company. Certainly he wouldn't have to break a sweat to scroll through the company staff roster or interoffice e-mail listing to find you. And should he not be as resourceful as you are...I imagine that he is a mother, sister, or female friend that could show him how, if he was really interested.

P.S.: Shame on you for using an eastern seaboard disaster as an excuse to call a guy up.

Have faith. You made an impression. Leave it at that. If he likes you, he'll still remember you after the tsunami flood, or Red Sox loss. If he doesn't, he's not worth your time. Know why? You are great.(Now, don't get cocky.)

长难句解析

He's recently divorced, and in AA.
他最近离婚了，并且双方都达成了共识。

"AA"这里表示"双方的"，根据文章可以理解为达成共识。

No flirting or making out or anything, but fun.
没有调情，没有偷食禁果或者其他的事，除了欢乐。

这里"but"理解为除了……的意思。

What the hell should I do with this guy?
我到底该怎么处理和这个男人的关系呢？

"the hell"用于句中加强语气，表示到底，究竟。

He won't keep you guessing, because he'll want to make sure you don't get frustrated and or away.
他不会让你胡思乱想，因为他想要确认你是否会为此沮丧或者想要转身离开。

“keep you guessing”中的“keep sb. doing”表示让某人不停地做某事。

Did he give you control, or did he just get you to do the heavy lifting?

他是否想要控制你或者是仅仅让你去承担更多？

give sb. control 控制。

读书笔记

072 Tess of the D'Urbervilles 苔丝

今日关键语导读 Today's Key Points

《苔丝》是托马斯·哈代的代表作，是“维塞克斯系列”中的一部。它描写了一位农村姑娘的悲惨命运。哈代在小说的副标题中称女主人公为“一个纯洁的女人”，公开地向维多利亚时代虚伪的社会道德发起挑战。

女主人公苔丝出生于一个贫苦的小贩家庭，父母要她到一个富老太婆家去攀亲戚，结果她被少爷亚力克诱奸，后来她与牧师的儿子克莱尔恋爱并订婚，在新婚之夜她把昔日的不幸坦白，却没能得到原谅，后来两人分居，丈夫去了巴西，几年后，苔丝再次与亚力克相遇，后者纠缠她，这时候她因家境窘迫不得不与仇人同居，不久克莱尔从国外回来，向妻子表示悔恨自己以往的冷酷无情，在这种情况下，苔丝痛苦地觉得是亚力克·伯德使他第二次失去了安吉尔，便愤怒地将他杀死。最后她被捕并被处以绞刑。

障碍词先听为快 Words and Expressions

chamber ['tʃeimb] n. （身体或器官内的）室，膛；房间；会所 adj. 室内的；私人的，秘密的

indescribable [ˌindi'skraibəbl] adj. 难以形容的；莫名其妙的；不能用语言表达的

insulted [ɪn'sʌlt] vt. 侮辱；辱骂；损害 n. 侮辱；凌辱；无礼

fixedly ['fiksidli] adv. 固定地；不动，不变

occasionally [ə'keiʒənəli] adv. 偶尔；间或

endearment [in'diəmənt] n. 钟爱；亲爱；亲爱的表示

somnambulistic [səm'næmbjʊ'lɪstɪk] adj. 梦游的

loyal ['lɔiəl] adj. 忠诚的，忠心的；忠贞的 n. 效忠的臣民；忠实信徒

combat ['kɔmbət] vt. 反对；与……战斗 vi. 战斗；搏斗 n. 战斗；争论 adj. 战斗的；为……斗争的

desirable [di'zaiərəbl] adj. 令人满意的；值得要的 n. 合意的人或事物

好英文娓娓动听 Beautiful stories

Midnight came and passed silently, for there was nothing to announce it in the Valley of the Froom.

Not long after one o'clock there was a slight creak in the darkened farm-house once the mansion of the d'Urbervilles. Tess, who used the upper chamber, heard it and awoke. It had come from the corner step of the staircase, which, as usual, was loosely nailed. She saw the door of her bedroom open, and the figure of her husband crossed the stream of moonlight with a curiously careful tread. He was in his shirt and trousers only, and her first flush of joy died when she perceived that his eyes were fixed in an unnatural stare on vacancy. When he reached the middle of the room he stood still and murmured, in tones of indescribable sadness—

"Dead! Dead! Dead!

Under the influence of any strongly-disturbing force clare

would occasionally walk in his sleep, and even perform strange feats, such as he had done on the night of their return from market just before their marriage, when he reenacted in his bedroom his combat with the man who had insulted her. Tess saw that continued mental distress had wrought him into that somnambulistic state now.

Her loyal confidence in him lay so deep down in her heart that, awake or asleep, he inspired her with no sort of personal fear. If he had entered with a pistol in his hand he would scarcely have disturbed her trust in his protectiveness.

Clare came close, and bent over her. "Dead, dead, dead!" he murmured.

After fixedly regarding her for some moments with the same gaze of unmeasurable woe he bent lower, enclosed her in his arms, and rolled her in the sheet as in a shroud. Then lifting her from the bed with as much respect as one would show to a dead body, he carried her across the room, murmuring—

"My poor, poor Tess—my dearest, darling Tess! So sweet, so good, so true!"

The words of endearment, withheld so severely in his waking hours, were inexpressibly sweet to her forlorn and hungry heart. If it had been to save her weary life she would not, by moving or struggling, have put an end to the position she found herself in. Thus she lay in absolute stillness, scarcely venturing to breathe, and, wondering what he was going to do with her, suffered herself to be borne out upon the landing

"My wife—dead, dead!" he said.

He paused in his labours for a moment to lean with her against the banister. Was he going to throw her down? Self solicitude was near extinction in her, and in the knowledge that he had planned to depart on the morrow, possibly for always, she lay in his arms in this precarious position with a sense rather of luxury than of terror. If they could only fall together, and both be dashed to pieces, how fit, how desirable.

However, he did not let her fall, but took advantage of the support of the handrail to imprint a kiss upon her lips-lips in the daytime scorned. Then he clasped her with a renewed firmness of hold, and they reached the ground-floor safely. Freeing one of his hands from his grasp of her for a moment, he slid back the doorbar and passed out, slightly striking his stockinged toe against the edge of the door. But this he seemed not to mind, and, having room for extension in the open air, he lifted her against his shoulder, so that he could carry her with ease, the absence of clothes taking much from his burden. Thus he bore her off the premises in the direction of the river a few yards distant.

长难句解析

He was in his shirt and trousers only, and her first flush of joy died when she perceived that his eyes were fixed in an unnatural stare on vacancy. When he reached the middle of the room he stood still and murmured, in tones of indescribable sadness—"Dead! Dead! Dead!

他只穿着衬衣和衬裤，当她注意到他空洞的眼神时，她原先的欣喜一下子消失了。走到房间的中央后，他站着，用一种难以形容的悲切的声音低声说道："死了！死了！死了！"

当表示穿着某种衣物时，应该用介词"in"；flush of joy可译为"一闪而过的欣喜"；when引导时间状语从句；the middle of 表示在……的中间；in tones of有"深浅不同的"的意思，如：In various tones of blue，以各种蓝色调。

Her loyal confidence in him lay so deep down in her heart that, awake or asleep, he inspired her with no sort of personal fear. If he had entered with a pistol in his hand, he would scarcely have disturbed her trust in his protectiveness.

她打心底是如此地相信他，不管是醒着还是睡着了，他总是让她丝毫感觉不到恐惧。即使他拿着一把手枪进来了，也绝不会影响她对他的信任。

so...that表"如此……以至于"；no sort of译为"毫无"；if后接虚拟语气，与过去事实相反，从句用过去完成时，主句为would(could)+v.原形。

Self solicitude was near extinction in her, and in the knowledge that he had planned to depart on the morrow, possibly for always, she lay in his arms in this precarious position with a sense rather of luxury than of terror. If they could only fall together, and both be dashed to pieces, how fit, how desirable.

她渐渐不再关心自己，她知道，他明天就要离开她了，可能是永远的离开。她怀着不安的心躺在他怀里，与其说是恐惧，她更多的感受到了不舍。要是他们能一起坠下，甚至一起粉身碎骨，那该多好啊！

for always 译为“永远的”；that 此句中引导同位语从句，对“knowledge”进行解释说明；rather than而不是；宁可……也不愿；if 引导条件状语从句，表假设；how 在此处引导感叹句。

Then he clasped her with a renewed firmness of hold, and they reached the ground-floor safely.

他搂她搂得很紧，后来，他带着她安全地到达底层。

safely为副词，修饰reach，放在动词后面。

“My poor, poor Tess—my dearest, darling Tess! So sweet, so good, so true!”

The words of endearment, withheld so severely in his waking hours, were inexpressibly sweet to her forlorn and hungry heart.

“我可怜的苔丝！我亲爱的苔丝！你是那么的甜美，那么的真实！”

这爱慕的话语，在他醒着的时候是绝对无法说出来的，对于她绝望和饥渴的心来说是难以言语的甜蜜。

the words of...，……的话语；副词修饰形容词，一般放在形容词前面，例如 inexpressibly sweet。

---

073 Uncle Tom's Cabin 汤姆叔叔的小屋

今日关键语导读 Today's Key Points

《汤姆叔叔的小屋》是美国作家哈里特·比彻·斯托于1852年发表的一部反奴隶制小说。全书围绕着一位久经苦难的黑奴——汤姆叔叔的故事展开，并描述了他与他身边奴隶与奴隶主的经历。这部小说深刻地描绘出了奴隶制度残酷的本质；并认为基督徒的爱可以战胜由奴役人类同胞所带来的种种伤害。另外，小说中关于非裔美国人与美国奴隶制度的观点曾产生过意义深远的影响，并在某种程度上激化了导致美国内战的地区局部冲突。

障碍词先听为快 Words and Expressions

impudent ['impjudənt] adj. 粗鲁的，无礼的；鲁莽的，厚颜无耻的，冒失的

rascally ['rɑːskəli] adj. / adv. 无赖的（地）；卑鄙的（地）

prevalence ['prevələns] n. 流行；普遍；广泛

gradual ['grædjuəl] adj. 逐渐的；平缓的

frail [freil] n. 灯芯草篓；少妇 adj. 脆弱的

counterpoise ['kauntəpɔiz] n. 平衡；抗衡力 v. 使平衡

indulgence [in'dʌldʒ(ə)ns] n. 嗜好；放纵；纵容；沉溺

portentous [pɔː'tentəs] adj. 不祥的；预兆的；令人惊讶的

periodic [piəri'ɔdik] adj. 周期的；定期的

hardheartedness n. 冷酷的性质

"I'd like to have been able to kick the fellow down the steps," said he to himself, as he saw the door fairly closed, "with his impudent assurance; but he knows how much he has me at advantage. If anybody had ever said to me that I should sell Tom down south to one of those rascally traders, I should have said, 'Is thy servant a dog, that he should do this thing?' And now it must come, for aught I see. And Eliza's child, too! I know that I shall have some fuss with wife about that; and, for that matter, about Tom, too. So much for being in debt, heigho! The fellow sees his advantage, and means to push it."

Perhaps the mildest form of the system of slavery is to be seen in the State of Kentucky. The general prevalence of agricultural pursuits of a quiet and gradual nature, not requiring those periodic seasons of hurry and pressure that are called for in the business of more southern districts, makes the task of the negro a more healthful and reasonable one; while the master, content with a more gradual style of acquisition, has not those temptations to hardheartedness which always overcome frail human nature when the prospect of sudden and rapid gain is weighed in the balance, with no heavier counterpoise than the interests of the helpless and unprotected.

Whoever visits some estates there, and witnesses the good-humored indulgence of some masters and mistresses, and the affectionate loyalty of some slaves, might be tempted to dream the oft-fabled poetic legend of a patriarchal institution, and all that;

but over and above the scene there broods a portentous shadow—the shadow of law. So long as the law considers all these human beings, with beating hearts and living affections, only as so many things belonging to a master, so long as the failure, or misfortune, or imprudence, or death of the kindest owner, may cause them any day to exchange a life of kind protection and indulgence for one of hopeless misery and toil, so long it is impossible to make anything beautiful or desirable in the best regulated administration of slavery.

长难句解析

Perhaps the mildest form of the system of slavery is to be seen in the State of Kentucky.

奴隶制表现得最温和的地方恐怕要算肯塔基州了。

这句话在英译汉过程中使用了转化法，将被动语态转化成了主动语态。the mildest form of 最温和的形式；the system of，……制度。

"I'd like to have been able to kick the fellow down the steps," said he to himself, as he saw the door fairly closed," with his impudent assurance; but he knows how much he has me at advantage.

"我恨不得把这个放肆的家伙一脚踢下楼去，" 房门关上之后，谢尔贝自言自语道，"可是，他知道在我身上有机可乘啊。"

would like to do sth. 想要做某事；be able to do 能够做某事；as在这里引导时间状语从句，表示当……时候；with引导的介词短语表伴随。

And now it must come, for aught I see. And Eliza's child, too! I know that I shall have some fuss with wife about that; and, for that matter, about Tom, too. So much for being in debt, —heigho! The fellow sees his advantage, and means to push it.

可是现在，我却束手无策，非做不可了。唉，还有伊丽莎的孩子呢！我知道太太一定不肯依我；就是汤姆他也不会答应啊。想不到债务竟把我逼到这步田地，咳！这家伙看见有机可乘，竟然还想得寸进尺呢。

that引导宾语从句，have some fuss with有一些过分讲究；be in debt 欠债；mean to do sth. 打算做某事。

Whoever visits some estates there, and witnesses the good-humored indulgence of some masters and mistresses, and the affectionate loyalty of some slaves, might be tempted to dream the oft-fabled poetic legend of a patriarchal institution.

谁要是到那些庄园去参观一下，亲眼看到庄园男女主人是那么和蔼可亲，黑奴们又那么忠心耿耿，也许容易引起幻想，联想起那些富于诗意的氏族社会的传奇来。

这是whoever引导的主语从句，and连接了几个小分句，看似结构复杂，其实是并列短语做主语，might be 为句子谓语，抓住主线句子就容易分析了。

So long it is impossible to make anything beautiful or desirable in the best regulated administration of slavery.

即使在奴隶制施行得最完善的地方，黑奴的处境也不可能达到美满或令人向往的地步。

it在这里作形式主语，真正的主语是后面的动词不定式；it is impossible to do sth. 做……是不可能的；best是good的最高级形式。

读书笔记

074 Childhood 童年

今日关键语导读 Today's Key Points

《童年》是前苏联作家高尔基以自身经历为原型创作的自传体小说三部曲中的第一部（其他两部分别为《在人间》《我的大学》）。讲述了阿廖沙（高尔基的乳名）三岁到十岁这一时期的童年生活，生动地再现了十九世纪七八十年代前苏联下层人民的生活状况，写出了高尔基对苦难的认识，对社会人生的独特见解，字里行间涌动着一股生生不息的热望与坚强。

障碍词先听为快 Words and Expressions

vanish ['væniʃ] vi. 消失；突然不见；成为零 vt. 使不见，使消失 n. 弱化音

innocent ['inəsnt] adj. 无辜的；无罪的；无知的 n. 天真的人；笨蛋

gaiety ['geiəti] n. 快乐，兴高采烈；庆祝活动，喜庆；（服饰）华丽，艳丽

envious ['enviəs] adj. 羡慕的；嫉妒的

gaze [geiz] vi. 凝视；注视 n. 凝视；注视

shed [ʃed] vt. 流出；摆脱；散发；倾吐 vi. 流出；脱落；散布 n. 小屋，棚；分水岭

lisp [lisp] n. 口齿不清；咬舌发音 v. 咬着舌说；口齿不清地说

rapturous ['ræptʃərəs] adj. 狂喜的；兴高采烈的；欢天喜地的

vague [veig] adj. 模糊的；含糊的；不明确的；暧昧的

No envious gaze sees her now. She is not afraid to shed upon me the whole of her tenderness and love. I do not wake up, yet I kiss and kiss her hand.

"Get up, then, my angel."

She passes her other arm round my neck, and her fingers tickle me as they move across it. The room is quiet and in half-darkness, but the tickling has touched my nerves and I begin to awake. Mamma is sitting near me—that I can tell—and touching me; I can hear her voice and feel her presence. This at last rouses me to spring up, to throw my arms around her neck, to hide my head in her bosom, and to say with a sigh:

"Ah, dear, darling Mamma, how much I love you!"

She smiles her sad, enchanting smile, takes my head between her two hands, kisses me on the forehead, and lifts me on to her lap.

"Do you love me so much, then?" she says. Then, after a few moments' silence, she continues: "And you must love me always, and never forget me. If your Mamma should no longer be here, will you promise never to forget her—never, Nicolinka? and she kisses me more fondly than ever.

"Oh, but you must not speak so, darling Mamma, my own darling Mamma!" I exclaim as I clasp her knees, and tears of joy and love fall from my eyes.

How, after scenes like this, I would go upstairs, and stand before the ikons, and say with a rapturous feeling, "God bless

Papa and Mamma!" and repeat a prayer for my beloved mother which my childish lips had learnt to lisp-the love of God and of her blending strangely in a single emotion!

After saying my prayers I would wrap myself up in the bedclothes. My heart would feel light, peaceful, and happy, and one dream would follow another. Dreams of what? They were all of them vague, but all of them full of pure love and of a sort of expectation of happiness. I remember, too, that I used to think about Karl Ivanitch and his sad lot. He was the only unhappy being whom I knew, and so sorry would I feel for him, and so much did I love him, that tears would fall from my eyes as I thought, "May God give him happiness, and enable me to help him and to lessen his sorrow. I could make any sacrifice for him!" Usually, also, there would be some favorite toy—a china dog or hare—stuck into the bed-corner behind the pillow, and it would please me to think how warm and comfortable and well cared-for it was there. Also, I would pray God to make every one happy, so that every one might be contented, and also to send fine weather to- morrow for our walk. Then I would turn myself over on to the other side, and thoughts and dreams would become jumbled and entangled together until at last I slept soundly and peacefully, though with a face wet with tears.

Do in after life the freshness and light-heartedness, the craving for love and for strength of faith, ever return which we experience in our childhood's years? What better time is there in our lives than when the two best of virtues—innocent gaiety and a boundless yearning for affection—are our sole objects of pursuit?

Where now are our ardent prayers? Where now are our best gifts—the pure tears of emotion which a guardian angel dries with a smile as he sheds upon us lovely dreams of ineffable childish joy? Can it be that life has left such heavy traces upon one's heart that those tears and ecstasies are for ever vanished? Can it be that there remains to us only the recollection of them?

长难句解析

He was the only unhappy being whom I knew, and so sorry would I feel for him, and so much did I love him, that tears would fall from my eyes as I thought, "May God give him happiness, and enable me to help him and to lessen his sorrow."

他是我所知道的唯一不幸的人，我为他感到难过，那么爱他，难过得替他掉下泪来，我想道："愿上帝赐给他幸福，使我能够帮助他，减轻他的痛苦；为了他，我情愿牺牲一切。"

whom 引导的定语从句修饰前面的unhappy being；feel sorry for sb"对…感到抱歉"；so…that"如此…以至于"；lessen为less的动词形式，表示"减轻"。

Also, I would pray God to make every one happy, so that every one might be contented.

接着我又祈祷，求上帝赐给大家幸福，让大家都称心如意。

pray god to do sth.，表示祈求上帝赐予某物，后面so that 引导结果状语从句。

Then I would turn myself over on to the other side, and thoughts and dreams would become jumbled and entangled together until at last I slept soundly and peacefully, though with a face wet with tears.

然后我翻个身，思绪和梦想就混成一片，脸上还带着湿漉漉的泪水，便平静而安然地进入了梦乡。

the other side 另一边；at last 最后、最终；though 一句引导的让步状语从句表示一种转折的关系。

What better time is there in our lives than when the two best of virtues—innocent gaiety and a boundless yearning for affection—are our sole objects of pursuit?

当天真的喜悦和对爱的无限需求这两种至上的美德是人生唯一的愿望时，有什么时候会比它更美好呢?

than 表比较，when引导时间状语从句；sole objects of 唯一的对象、目标、追求。

Do in after life the freshness and light-heartedness, the craving for love and for strength of faith, ever return which we experience in our childhood's years?

童年时代所具有的那种朝气蓬勃的精神，无忧无虑的心情，对爱的要求和信仰的力量，将来还会复返吗？

which 引导的定语从句修饰前面的the freshness，light-heartedness，the craving for love and faith.

读书笔记

075 Five Children and It 五个孩子和沙精

今日关键语导读 Today's Key Points

《五个孩子和沙精》是伊迪丝·内斯比特编著的一本图书。讲述了有一天孩子们在砾石坑中挖沙时发现了沙精。它已经几千岁了。当然了，沙精们可以帮人们实现他们的愿望——愿望每天只能实现一个，而且当太阳落山时一切也就结束了。安西娅、西里尔、罗伯特和简觉得这棒极了。他们的小弟弟还太小，不会许愿，而且大部分时间都呆在家里；可其他几个孩子却在盘算着些激动人心的东西。

障碍词先听为快 Words and Expressions

silent ['sailənt] n. 无声电影 adj. 沉默的；寂静的；无记载的

happen ['hæpən] vi. 发生；碰巧；偶然遇到

second ['sekənd] n. 秒；第二名

difficult ['difikəlt] adj. 困难的；不随和的；执拗的

remember [ri'membə] vi. 记得，记起 vt. 记得；记牢；纪念

bottom ['bɔtəm] n. 底部；末端；臀部；尽头

hole [həul] n. 洞，孔；洞穴；突破口

suddenly ['sʌdənli] adv. 突然地；忽然

stranger ['streindʒə] n. 陌生人；外地人；局外人

The Psammead looked a little happier when it heard that, and it said, "Well, you can talk to me , if you want to. Perhaps I'll answer you and perhaps I won't. Now say something."

At first the children could not think of anything to say, but then Robert asked, "How long have you lived here?"

"Oh, thousands of years," the Psammead answered.

The children waited, but the Psammead was silent.

"Please tell us more," Robert said.

"Well, all right, then," the Pasammead said. "There were lots of us then," it went on "People sent their children out to look for Pasammead, and when they found us, we gave them a wish."

"Well, if they get wet, they get ill and they usually die, and that's what happened. Most of them got wet and die. And I'm not going to tell you another thing."

"Oh, just one more question, please," said Robert. "Do you give wishes now?"

"You have had one," said the Psammead. "You wished to see me, and here I am."

"Oh, please. Just one more" Anthea cried.

"Well, all right, but be quick! I'm tired of you!"

It is very difficult to think of a really good wish, in just a second or two. Then Anthea remembered a wish of hers and Jane's. She knew that the boys wouldn't like it, but it was better than nothing.

"I wish we were all very, very beautiful," she said.

The Psammead pushed out its long year eyes and got bigger

and fatter, and the children waited. Then it said, "I'm sorry. I have not done this for a long time. I'll try again, but I can only do one with a day for you.Do you agree to that?"

"Yes, oh yes!" the children cried.

"But remember, the wish is only for a day." said the Psammead. "When the sun goes down, everything goes back to what it was."

The Psammead slowly got bigger, then suddenly went small again "That's all right!" it said. At once it turned and went back into the sand at the bottom of the hole.

The children stood there for a second, and then Anthea turned to speak to the others. But they were not there! She was looking at three strangers —a girl with beautiful red hair and big blue eyes, and two very good-looking boys. Suddenly she understood. They had their wish. The strangers were Robert and Cyril and Jane—but now they were beautiful. Cyril's hair was golden now, and Robert was black.

"I liked you better before!" Robert cried angrily to his brother and sisters. "Jane's hair looks like carrots, and Cyril looks really stupid with long golden hair."

They went to find Baby, but he was just the same as he was before.

"Perhaps it's because he is young. He can't have wishes. We'll have to remember that next time," Anthea said, and she held out her arms to him. But Baby's mouth turned down at the corners and then he began to cry loudly. He did not know them!

"It took an hour to stop him crying and then, very tired and cross, they took him home. Martha, Baby's nursemaid, was waiting at the front door. She took Baby from them quickly.

长难句解析

The Psammead looked a little happier when it heard that, and it said,'Well, you can talk to me , if you want to.

听到了那个赛米德看起来高兴了一些，它说："好吧，如果你们愿意，你们可以和我说说话。"

when 引导时间状语从句，if引导条件状语从句。

Well, if they get wet, they get ill and they usually die, and that's what happened.

噢，要是它们弄湿了自己，就会生病，常常会死的，事情就是那样。

if引导条件状语从句；what 引导的句子作表语成分。

When the sun goes down, everything goes back to what it was.

太阳落山时，一切都恢复了原样。

when 引导时间状语从句，what 引导的句子作宾语成分；go back to有"回去，返回，追溯到"的意思。

But Baby's mouth turned down at the corners and then he began to cry loudly.

可小弟弟撇着嘴开始大哭起来。

turn down 是"减小，关小，调低"的意思在原文中

"Baby's mouth turned down at the corners"可理解为"小弟弟撇着嘴"的意思。

It took an hour to stop him crying and then, very tired and cross, they took him home.

花了一个小时才哄他不哭了。他们又累又气，把他带回家。

It takes sometime to do sth. 花时间做某事，stop doing sth. 停下正在做的事，注意与stop to do sth.（停下来去做某事）区分。

读书笔记

076 Oliver Twist 雾都孤儿

今日关键语导读 Today's Key Points

《雾都孤儿》是狄更斯的第一部社会批判小说。主人公奥利弗是个孤儿，在济贫院长大，因饥饿向伙房师傅要粥喝而被送到棺材店当学徒。受尽凌辱后，奥利弗逃往伦敦谋生。在伦敦，他误入贼窟，受费金教唆去偷一个老绅士的东西，失败后被抓。好心的老绅士收养了他，奥利弗决心向善，但不久又被女贼南希抓回，跟随希克斯等人到玛丽叶夫人家行窃，被枪击中。希克斯等人弃他而去，奥利弗被玛丽叶夫人收养。此时，南希听到歹徒蒙克斯和费金的谈话，得知了奥利弗的身世秘密……

障碍词先听为快 Words and Expressions

miserable ['mizərəbl] adj. 悲惨的；令人痛苦的；太少的；卑鄙的

dreadful ['dredful] adj. 可怕的；令人畏惧的；讨厌的，糟透了的，丑陋的；糟糕的

rapidly ['ræpidli] adv. 很快地，迅速地；立即

vision ['viʒən] n. 视力，视觉；美景，绝妙的东西；幻影；想像力 vt. 在幻觉中看到；幻想，想象；梦见

suspicion [səs'piʃən] n. 怀疑；嫌疑；疑心；〈口〉一点儿 vt. 怀疑

curtain ['kəːtən] n. 窗帘，门帘；帐幕之物，幕布；启幕，落幕 vt. 给（窗户或房间）装上帘子；掩蔽

stiffly ['stifli] adv. 僵硬地；顽固地；坚硬地；生硬地

murder ['mə:də] n. 谋杀；杀戮；极艰难的经历 vt. 凶杀；糟蹋；打垮

disturbed [dis'tə:bd] adj. 被扰乱的；心理失常的；为心理失常者服务的 v. 干扰

flame [fleim] n. 火焰；热情，激情；〈俚〉爱人，情人 v. 燃烧，发出火焰；激怒

好英文娓娓动听 Beautiful stories

The sun burst upon the crowded city in all its brightness. It lit up every corner of London, the great houses of the rich, and the miserable homes of the poor. Its hone everywhere, even into the room where the murdered woman lay. The horror of that scene was even more dreadful in the clear morning light.

Sikes sat there, unable to move, looking at the body. He had thrown the blood-covered stick into the fire, then washed himself and his clothes. He had cut out the bits of his clothes that were stained and burnt them too, but there were still bloodstains all over the floor. Even the dog's feet were bloody.

Finally, he forced himself to leave the room, pulling the dog out with him and locking the door behind him. He walked rapidly north, towards High gate, then on to Hampstead. On the open land of Hampstead Heath, away from people and houses, he found a place in a field where he could sleep with out being disturbed.

But before long he was up again and running. This time he ran back towards London for a while. Then he turned and went north again, sometimes walking, sometimes running, with no clear purpose in his mind. Eventually, he felt hungry, and changed direction towards Hendon, a quiet place away from the crowds, where he could buy food. But even the children and chickens there seemed to look at him with suspicion. So he turned back towards Hampstead Heath again, without having eaten, uncertain where to go.

At last he turned north again, his dog still running at his heels, and set off to a village just outside London. He stopped at a small, quiet pub and bought a meal, then went on again. It was now dark and as he continued walking, he felt as if Nancy were following him, her shadow on the road, her last low cry in the wind. If he stopped, the ghostly figure did the same. If he ran, it ran too, moving stiffly, like a corpse. Sometimes he turned, determined to drive the ghost away, but his blood ran cold with terror. Every time he turned, the ghost turned too, and was still behind him.

Finally, he found another field where he could hide. He lay down, unable to sleep, his mind filled with visions of the dead girl. Her wide, dead eyes stared at him, watching him through a curtain of blood.

Suddenly he heard shouting in the distance. He jumped to his feet and saw that the sky seemed on fire. Sheets of flame shot into the air, driving clouds of smoke in his direction. He heard an alarm bell, and more shouts of 'Fire!' Running with his dog across the fields, he joined the crowds of men and women fighting the fire. He could forget his own terror in this new danger, and he worked all night with the crowd, shouting, running and working together to stop the flames destroying more buildings.

In the morning the mad excitement was over, and the dreadful memory of his crime returned-more terrifying than ever. In desperation, he decided to go back to London.

长难句解析

The sun burst upon the crowded city in all its brightness. It lit up every corner of London, the great houses of the rich, and the miserable homes of the poor.

喷薄而出的太阳悬挂在这座拥挤的城市的上空，光芒四射，它照亮了伦敦的每一个角落，照亮了有钱人家的宅院，也照亮了穷人家的陋室。

lit up，点火，点灯，light up的过去式；the rich和the poor指“有钱人”和“穷人”。

On the open land of Hampstead Heath, away from people and houses, he found a place in a field where he could sleep with out being disturbed.

在汉普斯泰德荒原空阔的野地里，远离人群和房屋的地方，他找到了一个能够不受惊扰睡一觉的地方。

where引导地点状语从句。

Finally, he forced himself to leave the room, pulling the dog out with him and locking the door behind him.

最后，他强迫自己离开了这屋子，拉出了狗，将房门上了锁。

force sb. to do...，强迫某人做某事；pulling、locking为现在分词作状语，表伴随。

Eventually, he felt hungry, and changed direction towards Hendon, a quiet place away from the crowds, where he could buy food. But even the children and chickens there seemed to look at him with suspicion. So he turned back towards Hampstead Heath again, without having eaten, uncertain where to go.

最后他感觉到肚子饿了，又掉转方向朝亨顿走去。这是个人不多的僻静的小地方，他可以在这儿买点东西吃。可是，连这里的孩子和鸡都好像在怀疑地看着他，所以他什么也没吃，又转身朝汉普斯泰德荒原走去，心里还是不知该往哪儿去。

crowds意为“人群”，故away from crowds意为“远离喧嚣”;where引导地点状语从句，look at sb with 用某种眼神看某人；turned back towards返回。

Suddenly he heard shouting in the distance. He jumped to his feet and saw that the sky seemed on fire. Sheets of flame shot into the air, driving clouds of smoke in his direction. He heard an alarm bell, and more shouts of 'Fire!'

他突然听见远处的叫喊声，便一跃而起，看见天空好像着了火。一片片火舌喷向空中，翻滚的浓烟朝他这边刮来。他听见了报警的铃声，还有更多的人喊叫着：“火！”

in the distance 在远处，that引导宾语从句；on fire “着火”；sheets of flame用来形容火的状态；shot into 迅速进入，如shot flames into the sky 火光冲天，shot gravel into the hole 把石子倒入洞中，driving为现在分词表伴随。

读书笔记

077 Time Machine 时间机器

今日关键语导读 Today's Key Points

《时间机器》是英国科幻小说大师H. G.威尔斯最早获得成功的一部科幻小说，也是他最负盛名的科幻作品之一。本书讲述了一个时间旅行家发明了一种能穿越时空的时间机器，并乘坐此机器穿越到公元802701年。在未来世界里，他发现人类正逐渐走向没落，并互相残杀。这难道是人类的终极命运？本书将“19世纪阶级斗争和人类进化相结合”，警示未来，发人深省。

障碍词先听为快 Words and Expressions

fragile ['frædʒail] adj. 脆的；易碎的

futurity [fjuː'tjuəriti] n. 未来；来世；后世的人

exquisite ['ekskwizit] adj. 精致的；细腻的；高雅的

tentacle ['tentəkl] n. 触手，触须， 触角

alarming [ə'lɑːmiŋ] adj. 令人担忧的；使人惊恐的 v. 使惊恐（alarm的ing 形式）

unscrew ['ʌn'skruː] vt. 旋开；旋松；从……旋出螺丝

singularly ['siŋgjuləli] adv. 异常地；非常地；令人无法理解地

egotism ['iːgətiz(ə)m] n. 自负；自我中心

In another moment we were standing face to face, I and this fragile thing out of futurity. He came straight up to me and laughed into my eyes. The absence from his bearing of any sign of fear struck me at once. Then he turned to the two others who were following him and spoke to them in a strange and very sweet and liquid tongue.

There were others coming, and presently a little group of perhaps eight or ten of these exquisite creatures were about me. One of them addressed me. It came into my head, oddly enough, that my voice was too harsh and deep for them. So I shook my head, and, pointing to my ears, shook it again. He came a step forward, hesitated, and then touched my hand. Then I felt other soft little tentacles upon my back and shoulders. They wanted to make sure I was real. There was nothing in this at all alarming. Indeed, there was something in these pretty little people that inspired confidence—a graceful gentleness, a certain childlike ease. And besides, they looked so frail that I could fancy myself flinging the whole dozen of them about like nine-pins. But I made a sudden motion to warn them when I saw their little pink hands feeling at the Time Machine. Happily then, when it was not too late, I thought of a danger I had hitherto forgotten, and reaching over the bars of the machine I unscrewed the little levers that would set it in motion, and put these in my pocket. Then I turned again to see what I could do in the way of communication.

And then, looking more nearly into their features, I saw some further peculiarities in their Dresden-china type of prettiness. Their hair, which was uniformly curly, came to a sharp end at the neck and cheek; there was not the faintest suggestion of it on the face, and their ears were singularly minute. The mouths were small, with bright red, rather thin lips, and the little chins ran to a point. The eyes were large and mild; and—this may seem egotism on my part—I fancied even that there was a certain lack of the interest I might have expected in them.

长难句解析

Then he turned to the two others who were following him and spoke to them in a strange and very sweet and liquid tongue.

接着他转身对跟着他的两个家伙讲话，他讲的话听起来很古怪，却清脆悦耳。

who 引导的定语从句，修饰two others。

It came into my head, oddly enough, that my voice was too harsh and deep for them.

真是奇怪，我想我的声音对于他们怕是太刺耳、太低沉了。

it 作形式主语，that引导宾语从句。

So I shook my head, and, pointing to my ears, shook it again.

于是我摇了摇头，用手指指自己的耳朵，又摇了摇头。

pointing 做伴随状语，表示shook my head 和pointing to my ears 两个动作几乎同时发生。

And besides, they looked so frail that I could fancy myself flinging the whole dozen of them about like nine-pins.

此外，他们又是这样脆弱，我完全可以像玩九柱戏那样一下子打倒他们十几个。

so ...that 如此……以至于。

读书笔记

078 Bridge to Terabithia 仙境之桥

今日关键语导读 Today's Key Points

《仙境之桥》是作者凯塞琳·帕特森为了纪念她的儿子的最亲密朋友莉萨而著。故事的主人公杰西开始是个不怎么快乐的孩子。他在学校里受同学欺负，在家中又无法得到父母的宠爱。只有两个人能为他的童年带来亮光——一个是音乐老师，另一个便是刚转校来到班上的莱斯利。后来杰西与莱斯利成为了亲密无间的朋友，一起虚构了一个树林里的特雷比西亚王国，快乐地在一起，直到一个悲剧的发生，使杰西必需鼓起勇气独自面对生活。

障碍词先听为快 Words and Expressions

tiptoe ['tiptəu] vi. 用脚尖走

rattly ['rætli] adj. 吵闹的；格格响的

screech [skriːtʃ] vi. 发出尖锐的声音；发出恐惧或痛苦的叫喊声

smash [smæʃ] vi. 粉碎；打碎

despise [dis'paiz] vt. 轻视，鄙视

rusty ['rʌsti] adj. 生锈的，腐蚀的；铁锈色的，锈色的

trot [trɔt] vi. （人）慢跑；快步走

soothingly [suiːðɪŋlɪ] adv. 安慰地

yank [jæŋk] vi. 猛地一拉

stroll [strəul] vi. 散步；闲逛

He tiptoed out of the house. The place was so rattly that it screeched whenever you put your foot down, but Jess had found that if you tiptoed, it gave only a low moan, and he could usually get outdoors without waking Momma or Ellie or Brenda or Joyce Ann. May Belle was another matter. She was going on seven, and she worshiped him, which was OK sometimes. When you were the only boy smashed between four sisters, and the older two had despised you ever since you stopped letting them dress you up and wheel you around in their rusty old doll carriage, and the littlest one cried if you looked at her cross-eyed, it was nice to have somebody who worshiped you. Even if it got unhandy sometimes.

He began to trot across the yard. His breath was coming out in little puffs—cold for August. But it was early yet. By noontime when his mom would have him out working, it would be hot enough.

Miss Bessie stared at him sleepily as he climbed across the scrap heap, over the fence, and into the cow field. "Moo—oo, " she said, looking for all the world like another May Belle with her big, brown droopy eyes.

"Hey, Miss Bessie," Jess said soothingly. "Just go on back to sleep."

Miss Bessie strolled over to a greenish patch—most of the field was brown and dry—and yanked up a mouthful.

"That' a girl. Just eat your breakfast. Don't pay me no mind."

He always started at the northwest corner of the field, crouched over like the runners he had seen on Wide World of

Sports.

"Bang," he said, and took off flying around the cow field. Miss Bessie strolled toward the center, still following him with her droopy eyes, chewing slowly. She didn't look very smart, even for a cow, but she was plenty bright enough to get out of Jess's way.

长难句解析

The place was so rattly that it screeched whenever you put your foot down, but Jess had found that if you tiptoed, it gave only a low moan, and he could usually get outdoors without waking Momma or Ellie or Brenda or Joyce Ann.

他家如此破旧，他不管在哪落脚，地板都会发出尖锐刺耳的声音。但杰西发现，如果他踮着脚尖，它只会发出很小的声音，能够让他在不吵醒妈妈或埃莉或布伦达或乔伊斯·安的情况下走到室外。

so...that，"如此……以至于……"，whenever引导时间状语从句；put down"落下"，that 引导宾语从句，if引导条件状语从句。

When you were the only boy smashed between four sisters, and the older two had despised you ever since you stopped letting them dress you up and wheel you around in their rusty old doll carriage, and the littlest one cried if you looked at her cross-eyed, it was nice to have somebody who worshiped you.

当你是被夹在四个姐妹中的唯一一个男孩，并且两个姐姐自从你不让她们像芭比娃娃一样给你打扮打扮，再把你放在她们的老旧的婴儿车里推来推去的时候就轻视你，还有那个最小的妹妹因为你盯着她看她就会嚎啕大哭的时候，有人崇拜你的感觉确实不错。

when 引导时间状语从句；ever since 自从；stop doing sth. 停止做某事（正在做的事），stop to do sth. 停下来去做某事；if引导条件状语从句；dress up“打扮”，wheel around“使……转来转去”，look at“注视”；be nice to do sth. 做某事感觉好；who引导定语从句修饰somebody。此句两处用到虚拟语气，you were...和looked at...，与现在事实相反，谓语动词用一般过去式。

Miss Bessie stared at him sleepily as he climbed across the scrap heap, over the fence, and into the cow field.

贝茜小姐睡眼惺忪地看着他跑过杂物堆，翻越篱笆，最终进入牛圈。

stare at“盯着，注视着”，as 引导时间状语从句。across 穿过，横穿；over“在……之上越过”；into“到……里，深入……之中”。

---

079 The Elephant Man
象人

今日关键语导读 Today's Key Points

《象人》的主人公约翰·梅力因为脑袋硕大无比，身体畸形酷似大象而被人称为“象人”，不过这个人物并不是剧作家杜撰出来的，而是真实存在于19世纪的伦敦。1923年，以他为研究对象的医生弗瑞迪·崔佛士出版了《象人和他的回忆》的手记。一百年前的世界与现在截然不同。大多数人生活在没有电的阴冷、潮湿的环境中。他们从不上医院，往往死得很惨。

本书讲述了一个贫穷、丑陋的人的故事。没有人喜欢他，大家都嘲笑他。人们将他放在笼子里，当作动物一样展览。直到有一天一位医生发现了他，觉得他很有趣，想研究他。象人就这样出了名，每个人都想去拜访他，甚至女王都来看望他。

为什么刚开始人们逃避他，后来又接近他？看了这本书，你便会明白。

障碍词先听为快 Words and Expressions

theater ['θiətə(r)] n. 电影院，戏院；戏剧工作；演戏；手术室

prison ['prizn] n. 监狱；牢笼；监禁；入狱

country ['kʌntri] n. 国家；国民；乡下；地区

wonderfully ['wʌndəfəli] adv. 精彩地；极好地；惊人地；奇妙地

strange [streindʒ] adj. 陌生的，生疏的；奇怪的，古怪的；疏远的；外国的 adv. 奇怪地；陌生地；冷淡地

difficult ['difikəlt] adj. 困难的；难做的；难解的；不易相处的

perhaps [pə'hæps] adv. 或许；（表示不确定）也许；（用于粗略的估计）或许；（表示勉强同意或其实不赞成）也许

remember [ri'membə] vt. & vi. 记得；牢记

back [bæk] n. 背，背部；背面，反面；后面，后部；（椅子等的）靠背 v. 使后退；支持；加背书于；以前的；拖欠的 adv. 以前；向后地

afraid [ə'freid] adj. 害怕的；担心的；恐怕；畏惧，害怕

好英文娓娓动听 Beautiful stories

Outside the Hospital

Merrick had a lot of friends now, but he was more like a child than a man. He could read about things, and talk to his visitors, but he could not go out of the hospital by himself. He thought and played like a child.

After Christmas, he wanted to go to the theater. This was very difficult, because I did not want the people in the theater to see him. But a kind lady from the theater—Mrs Kendal—helped us. We bought tickets for a box at the side of the theater We went to the theater in a cab with dark windows, and we went into the theater by a door at the back—the Queen's door. Nobody saw us.

Three nurses sat at the front of the box, and Merrick and I sat in the dark behind them. Nobody in the theater could see us, but we could see the play.

It was a children's Christmas play. Merrick loved it. It was a most wonderful, exciting story. Often he laughed, and sometimes he tried to sing like the children in the theater. He was like a child. For him, everything in the story was true.

Once he was very afraid, because the bad man in the play was angry and had a knife. At first Merrick wanted to leave the theater, but I stopped him. Then he was very angry with this bad man in the play. He hit his hand on his chair, and stood up and talked to the man. But nobody heard him. When the bad man went to prison, Merrick laughed.

Merrick thought the beautiful young lady in the play was wonderful. He wanted to talk to her too. At the end of the play he was very happy because she married a good young man.

He remembered this play for a long time, and he talked a lot about the people in it. "What do you think they did after we left?" he asked me. "Where do the young lady and the young man live? What are they doing now?"

"I don't know, I said. 'Perhaps they live in the country."

Merrick thought about this for a long time. Then he said: "Dr Treves, can I go to the country, please? I saw the country once from a train, but I never went there. I often read about it in books. It's very beautiful, isn't it? I would like to see it."

The visit to the theater was difficult but a visit to the country was more difficult. But again, one of his new friends helped us. She had a small house in the country, and Merrick could stay in it for the summer, she said.

I took Merrick to the country in a train with dark windows, so nobody could see him. Then we went in a cab to the country house.

There were a lot of trees near the house, but no people lived near it. A countryman brought food to the house everyday, but no people came near it.

I stayed with him that night. At night, it was very dark and quiet. In the morning, hundreds of birds sang in the trees, and everything outside the house was green. Merrick walked under the big trees, looking at things happily, and singing his strange song.

I went back to London, but Merrick stayed there for six weeks. He was wonderfully happy. Every week, he wrote me a letter.

Apple Tree House,
West Wickham,
Berkshire.
21st July 1889

长难句解析

It was a children's Christmas play. Merrick loved it. It was a most wonderful, exciting story. Often he laughed, and sometimes he tried to sing like the children in the theater. He was like a child. For him, everything in the story was true.

这是一部儿童圣诞剧，麦里克喜欢看。这是一个极精彩并令人激动的故事。他常常笑出声来，有时他也想像剧中的孩子们一样歌唱，他像个孩子似的，在他看来，故事里的每件事都是真实的。

often he laughed 也可以写成 he often laughed；try to

do sth. 表示尽力做某事，try doing sth. 表示尝试做某事，注意二者区分；for him 在此处不是“为了他”的意思，而是“在他看来”。

Once he was very afraid, because the bad man in the play was angry and had a knife. At first Merrick wanted to leave the theater, but I stopped him. Then he was very angry with this bad man in the play. He hit his hand on his chair, and stood up and talked to the man. But nobody heard him. When the bad man went to prison, Merrick laughed.

剧中有个坏男人生气地拿着刀，他一度害怕起来，要离开剧院，我拉住了他。他非常生那个坏男人的气，击打着椅子，站起来骂那个坏男人，但无人听见。当那个坏男人被投进监狱时，麦里克高兴地大笑起来。

be angry with 为固定句型，对……感到生气；at first 起初、首先；stand up起身、站立；when 引导时间状语从句。

He remembered this play for a long time, and he talked a lot about the people in it. "What do you think they did after we left?' he asked me. 'Where do the young lady and the young man live? What are they doing now?"

他好长时间都没有忘记这出戏，他叙述了许多有关剧中人的事。他问我：“我们离开以后他们怎么办？那个年轻人和那个姑娘在哪儿生活？现在他们在干什么？”

remember sth for a long time 意为“很长一段时间记得

某事”；talk about sth.“谈论某事”；此处“it”代指戏剧。

Merrick thought about this for a long time. Then he said: "Dr Treves, can I go to the country, please? I saw the country once from a train, but I never went there. I often read about it in books. It's very beautiful, isn't it? I would like to see it."

这件事麦里克想了很久。后来他问我：“特里维斯博士，我可以到乡下去吗？我坐火车时曾看到过乡间，但我从来没去过那里。我在书上读到过有关乡间的事，很美，是不是？我想去看看。”

please在句末含请求之意；It's very beautiful, isn't it? 此句中“isn't it?”为反义疑问句，加强语气；would like to do sth. 表示想要做某事。

I stayed with him that night. At night, it was very dark and quiet. In the morning, hundreds of birds sang in the trees, and everything outside the house was green. Merrick walked under the big trees, looking at things happily, and singing his strange song.

那天晚上我与他待在一起。晚上天很黑，但很安静，清晨许多小鸟在树上歌唱。屋子外面一片翠绿。麦里克在树下散步，开心地欣赏着这里的一切，唱着他那奇怪的歌。

hundreds of...译为“成百上千的”，在此处泛指数量多，look at 注视，此处looking，singing为现在分词作状语，表伴随。

080 Little Women 小妇人

今日关键语导读 Today's Key Points

这部小说以家庭生活为描写对象，以家庭成员的感情纠葛为线索，描写了马奇一家的天伦之爱。马奇家的四姐妹中，无论是为了爱情甘于贫困的梅格，还是通过自己奋斗成为作家的乔，以及坦然面对死亡的贝思和以扶弱为己任的艾米，都具有自强自立的共同特点。本书描写了她们对家庭的眷恋，对爱的忠诚以及对亲情的渴望。在这本书中可以找到：初恋的甜蜜和烦恼，感情与理智的差异，理想和现实的距离，贫穷与富有的矛盾。

障碍词先听为快 Words and Expressions

husky ['hʌski] adj. 沙哑的；强壮的 n. 哈士奇

comforter ['kʌmfətə] n. 安慰者，圣灵，被子

russet ['rʌsit] adj. 枯叶色的，红褐色的，手织的 n. 红褐色

particle ['pɑːtikl] n. 微粒，颗粒，极小量，粒子，质点

whisk [(h)wisk] n. 搅拌机，扫帚，毛毯子 v. 飞奔，疾过，搅

girlish ['gəːliʃ] adj. 少女的，少女似的，适于女子的

ribbon ['ribən] n. 带；绸缎；带状物 v. 用绸带装饰

好英文娓娓动听 Beautiful stories

"Here!" answered a husky voice from above, and, running

up, Meg found her sister eating apples and crying over the Heir of Redclyffe, wrapped up in a comforter on an old three-legged sofa by the sunny window.

This was Jo's favorite refuge, and here she loved to retire with half a dozen russets and a nice book, to enjoy the quiet and the society of a pet rat who lived near by and didn't mind her a particle. As Meg appeared, Scrabble whisked into his hole. Jo shook the tears off her cheeks and waited to hear the news.

"Such fun! Only see! A regular note of invitation from Mrs. Gardiner for tomorrow night!" cried Meg, waving the precious paper and then proceeding to read it with girlish delight.

"Mrs. Gardiner would be happy to see Miss March and Miss Josephine at a little party on New Year's Eve. Marmee is willing we should go, now what shall we wear?"

"What's the use of asking that, when you know we shall wear our poplins, because we haven't got anything else?" answered Jo with her mouth full.

"If I only had a silk!" sighed Meg. "Mother says I may when I'm eighteen perhaps, but two years is an everlasting time to wait."

"I'm sure our pops look like silk, and they are nice enough for us. Yours is as good as new, but I forgot the burn and the tear in mine. Whatever shall I do? The burn shows badly, and I can't take any out."

"You must sit still all you can and keep your back out of sight. The front is all right. I shall have a new ribbon for my hair, and Marmee will lend me her little pearl pin, and my new slippers are lovely, and my gloves will do, though they aren't as nice as I'd like."

长难句解析

"Here!" answered a husky voice from above, and, running up, Meg found her sister eating apples and crying over the Heir of Redclyffe, wrapped up in a comforter on an old three-legged sofa by the sunny window.

"在这里！"上面一个嘶哑的声音应道。梅格跑上去，只见自己的妹妹身上裹着一条羊毛围巾，坐在靠着向阳窗户的一张旧三脚沙发上，一边吃苹果一边抹着眼泪读《莱德克力夫的继承人》。

run up 匆匆制成、迅速积累、向上跑、高涨；find sb. doing sth. 发现某人正在做某事；wrap up包裹、圆满完成，comforter 被子、羊毛围巾，安慰者。

This was Jo's favorite refuge, and here she loved to retire with half a dozen russets and a nice book, to enjoy the quiet and the society of a pet rat who lived near by and didn't mind her a particle.

这里是乔最钟爱的避护所；她喜欢带上五六个苹果和一本好书在此逍遥，享受这里的宁静以及和爱鼠作伴的滋味。

half a dozen，半打，六个；russets，赤褐色，黄褐色；冬季粗皮苹果（黄色苹果之一种），在这里代指苹果；who引导定语从句，修饰前面的a pet rat。

"Such fun! Only see! A regular note of invitation from Mrs. Gardiner for tomorrow night!" cried Meg, waving the precious paper and then proceeding to read it with girlish delight.

“多有趣！加德纳夫人正式邀请我们参加明天的晚会。你瞧，这是邀请函！”梅格一边叫一边扬扬那张宝贝字条，以女孩子特有的兴致读起来。

waving为现在分词作状语，表伴随；with girlish delight在这做方式状语。

I shall have a new ribbon for my hair, and Marmee will lend me her little pearl pin, and my new slippers are lovely, and my gloves will do, though they aren't as nice as I'd like.

我要用一条新丝带扎头发，妈妈会把她的小珍珠发夹借给我，我的新鞋子很漂亮，手套虽然没有我希望的那么漂亮，但也算可以出出场面。

这里的and... and...连接几个并列句；though引导让步状语从句；as...as像……一样。

读书笔记

081 Stuart Little 小老鼠斯图亚特

今日关键语导读 Today's Key Points

《小老鼠斯图亚特》是怀特的第一部享有世界声誉的作品。英国儿童文学史家把它视为美国20世纪40年代的童话代表作，认为它反映了西方现代童话的创作特色。这部充满童趣的作品生动地叙述了可爱的小鼠孩斯图亚特的生活趣闻和冒险经历。

障碍词先听为快 Words and Expressions

falcon ['fælkən,'fɔːlkən] n. 猎鹰

kidnap ['kidnæp] v. 绑架；诱拐

miniature ['miniətʃə] adj. 微型的，小规模的

capture ['kæptʃə] v. 俘获；夺得

reluctant [ri'lʌktənt] adj. 不情愿的，勉强的；顽抗的；难处理的；厌恶的

headquarter [ˌhed'kwɔːtə] vi. 设总部 vt. 将……的总部设在；把……放在总部里

parachute ['pærəʃuːt] n. 降落伞；降落伞状物； vt. & vi. 用降落伞投送；用降落伞降落 vi. 跳伞；第三人称单数

好英文娓娓动听 Beautiful stories

When the Littles see that the ring is missing, they think it has fallen down the sink drain. Stuart offers to be lowered down the drain on a string to get it, but can't quite find it. When the string breaks Margalo saves him, and Stuart's thanks to Margalo only makes her feel even more guilty, so she decides to leave. When Stuart can't find her, he assumes she has been kidnapped—and that Falcon is somehow involved. He leaves on a quest to rescue her with the household's reluctant cat Snowbell, but not before setting up a plan with George. Stuart travels with Snowbell in his miniature car, but his car overheats and breaks down.

Stuart and Snowbell enlist the help of Monty (Snowbell's old friend from the first movie), who tells them that Falcon's headquarters is at the disused observation deck of the nearby Pishkin Building. They attach a balloon to a popcorn box to get Stuart to the top, where he finds out that Margalo is Falcon's slave, and was forced to take the ring. He tries to save her, but Falcon captures him, and drops him on to the street, but is accidentally saved by a passing garbage truck. Falcon then shuts Margalo inside a paint can as punishment for rebelling against him. Meanwhile, Snowbell makes his way to the top of the building while the Falcon is absent and frees Margalo, who tearfully tells Snowbell that Falcon killed Stuart. Distraught and outraged, Snowbell vows revenge.

On a garbage barge where he has ended up, Stuart blames himself for everything, and has almost lost all hope. Suddenly, he finds George's broken plane, fixes it up, and flies to save Margalo. Falcon returns and almost pushes Snowbell in the paint can off the building, but Margalo defies him by taking the ring and fleeing. Falcon gives chase, but Stuart catches up in the plane and saves

Margalo while trying to evade the Falcon. The Littles, who have discovered his absence and whereabouts follow him by taxi as he begins an aerial adventure through the park, with Margalo at his side. They lose Falcon, but he catches up and makes an attempt to kill Stuart, when he detaches the plane's upper wing, damaging the main one and causing it to enter a steep nose dive, which fails when Stuart recovers from the dive, narrowly missing the Littles. Unable to run from Falcon, he lets Margalo off. He turns and flies the damaged plane in a kamikaze run while Falcon goes into an attack dive. He uses Mrs. Little's ring to temporarily blind him, and jumps out using a bandana as a parachute. The kamikaze attack works and Falcon is struck head on and defeated. Stuart falls when his parachute is sliced apart by the propeller of the shattered plane, and then is rescued by Margalo. Although Falcon survives the attack, he is injured and falls out of the sky, and lands in a garbage can next to Monty, who mocks him.

Stuart is congratulated by his family, and Margalo, who gives Mrs. Little her ring back, and Snowbell reunites with them as well. Soon after, Margalo says goodbye to her friends and leaves with the other birds to migrate south for the winter. Before flying away, she turns around and says "Little High little low" to which the Littles reply with "Little Hey, little hoe." which is the family's greeting. Stuart says the "silver lining" is that she'll be back in the spring, and his baby sister, Martha says her first words: "Bye bye, birdie", which the family then celebrates and then head inside to the comfort of their home.

长难句解析

When the Littles see that the ring is missing, they think it has fallen down the sink drain. Stuart offers to be lowered down the drain on a string to get it, but can't quite find it.

当小老鼠看到戒指丢失，他们认为这已经倒入了水槽排水管。斯图亚特拉住一根细绳下到排水管底试图找到它，但是怎么也找不到。

句中when引导时间状语从句，that 引导宾语从句；fall down 表示掉下，掉入，offer to do sth 主动做某事；quite doing sth. 停止做……。

Stuart is congratulated by his family, and Margalo, who gives Mrs. Little her ring back, and Snowbell reunites with them as well.

斯图尔特的家人向它表示祝贺，玛戈把戒指送还给它，雪铃也和他们团聚了。

句中who引导定语从句；give back 归还；reunite with sb 表示和某人重聚；as well表示“也，又，还”。

On a garbage barge where he has ended up, Stuart blames himself for everything, and has almost lost all hope.

在垃圾场上，斯图亚特把所有的事情都归咎在自己身上，几乎失去了所有的希望。

句中where引导地点状语从句；blame sb. for sth. 因某事而责备某人；lost hope失去希望。

Stuart falls when his parachute is sliced apart by the propeller of the shattered plane, and then is rescued by Margalo.

当斯图亚特的降落伞被破碎飞机的螺旋桨划破的时候，它掉下来了，然后被玛戈救了。

句中when引导时间状语从句，slice apart 切开，be rescued by 被解救。

Before flying away, she turns around and says "Little High little low" to which the Littles reply with "Little Hey, little hoe. " which is the family's greeting.

在飞走之后，她转身说“小老鼠高一点小老鼠低一点，小老鼠回复说“嘿，小锄头”，这是家庭间的问候。

句中fly away 飞走，turn around 转身，to which引导定语从句，which 引导定语从句。

读书笔记

082 Little House 小木屋

今日关键语导读 Today's Key Points

书中描述罗兰一家离开威斯康星大森林，坐着篷车迁徙到堪萨斯大草原的经过，这正是当时美国西部垦荒者的典型写照。这次搬家，罗兰一家惊险万分地渡过涨水的河流，到了大草原以后，他们也曾遇到印第安人，并遭受狼群包围、草原大火以及热病的侵袭，但最后他们还是住进了爸爸亲手所盖的小木屋中，在草原上度过了一段靠打猎维生的甜美时光。

障碍词先听为快 Words and Expressions

fiddle ['fidl] n. 小提琴 vi. 瞎搞；拉小提琴

elbow ['elbəu] n. 肘部；弯头；扶手 vt. 推挤；用手肘推开

rollicking ['rɔlikiŋ] adj. 欢乐的；喧闹的 n. 申斥；责骂

creek [kriːk] n. 小溪；小湾

prairie ['prɛəri] n. 大草原；牧场

lonesome ['ləunsəm] adj. 寂寞的；人迹稀少的

shadowy ['ʃædəui] adj. 朦胧的；有阴影的；虚无的；暗黑的

mellowness ['meləʊnɪs] n. 芳醇；肥沃；怡然；老练

rustle ['rʌs(ə)l] vi. 发出沙沙声 vt. 使……沙沙作响 n. 沙沙声；急忙

overturn [ˌəuvə'təːn] adj. 倾覆的，倒转的

"Oh, sing it again, Pa! Sing it again!" she cried, before she remembered that children must be seen and not heard. Then she was quiet. Pa went on playing, and everything began to dance. Mr. Edwards rose up on one elbow, then he sat up, then he jumped up and he danced. He danced like a jumping-jack in the moonlight, while Pa's fiddle kept on rollicking and his foot kept tapping the ground, and Laura's hands and Mary's hands were clapping together and their feet were patting, too. "You're the fiddlin'est fool that ever I see!" Mr. Edwards shouted admiringly to Pa. He didn't stop dancing, Pa didn't stop playing. He played "Money Musk" and "Arkansas Traveler", "Irish — Washerwoman" and the "Devil's Hornpipe." Baby Carrie couldn't sleep in all that music. She sat up in Ma's lap, looking at Mr. Edwards with round eyes, and clapping her little hands and laughing.

Even the firelight danced, and all around its edge the shadows were dancing. Only the new house stood still and quiet in the dark, till the big moon rose and shone on its gray walls and the yellow chips around it. Mr. Edwards said he must go. It was a long way back to his camp on the other side of the woods and the creek. He took his gun, and said good night to Laura and Mary and Ma. He said a bachelor got mighty lonesome, and he surely had enjoyed this evening of home life.

……

When Pa's fiddle stopped, they could not hear Mr. Edwards any more. Only the wind rustled in the prairie grasses. The big, yellow moon was sailing high overhead. The sky was so full of light that not one star twinkled in it, and all the prairie was a shadowy mellowness. —Then from the woods by the creek —a nightingale began to sing.

Everything was silent, listening to the nightingale's song. The bird sang on and on. The cool wind moved over the prairie and the song was round and clear above the grasses' whispering. The sky was like a bowl of light overturned on the flat black land.

The song ended. No one moved or spoke. Laura and Mary were quiet, Pa and Ma sat motionless. Only the wind stirred and the grasses sighed. Then Pa lifted the fiddle to his shoulder and softly touched the bow to the strings. A few notes fell like clear drops of water into the stillness. A pause, and Pa began to play the nightingale's song. The nightingale answered him. The nightingale began to sing again. It was singing with Pa's fiddle.

When the strings were silent, the nightingale went on singing. When it paused, the fiddle called to it and it sang again. The bird and the fiddle were talking to each other in the cool night under the moon.

长难句解析

He danced like a jumping-jack in the moonlight, while Pa's fiddle kept on rollicking and his foot kept tapping the ground.

当爸爸欢乐地拉着小提琴，他的脚不停地拍打着地面，在月光下跳得像一个跳爆竹。

jumping-jack跳爆竹（一种跳跃运动，跳起时双腿展开，双手在头顶接触，然后恢复到双脚并拢，手臂垂放在身体两侧的姿势）。while连词，引导时间状语从句，表动作同时发生；keep on doing sth 一直做某事。

Even the firelight danced, and all around its edge the shadows were dancing. Only the new house stood still and quiet in the dark, till the big moon rose and shone on its gray walls and the yellow chips around it.

炉火甚至在跳舞，围绕它边缘的阴影也在舞动。只有新房子在黑暗中寂静不动，直到月亮升起来光照在灰色的墙上，和淡黄的火光萦绕。

stand still 站着不动，固步自封，一直站着；rise 上升；起立；高耸，注意与raise区分。

The sky was so full of light that not one star twinkled in it, and all the prairie was a shadowy mellowness.

天空充满了亮光没有一颗星星闪烁，所有的草原陷入了神秘的怡然。

So...that...如此……以至于……，引导结果状语从句。

Everything was silent, listening to the nightingale's song. The bird sang on and on. The cool wind moved over the prairie and the song was round and clear above the grasses' whispering.

所有的一切都归于沉寂，鸟儿听到了夜莺的歌声也跟着唱了起来。寒风刮过了大草原，歌声是那么明亮，萦绕在草地的低声细语中。

listening 为现在分词作状语，表伴随；on and on继续不停地。

Then Pa lifted the fiddle to his shoulder and softly touched the bow to the strings. A few notes fell like clear drops of water into the stillness.

然后爸爸举起了小提琴，轻轻地从弓抚摸到了琴弦，几个音符像掉落的水珠打破了寂静。

like后是比喻，将notes比作water 。

读书笔记

083 The Little Prince 小王子

今日关键语导读 Today's Key Points

《小王子》是一部充满诗意而又温馨的美丽童话。讲述了“我”在浩瀚的撒哈拉大沙漠上遇到了一个古怪奇特而又天真纯洁的小王子——他来自一颗遥远的小星球，游历了分别住着国王、爱慕虚荣的人、酒鬼、商人、地理学家的几个星球。作者通过小王子的游历暗讽了成人世界的荒唐和虚伪，情节别致而曲折，行文富于诗情和哲理，字里行间蕴含着作者对于爱、人生等重大命题的深刻体会与感悟，让人读后回味无穷。

障碍词先听为快 Words and Expressions

tame [teim] adj. 驯服的；平淡的；乏味的；顺从的 v. 驯养；使变得平淡

disturbing [di'stəːbiŋ] adj. 令人不安的；烦扰的

neglect [ni'glekt] n. 疏忽，忽视；怠慢 vt. 疏忽，忽视；忽略

establish [is'tæbliʃ] vi. 植物定植 vt. 建立；创办；安置

unique [juː'niːk] n. 独一无二的人或物 adj. 独特的，稀罕的

monotonous [mə'nɔtənəs] adj. 单调的，无抑扬顿挫的；无变化

consequence ['kɔnsikwəns] n. 结果；重要性；推论

burrow ['bʌrəu] n. （兔、狐等的）洞穴，地道；藏身处，住处 vt. 挖掘

yonder ['jɔndə] adj. 那边的，远处的 adv. 在那边；在远处 pron. 那边

gaze [geiz] *n.* 凝视；注视 *vi.* 凝视；注视

好英文娓娓动听 Beautiful stories

"Ah! Please excuse me," said the little prince. But, after some thought, he added, "What does that mean—'tame'?"

"You do not live here," said the fox. "What is it that you are looking for?"

"I am looking for men," said the little prince. "What does that mean—'tame'?"

"Men," said the fox. "They have guns, and they hunt. It is very disturbing. They also raise chickens. These are their only interests. Are you looking for chickens?"

"No," said the little prince. "I am looking for friends. What does that mean—'tame'?"

"It is an act too often neglected," said the fox. "It means to establish ties."

"To establish ties?"

"Just that," said the fox. "To me, you are still nothing more than a little boy who is just like a hundred thousand other little boys. And I have no need of you. And you, on your part, have no need of me. To you, I am nothing more than a fox like a hundred thousand other foxes. But if you tame me, then we shall need each other. To me, you will be unique in all the world. To you, I shall be unique in all the world."

"I am beginning to understand," said the little prince. "There is a flower... I think that she has tamed me."

"It is possible," said the fox. "On the Earth one sees all sorts of things... "

......

"My life is very monotonous," the fox said. "I hunt chickens; men hunt me. All the chickens are just alike, and all the men are just alike. And, in consequence, I am a little bored. But if you tame me, it will be as if the sun came to shine on my life. I shall know the sound of a step that will be different from all the others. Other steps send me hurrying back underneath the ground. Yours will call me, like music, out of my burrow. And then look: you see the grain-fields down yonder? I do not eat bread. Wheat is of no use to me. The wheat fields have nothing to say to me. And that is sad. But you have hair that is the colour of gold. Think how wonderful that will be when you have tamed me! The grain, which is also golden, will bring me back the thought of you. And I shall love to listen to the wind in the wheat..." The fox gazed at the little prince, for a long time. "Please—tame me!" he said.

长难句解析

"You do not live here," said the fox. "What is it that you are looking for?"

"你不是本地人，"狐狸说道，"你来这儿寻找什么呢？"

What is it that ...?强调句型的特殊疑问句，look for 寻找。

To me, you are still nothing more than a little boy who is just like a hundred thousand other little boys. And I have no need of you.

对我来说，你与其他成千上万个小男孩没什么区别。我不需要你，你也不需要我。

nothing more than...“仅仅、不过是”，who引导定语从句；a hundred thousand 成千上万；have no need of 不需要。

I shall know the sound of a step that will be different from all the others. Other steps send me hurrying back underneath the ground.

我将会分辨出一种与众不同的脚步声。听到别的脚步声，我会急急忙忙躲进地下。

the sound of...的声音；that引导宾语从句；be different from 与……不同；hurrying 为v-ing做宾语补足语；underneath为介词，意为在……下面。

The grain, which is also golden, will bring me back the thought of you. And I shall love to listen to the wind in the wheat...

那金黄色的小麦会让我联想起你。于是，我也会喜欢听穿过麦田的风声……

which 引导的非限制性定语从句；the thought of 想起。

---

084 Swallows and Amazons 燕子与鹦鹉

今日关键语导读 Today's Key Points

《燕子与鹦鹉》著名作家亚瑟·莱瑟姆的一部经典儿童小说，讲述了20世纪20年代的英国乡村，六名年龄相仿的儿童在父母的允许之下，到湖区的小岛上过一段自由自在的独立生活。在小岛上，他们遇到了上校约翰以及船员，并在他们的带领下打败了野人和海盗，度过了这段惊险而美好的少年时光。

障碍词先听为快 Words and Expressions

zigzags ['zɪgzæg] n. 之字形；Z字形

steep [stiːp] adj. 陡峭的；不合理的

hedge [hedʒ] n. 树篱；障碍

vessel ['vesl] n. 船，舰

clipper ['klipə] n. 快速帆船

anchor ['æŋkə] v. 抛锚；使固定

harbour ['haːbə] n. 海港

caper ['keipə] v. 雀跃

好英文娓娓动听 Beautiful stories

ROGER, aged seven, and no longer the youngest of the family, ran in wide zigzags, to and fro, across the steep field that sloped up from the lake to Holly Howe, the farm where they were staying for part of the summer holidays. He ran until he nearly reached the hedge by the footpath, then turned and ran until he nearly reached the hedge on the other side of the field. Then he turned and crossed the field again. Each crossing of the field brought him nearer to the farm. The wind was against him, and he was tacking up against it to the farm, where at the gate his patient mother was awaiting him. He could not run straight against the wind because he was a sailing vessel, a tea clipper, the Cutty Sark. His elder brother John had said only that morning that steamships were just engines in tin boxes. Sail was the thing, and so, though it took rather longer, Roger made his way up the field in broad tacks.

When he came near his mother, he saw that she had in her hand a red envelope and a small piece of white paper, a telegram. He knew at once what it was. For a moment he was tempted to run straight to her. He knew that telegrams came only from his father, and that this one must be the answer to a letter from his mother, and letters from John, Susan, Titty, and himself, all asking the same thing, but asking it in different ways. His own letter had been very short. "Please, Daddy, may I too? With love. Roger." Titty's had been much longer, longer even than John's. Susan, though she was older than Titty, had not written a letter of her own. She had put her name with John's at the end of his, so that these two had sent one letter between them. Mother's letter had been the longest of all, but Roger did not know what she had said in it. All the letters had gone together, a very long way, to his father, whose ship was at Malta but under orders for Hong Kong. And there, in his mother's hand, was the red envelope that had brought the answer. For a moment Roger wanted to run straight to her. But sail was the thing, not steam, so he tacked on, heading, perhaps, a little closer to the wind. At last he headed straight into the wind, moved slower and slower, came to a stop at his mother's side, began to move backwards, and presently brought up with a little jerk, anchored, and in harbour.

"Is it the answer?" he panted, out of breath after all that beating up against the wind. "Does he say Yes?"

Mother smiled, and read the telegram aloud:

BETTER DROWNED THAN DUFFERS IF NOT DUFFERS WONT DROWN.

"Does that mean Yes?" asked Roger.

"I think so."

"Does it mean me, too?"

"Yes, if John and Susan will take you, and if you promise to do whatever they tell you."

"Hurrah," shouted Roger, and capered about, forgetting for a moment that he was a ship, and anchored in a quiet harbour.

"Where are the others?" asked Mother.

"In Darien," said Roger.

"Where?"

"On the peak, you know. Titty called it that. We can see the island from there."

长难句解析

ROGER, aged seven, and no longer the youngest of the family, ran in wide zigzags, to and fro, across the steep field that sloped up from the lake to Holly Howe, the farm where they were staying for part of the summer holidays.

七岁的罗杰已经不是家中最年幼的孩子了，他来回地沿着“Z”字型街道狂奔，穿过通向Holly Howe的河流延伸的陡峭田地，Holly Howe是他们度过部分暑假时光的农场。

no longer，不再；to and fro，表示来回地，往返地；that引导定语从句；where引导地点状语从句。

The wind was against him, and he was tacking up against it to the farm, where at the gate his patient mother was awaiting him.

风逆着他吹，他顶着风来到农场，农场大门处，好脾气的妈妈正在等他。

where 在此处引导地点状语从句。

"Is it the answer?" he panted, out of breath after all that beating up against the wind. "Does he say Yes?"

“这就是答案?”经过与风的斗争，他上气不接下气，喘息道，“他同意了吗?”

out of breath“上气不接下气”；after all“毕竟”。

085 Butterball 羊脂球

今日关键语导读 Today's Key Points

法国文学家莫泊桑的中篇小说代表作，福楼拜称之为“可以流传于世的杰作”。这篇小说以1870年普法战争为背景，描写普鲁士军队向巴黎大举进攻后，被敌军占领下的卢昂（Rouen）十名居民出逃到法军还据守着的勒阿弗尔港（Le Havre）的故事。

主人公是一名妓女，身材丰满圆润，所以有“羊脂球”的浑名。羊脂球一个人带了一篮子的食物，足够她吃上三天，她知道这些上层人物看不起自己，可是她还是慷慨地请大家一起吃。马车在行经中途被一普军军官扣留，放行的条件是要车中的羊脂球陪他睡觉，羊脂球大声斥骂这个无耻之徒。但是车上的那些人为了个人安危而逼迫羊脂球作出自我牺牲，在需要羊脂球帮助时用尽华丽的词句来赞美她，修女们甚至引用圣经的故事，劝羊脂球屈服；于是羊脂球出于无奈被迫向敌人献身；当马车放行后，他们又对羊脂球横加唾弃、嘲笑。

最后马车伴着羊脂球的哭泣声扬长而去。

障碍词先听为快 Words and Expressions

veal [viːl] n. 小牛肉

string [striŋ] n. 绳子；串线，串绳；一串，一行，一列；（乐器的）弦；（植物的）纤维，筋

slice [slais] n. 薄片，片；部分，份额；锅铲

provision [prə'viʒən] n. 提供，供给，给养，供应品

garlic ['gɑːlik] n. sausage ['sɔsidʒ] n. 香肠，腊肠

shrug [ʃrʌg] v. 耸肩

nun [nʌn] n. 修女，尼姑

nonchalantly ['nɒnʃələntlɪ] adv. 不关心地；冷淡地

conscience ['kɔnʃəns] n. 良心，良知；内疚，愧疚；凭良心

scapegoat ['skeipgəut] n. 替罪羊

好英文娓娓动听 Beautiful stories

The next morning, the coach, ready at last, was standing at the door, bright in the winter sun. A flock of white pigeons were seeking food on the snow in and out between the legs of the six horses.

The driver, wrapped in his sheepskin, was smoking a pipe on the box, and the travellers with a glad air, were packing up provisions for the rest of the journey. The only passenger who had not yet appeared was Boule de Suif.

At last she appeared. She looked somewhat restless and ashamed, and timidly approached her fellow travellers, who all coldly turned their faces away from her. The Count, with a pompous air, took his wife's arm and drew her away as from something disgusting and repulsive. Boule de Suif stood for a moment, aghast; but then plucking up her courage, she said to the manufacturer's wife, "Good morning, Madame." The latter, however, only nodded at the greeting with a scornful glance. The rest of them kept aloof from her, as if she were carrying the germs of an infectious disease.

The time came for the coach to start. Boule de Suif got into it behind them and took the seat she had occupied during the first stage of the journey.

The coach lumbered off, and the journey was resumed. There was an awkward silence. Presently, turning to Madame Carré-Lamadon, the Countess said:

"I think you're acquainted with Madame d' Etrelles?" Madame Garré-Lamadon smiled and said: "Yes, I am."

Then ensued the following conversation. "She is a charming person, isn't she?"

"Yes, there's an indefinable charm about her."

"She talks beautifully and sings beautifully. She has received an excellent education, so I hear."

"She is a model of propriety, Countess."

When they had been three hours or so on the way, Loiseau, who had been playing cards with his wife, looked up and said, "I am hungry."

His wife produced a packet tied with strings, from which she took a piece of cold veal and cut it neatly into thin slices, and they both began to eat.

"What about doing the same?" the Countess said to her husband and unpacked the provisions, taking out a hare-pie. The two nuns took out a piece of sausage smelling of garlic, while Cornudet began to eat hard-boiled eggs with a crust of bread.

Boule de Suif tried, as best she might, to put a bold face on the matter, but soon tears glistened in her eyes and rolled down her cheeks. She sat erect and looked straight before her, so that her sorrow might pass unnoticed by those respectable people, but the Countess noticed it, and with a gesture drew her husband's attention to it.

The Count shrugged his shoulders, while Madame Loiseau laughed silently and murmured, "Serve her right! She disgraced herself."

Meanwhile, the two nuns nonchalantly wrapped up the remnants of their sausage, and said grace, seemingly with a clear conscience. Boule de Suif had been made the scapegoat for them all.

The shade of the evening began to close round the coach. Suddenly Cornudet whistled the Marseillaise and every passenger started as if seized by a sense of guilt.

长难句解析

The driver, wrapped in his sheepskin, was smoking a pipe on the box, and the travellers with a glad air, were packing up provisions for the rest of the journey.

赶车的披上羊皮大衣，坐在车子头里的坐位上安闲地衔着烟斗，所有的人全是喜笑颜开的，匆匆忙忙让人包好为了在剩下的路程上食用的食品。

pack up整理；把……打包；the rest of 其余的，剩下的，剩余的。

At last she appeared. She looked somewhat restless and ashamed, and timidly approached her fellow travellers, who all coldly turned their faces away from her.

她终于出现了。她像是有点不安定，不好意思，后来她胆怯地向她的旅伴们走过来，旅伴们却同时把身子偏向另一面，如同都没有望见她似的。

at last 最终，最后；who 在句中引导定语从句，turn one's face away from 把一个人的脸转向……。

"What about doing the same?" the Countess said to her husband and unpacked the provisions, taking out a hare-pie.

“我们是不是也照样做。”伯爵夫人说。有人同意了，于是她解开了那些为了两家而预备的食品。

unpack 从包（或箱）中取出，如He unpacked the doll carefully from its box. 他小心地将玩偶从盒中取出来；“taking out a hare－pie”作伴随状语。

Boule de Suif tried, as best she might, to put a bold face on the matter, but soon tears glistened in her eyes and rolled down her cheeks.

她最大程度地克制自己保持镇定，如同孩子一般吞住自己的呜咽，但是眼泪还是很快地流出来，润湿了她的眼睑边缘。

put a bold face镇定；bold大胆自信的；roll down滚下。

The Count shrugged his shoulders, while Madame Loiseau laughed silently and murmured, "Serve her right! She disgraced herself."

伯爵耸了耸肩，罗瓦索夫人心里笑着，接着低声慢气地说："活该，她是自取其辱。"

while引导时间状语从句；disgrace oneself以某人为耻。

读书笔记

086 The Call of Wild 野性的呼唤

今日关键语导读 Today's Key Points

《野性的呼唤》是杰克·伦敦最受欢迎的小说之一。它讲述了大狗巴克的曲折经历。巴克原来在加利福尼亚的富豪大院里过着养尊处优的日子。当淘金兴起时，贩卖雪橇狗的行业暗流涌动。巴克被人倒卖到北方，投入蛮荒之地，被迫在弱肉强食的环境中为生存而拼杀。原有的尊严荡然无存，原始的兽性慢慢回归。在受尽磨难、奄奄一息的时候，巴克被约翰·桑顿搭救，从此巴克感受到爱的温暖，并知恩图报。但是，在约翰·桑顿遇害后，巴克最终切断了与人类社会的纽带，在荒野的声声呼唤感召下，汇入狼群，重回归自然。

障碍词先听为快 Words and Expressions

primordial [prai'mɔːdjəl] *adj.* 初生的，初发的，原始的

demonstrative [di'mɔnstrətiv] *adj.* 公开表露感情的，感情外露的

supremacy [sju'preməsi] *n.* 支配地位；优势

antagonist [æn'tægənist] *n.* 敌手

merciless ['məːsilis] *adj.* 残忍的；冷酷无情的

forego [fɔː'gəu] *vt.* 放弃

mandate ['mændeit] *n.* 授权；命令

His face and body were scored by the teeth of many dogs, and he fought as fiercely as ever and more shrewdly. Skeet and Nig were too good-natured for quarreling—besides, they belonged to John Thornton; but the strange dog, no matter what the breed or valor, swiftly acknowledged Buck's supremacy or found himself struggling for life with a terrible antagonist. And Buck was merciless. He had learned well the law of club and fang, and he never forewent an advantage or drew back from a foe he had started on the way to death. He had lessoned from Spitz, and from the chief fighting dogs of the police and mail, and knew there was no middle course. He must master or be mastered; while to show mercy was a weakness. Mercy did not exist in the primordial life. It was misunderstood for fear, and such misunderstandings made for death. Kill or be killed, eat or be eaten, was the law; and this mandate, down out of the depths of Time, he obeyed.

He was older than the days he had seen and the breaths he had drawn. He linked the past with the present, and the eternity behind him throbbed through him in a mighty rhythm to which he swayed as the tides and seasons swayed. He sat by John Thornton's fire, a broad-breasted dog, white-fanged and long-furred; but behind him were the shades of all manner of dogs, half wolves and wild wolves, urgent and prompting, tasting the savor of the meat he ate, thirsting for the water he drank, scenting the wind with him, listening with him and telling him the sounds made by the wild life in the forest; dictating his moods, directing his actions, lying down to sleep with him when he lay down, and dreaming with him and beyond him and becoming themselves the stuff of his dreams.

So peremptorily did these shades beckon him, that each day mankind and the claims of mankind slipped farther from him. Deep in the forest a call was sounding, and as often as he heard this call, mysteriously thrilling and luring, he felt compelled to turn his back upon the fire and the beaten earth around it, and to plunge into the forest, and on and on, he knew not where or why; nor did he wonder where or why, the call sounding imperiously, deep in the forest. But as often as he gained the soft unbroken earth and the green shade, the love for John Thornton drew him back to the fire again.

Thornton alone held him. The rest of mankind was as nothing. Chance travelers might praise or pet him; but he was cold under it all, and from a too demonstrative man he would get up and walk away. When Thornton's partners, Hans and Pete, arrived on the long-expected raft, Buck refused to notice them till he learned they were close to Thornton; after that he tolerated them in a passive sort of way, accepting favors from them as though he favored them by accepting. They were of the same large type as Thornton, living close to the earth, thinking simply and seeing clearly; and ere they swung the raft into the big eddy by the saw-mill at Dawson, they understood Buck and his ways, and did not insist upon an intimacy such as obtained with Skeet and Nig.

长难句解析

His face and body were scored by the teeth of many dogs, and he fought as fiercely as ever and more shrewdly.

他的脸和身体被许多狗用牙齿报复着，而他一如继往的激烈战斗，愈发精明。

as...as 意为“像……一样，同……一样”。

He linked the past with the present, and the eternity behind him throbbed through him in a mighty rhythm to which he swayed as the tides and seasons swayed.

他将过去跟现在连接起来，背后的永恒以一种强有力的旋律震动了他的全身，使他像潮汐和季节一样随之摇晃。.

link with意为“与……有关；与……相连接”；to which 引导目的状语从句。

After that he tolerated them in a passive sort of way, accepting favors from them as though he favored them by accepting.

之后，他才采取一种消极的态度容忍了他们，接受他们的好意的时候仿佛是赏了他们的脸。

accepting作伴随状语，as though意为“仿佛，好像”，以as though引导的方式状语从句或表语从句，常用虚拟语气。

087 The Love of A King
一个国王的爱情故事

今日关键语导读 Today's Key Points

你想当国王，想拥有荣华富贵、名闻天下吗？你希望无论走到哪里都成为众人的中心吗？你希望自己每时每刻都是人们关注的对象吗？国王永远不会独自一人。每时每刻总有人注视着他——有时是他的保镖，有时是街上成千的民众。每个人都认识他的面孔，他做事必须检点，因为他的所做所为是无法保密的。

国王永远不会独自一人，但他总是感到孤独。谁会是国王的朋友呢？谁会与他共同分担那份孤独呢？

障碍词先听为快 Words and Expressions

crown [kraun] n. 王冠，花冠，王权 v. 加冕，表彰

Buckingham ['bʌkiŋəm] n. 白金汉宫

palace ['pælis] n. 宫殿，宅邸

empty ['empti] n. 空车，空的东西 adj. 空无意义的，的，无知的，徒劳的 vt. 使失去 使……成为空的

deep [diːp] n. 深处，深渊 adj. 深的，低沉的

hit [hit] n. 打击，（演奏等）成功；讽刺，偶然碰上

conversation [ˌkɔnvə'seiʃən] n. 交谈，会话，社交，交际

forgotten [fə'gɔtn] v. 忘记（forget 的过去分词）

"I have never met a more beautiful woman than Wallis," Edward wrote, "and I love giving her presents. She has given me so much happiness. I buy her jewels to say 'thank you'."

In May 1972 the Duke became ill. When the doctor arrived, he listened to Edward's heart and then said: "How many cigarettes do you have a day, Sir?"

"About forty or fifty," the Duke replied. "But please don't ask me to stop. I've smoked for sixty years and I cannot change now."

That night Edward called Wallis into the room. "I feel very tired," he said. "And I'm afraid. I love you. I have been very happy with you, and you have been a wonderful wife. When I die, I want you to take my body back to Windsor. Will you do that for me?"

"Yes, of course," she said. And they both began to cry.

The Duke of Windsor died one hour later with Wallis by his side.

Three days later, a blue aeroplane arrived in Paris. Wallis went back to England with the Duke's body and, for the first time in her life, she entered Buckingham Palace.

A week later the Duchess returned to France, and for the next fourteen years she lived alone in Paris. The big house was dark. The doors were locked and she did not go out.

In the afternoons she sat in the dining room with Edward's love letters. "They were so beautiful," she said. "I read them again and again."

But then, in 1986, Wallis became ill. She went to a small

hospital near the house, and a few days later she died. "Without Edward," she once wrote, "my life was empty."

She was buried in England next to her husband at Windsor. "It's a strange thing," one newspaper wrote. "When they were alive, the Duke and Duchess could never live in Britain. It was only in death that they could be there together."

In 1970, two years before his death, Edward said:

There are some people who think that I was wrong to give away my crown, but they don't understand true love.

When I was young, I lived in Buckingham Palace. I could have anything that I wanted. But I wasn't happy because my heart was empty.

Then I met Wallis and everything changed. For half of my life I have lived here with the most beautiful woman in the world. And she is everything to me.

When I sit in my garden with the Duchess by my side, I sometimes think about my early life. I remember the days alone in my bedroom. I remember the teacher who hit me with a stick. I remember the war and my travels around the world. And then I remember the crowds of people below my window, who shouted: "Long live love!"

On my last night in London I spoke with Winston Churchill. In the middle of our conversation he said: "I think, Sir, that the best things in life are free." I have never forgotten those words. And now, many years later, I understand what they mean. You cannot buy happiness. And you cannot buy love. To be happy deep inside your heart is the most wonderful thing in the world. I have been a lucky man. And so I say: "Thank God for Wallis, and LONG LIVE LOVE!"

长难句解析

There are some people who think that I was wrong to give away my crown, but they don't understand true love.

有些人认为我放弃王位是错误的。但他们不懂得真正的爱。

who 在这里引导的定语从句，修饰前面的people；that 引导宾语从句；give away放弃。

For half of my life I have lived here with the most beautiful woman in the world. And she is everything to me.

我的后半生都和这位世界上最美丽的女人在这里一起度过。她就是我的一切。

for half of my life 在这做时间状语；be everything to 某人的全部。

When I sit in my garden with the Duchess by my side, I remember the days alone in my bedroom. I remember the teacher who hit me with a stick. I remember the war and my travels around the world. And then I remember the crowds of people below my window, who shouted: "Long live love!'

我和公爵夫人一起坐在花园里时，有时会想起自己早年的生活。我想起自己孤零零待在卧室里的那些日子。我想起那个用棍子打我的老师。我想起战争和周游世界的旅行。我想起那些聚集在我窗下的人群，他们高呼着：“爱情万岁！”

when 引导时间状语从句，意为“当……的时候”；who引导定语从句。

In the middle of our conversation he said: “I think, Sir, that the best things in life are free.” I have never forgotten those words.

谈话中，他说：“陛下，我认为生活中最好的事情是无偿的。”我从未忘记这句话。

In the middle of 在……中；that 在这引导宾语从句。

To be happy deep inside your heart is the most wonderful thing in the world.

内心深处的幸福是世界上最美妙的。

to be happy deep inside your heart 是动词不定式做主语；most+adj. 表示形容词最高级。

088 Aesop's Fables 伊索寓言

今日关键语导读 Today's Key Points

《伊索寓言》原书名为《埃索波斯故事集成》，是古希腊、古罗马时代流传的讽喻故事，现存的《伊索寓言》经后人汇集，统归在伊索名下。《伊索寓言》是世界上最早的寓言故事集。同时也是世界文学史上流传最广的寓言故事之一，多次被选入中小学教材。

障碍词先听为快 Words and Expressions

leap [liːp] vi. 跳 n. 跳跃

merrily ['merili] adv. 快乐地，愉快地

pipe [paip] n. 管子 vt. 以管输送

aghast [ə'gɑːst] adj. 惊呆的；吓呆的

wagon ['wægən] n. 四轮的运货马车

bullock ['bulək] n. 阉牛

henceforth [hens'fɔːθ] adv. 从今以后，今后

好英文娓娓动听 Beautiful stories

The Wolf and The Crane

A WOLF who had a bone stuck in his throat hired a Crane, for a large sum, to put her head into his mouth and draw out the bone.

When the Crane had extracted the bone and demanded the promised payment, the Wolf, grinning and grinding his teeth, exclaimed:

"Why, you have surely already had a sufficient recompense, in having been permitted to draw out your head in safety from the mouth and jaws of a wolf."

In serving the wicked, expect no reward, and be thankful if you escape injury for your pains.

The Fisherman Piping

A FISHERMAN skilled in music took his flute and his nets to the seashore. Standing on a projecting rock, he played several tunes in the hope that the fish, attracted by his melody, would of their own accord dance into his net, which he had placed below. At last, having long waited in vain, he laid aside his flute, and casting his net into the sea, made an excellent haul of fish. When he saw them leaping about in the net upon the rock he said: "O you most perverse creatures, when I piped you would not dance, but now that I have ceased you do so merrily."

Hercules and the Wagoner

A CARTER was driving a wagon along a country lane, when the wheels sank down deep into a rut. The rustic driver, stupefied and aghast, stood looking at the wagon, and did nothing but utter loud cries to Hercules to come and help him. Hercules, it is said, appeared and thus addressed him: "Put your shoulders to the wheels, my man. Goad on your bullocks, and never more pray to me for help, until you have done your best to help yourself, or depend upon it you will henceforth pray in vain."

The Traveler and His Dog

A TRAVELER about to set out on a journey saw his Dog stand at the door stretching himself. He asked him sharply: "Why do you stand there gaping? Everything is ready but you, so come with me instantly." The Dog, wagging his tail, replied: "O, master! I am quite ready; it is you for whom I am waiting."

The Herdsman and the Lost Bull

A HERDSMAN tending his flock in a forest lost a Bull-calf from the fold. After a long and fruitless search, he made a vow that, if he could only discover the thief who had stolen the Calf, he would offer a lamb in sacrifice to Hermes, Pan, and the Guardian Deities of the forest. Not long afterwards, as he ascended a small hillock, he saw at its foot a Lion feeding on the Calf. Terrified at the sight, he lifted his eyes and his hands to heaven, and said: "Just now I vowed to offer a lamb to the Guardian Deities of the forest if I could only find out who had robbed me; but now that I have discovered the thief, I would.

长难句解析

Standing on a projecting rock, he played several tunes in the hope that the fish, attracted by his melody, would of their own accord dance into his net, which he had placed below.

他站在一块突出的岩石上，心想鱼儿如果被他的旋律所吸引，会自愿舞蹈跳进他放在下面的网中。

standing为非谓语动词，表状态；which引导非限制性定语从句。

At last, having long waited in vain, he laid aside his flute, and casting his net into the sea, made an excellent haul of fish. When he saw them leaping about in the net upon the rock he said:" O you most perverse creatures, when I piped you would not dance, but now that I have ceased you do so merrily."

最后，经过长时间徒劳地等待，他放下了长笛，把网投入大海，捕获了一大网鱼。当他看到鱼儿在岩石上跳跃的时候，说道:“啊，你们这些最执拗的生物，当我吹笛时你们不跳舞，但现在，我不吹了，你们却跳了起来。”

in vain徒劳地，when引导时间状语从句；have sb. do sth.，使某人做某事。

A CARTER was driving a wagon along a country lane, when the wheels sank down deep into a rut. The rustic driver, stupefied and aghast, stood looking at the wagon, and did nothing but utter loud cries to Hercules to come and help him.

一个运货马车夫沿着乡间小路行进，可车轮深陷入了车辙里。这个车夫愣住并惊呆了，站在那凝视着马车，不断地叫喊求大力神来帮忙。

when引导时间状语从句；look at“注视”。

"Put your shoulders to the wheels, my man. Goad on your bullocks, and never more pray to me for help, until you have done your best to help yourself, or depend upon it you will henceforth pray in vain."

将你的肩膀贴紧车轮吧，我的伙计。再抽打你的牛。在你竭尽全力自力更生之前不要祈祷我帮忙，否则今后你的祈求都会是徒劳。"

depend upon"依赖……"; never/not...until: 直到....才；in vain"徒劳地"。

After a long and fruitless search, he made a vow that, if he could only discover the thief who had stolen the Calf, he would offer a lamb in sacrifice to Hermes, Pan, and the Guardian Deities of the forest.

经过长时间和徒劳的搜索，他发了一个誓，只要能发现是谁偷了小牛，他将提供一头小羊来祭祀赫耳墨斯，还有守护森林的神灵。

if 引导条件状语从句；who引导定语从句；offer sth to sb.，给某人提供某物；in sacrifice"牺牲"。

---

089 English Traits 英国人的特质

今日关键语导读 Today's Key Points

《英国人的特质》是美国著名思想家，文学家，诗人爱默生的代表作之一。此书以朴实的语言，平静的叙述方式介绍了英国的人文地理特点。作品注重思想内容和纪实性，深入浅出，说服力强，其充满智慧的文字、深邃的思想赢得了越来越多读者的共鸣。

障碍词先听为快 Words and Expressions

ponderous ['pɔndərəs] adj. 呆板的；笨重的；沉闷的

endurance [in'djurəns] n. 忍耐力；持久；耐久

combatant ['kɔmbətənt] n. 战士；争斗者

sentiment ['sentimənt] n. 感情；观点；情绪；多愁善感

drowsy ['drauzi] adj. 催眠的；沉寂的；昏昏欲睡的

flagellate ['flædʒeleit] adj. 鞭状的；有鞭毛的

clinch [klintʃ] v. 扭住；敲弯

composition [kɔmpə'ziʃən] n. 作曲，作文；（材）构成；合成物

tenacity [ti'næsiti] n. 韧性；固执；不屈不挠；黏性

immoderate [i'mɔdərit] adj. 无节制的；过度的；不适中的

But conscious that no race of better men exists, they rely most on the simplest means; and do not like ponderous and difficult tactics, but delight to bring the affair hand to hand, where the victory lies with the strength, courage, and endurance of the individual combatants. They adopt every improvement in rig, in motor, in weapons, but they fundamentally believe that the best stratagem in naval war, is to lay your ship close alongside of the enemy's ship, and bring all your guns to bear on him, until you or he go to the bottom. This is the old fashion, which never goes out of fashion, neither in nor out of England.

It is not usually a point of honor, nor a religious sentiment, and never any whim that they will shed their blood for; but usually property, and right measured by property, that breeds revolution. They have no Indian taste for a tomahawk-dance, no French taste for a badge or a proclamation. The Englishman is peaceably minding his business, and earning his day's wages. But if you offer to lay hand on his day's wages, on his cow, or his right in common, or his shop,he will fight to the Judgment. Magna-charta, jury-trial, habeas-corpus, star-chamber, ship-money, Popery, Plymouth-colony, American Revolution, are all questions involving a yeoman's right to his dinner, and, except as touching that, would not have lashed the British nation to rage and revolt.

Whilst they are thus instinct with a spirit of order, and of calculation, it must be owned they are capable of larger views; but the indulgence is expensive to them, costs great crises, or accumulations of mental power. In common, the horse works best with blinders. Nothing is more in the line of English thought, than our unvarnished Connecticut question, “Pray, sir, how do you get your living when you are at home?” The questions of freedom, of taxation, of privilege, are money questions. Heavy fellows, steeped in beer and fleshpots, they are hard of hearing and dim of sight. Their drowsy minds need to be flagellated by war and trade and politics and persecution. They cannot well read a principle, except by the light of fagots and of burning towns.

Tacitus says of the Germans, “powerful only in sudden efforts, they are impatient of toil and labor.” This highly-destined race, if it had not somewhere added the chamber of patience to its brain, would not have built London. I know not from which of the tribes and temperaments that went to the composition of the people this tenacity was supplied, but they clinch every nail they drive. They have no running for luck, and no immoderate speed. They spend largely on their fabric, and await the slow return. Their leather lies tanning seven years in the vat. At Rogers's mills, in Sheffield, where I was shown the process of making a razor and a penknife, I was told there is no luck in making good steel; that they make no mistakes, every blade in the hundred and in the thousand is good. And that is characteristic of all their work, — no more is attempted than is done.

长难句解析

But conscious that no race of better men exists, they rely most on the simplest means; and do not like ponderous and difficult tactics, but delight to bring the affair hand to hand, where the victory lies with the strength, courage, and endurance of the individual combatants.

但意识到没有更好的人存在，他们最依赖最简单的方式，不喜欢沉闷、困难的战术，但喜欢将事件聚到一起，胜利属于有力量、勇气和耐力的个人战斗人员。

that引导宾语从句。形容词作状语。

This is the old fashion, which never goes out of fashion, neither in nor out of England.

这是古老的时尚，它永远是一种时尚，不管是否在英格兰，依旧如此。

which引导非限制定语从句。

This highly-destined race, if it had not somewhere added the chamber of patience to its brain, would not have built London.

这个高命数的种族，如果不是拥有足够的耐心就不会建立了伦敦。

if引导条件状语从句。

I know not from which of the tribes and temperaments that went to the composition of the people this tenacity was supplied, but they clinch every nail they drive.

我不知道是哪个部落能使人们养成这种坚韧的性格，但是他们的确解决了所遇到的每个问题。

that引导限制性定语从句。

At Rogers's mills, in Sheffield, where I was shown the process of making a razor and a penknife, I was told there is no luck in making good steel; that they make no mistakes, every blade in the hundred and in the thousand is good.

在罗杰斯的磨坊，在谢菲尔德，我看到了生产剃刀和小刀的过程，我被告知没有使用好的钢材；但他们没有出过差错，每个叶片在几百、几千的都是好的。

where引导非限制性定语从句，there is （no）luck in doing sth.（没）有运气做什么

读书笔记

090 A Farewell to Arms 永别了武器

今日关键语导读 Today's Key Points

《永别了武器》是美国文学大师欧内斯特·海明威以在意大利半年左右的战地生活为题材所写的长篇小说。小说主人公亨利自愿到意奥战场前线做救护车司机，结识并爱上护士凯瑟琳·巴克利小姐。由于战场混乱，亨利历经重重艰难，九死一生，两人的幸福也只是昙花一现，最后凯瑟琳母子双双死于难产，亨利悲痛欲绝。

障碍词先听为快 Words and Expressions

drown [draun] v. 淹没；溺死；把……淹死

grab [græb] v. 霸占；夺取；将……深深吸引 n. 夺取之物

branch [brɑːntʃ] v. 分支，出现分歧

crawl [krɔːl] v. 爬行，匍匐前进

track [træk] n. 轨道；足迹；踪迹；小道

guard [gɑːd] n. 守卫；后卫；护卫队；禁卫军 v. 守卫；看守

underneath [ˌʌndəˈniːθ] prep. 在……下面；在……的形式上；在……的支配下 adv. 在下面；在底下 n. 下面；底部 adj. 下面的；底层的

brand [brænd] v. 铭刻于；铭记；打烙印于；印……商标于 n. 商标；牌子；烙印

genius [ˈdʒiːnjəs] n. 天才；天赋精神

wetness [wetnəs] *n.* 湿润；下雨

好英文娓娓动听 Beautiful stories

I did not know how long I was in the river. I surely would have drowned if I had not found that piece of floating wood. I held on to it as gently as I could, for the water was cold and I did not want to get any pains in my arms or legs. That would certainly mean death. After a while, I managed to grab hold of some tree branches near the edge of the river. I pulled myself up into the tall grass that grew up out of the water, and crawled my way toward dry land.

I walked for a little while, keeping low to the ground. There was no one around. Feeling a little safer, I decided to rest for a while. I sat down on a stone, and took off my clothing to let it dry. Most importantly, I tore the stars from my shoulders so that no one would recognize me as an officer.

When I began to walk again, I found a road and decided to follow it. After several hours, I came to some railroad tracks. A little further down, I could see two guards keeping watch over the tracks. In the distance, the sound of an approaching train could be heard. I waited down at the bottom of the hill next to the tracks, and stayed out of sight from the guards. Eventually the train passed. It was not going very quickly so I felt it would be possible for me to jump aboard. Many cars passed in front of me, but it was not until I saw one with a cloth cover that I decided to take my chances and jump on. Luckily, the guards were not looking my way, and I managed to get on without being seen. Of course, there would be other guards on the train itself, so I climbed underneath the cloth cover to hide. Inside, I found myself lying upon a car full of brand new guns. I guessed that they were being sent to the town of Mestre, for it was the closest place in the area.

I was very uncomfortable. My clothes were still wet, and I had not eaten in quite a while. I thought about how well my leg had done during these last few days. I decided that Dr. Valentini was a genius. I began to miss Catherine again. I tried to imagine being with her in the future, but the cold wetness of the guns made it difficult. I thought about how I had lost my cars and my men just like a manager loses his goods when a fire destroys the store he works in. Then I thought, "Would a manager go back to work at that store if he knew the owners would shoot him for not speaking their language perfectly?" Of course he would not. That was when I decided I was finished fighting for the Italians. I had nothing against them.I was just finished.

Thoughts of returning to Catherine came back. When would I see her next? Tonight? No. At the very earliest it would be tomorrow evening. I decided that once I was with her again, I would never leave her side; not even for a business trip. But where would we live? We could go almost anywhere.

长难句解析

I held on to it as gently as I could, for the water was cold and I did not want to get any pains in arms or legs. That would certainly mean death.

我尽量小心地抱住它，河水冰冷刺骨，我不能让我的手和腿增加任何外伤，不然的话，也必死无疑。

as...as表示和……一样，for 一词在此表“因为”，引导原因状语从句。

Most importantly, I tore the stars from my shoulders so that no one would recognize me as an officer.

最重要的是，我把肩章上的几颗星撕掉，这样别人就认不出我是一名军官了。

so that是“以便”的意思；recognize sb. as...，认为某人是……。

Many cars passed in front of me, but it was not until I saw one with a cloth cover that I decided to take my chances and in front of.

许多车厢都过去了，当我看见有一节盖着帆布的车厢过来时，抓住机会，纵身一跃，攀上列车。

in front of，在……前面；not until...that 固定句式，意思是“直到……才”；decided to决定做某事；take chances

意为抓住机会；jump on跳上。

That was when I decided I was finished fighting for the Italians. I had nothing against them. I was just finished.

就是从那时起，我不再参与意大利的战事。我不反对他们，我只是同他们断绝来往。

when引导时间状语从句，fight for为……斗争。

I decided that once I was with her again, I would never leave her side; not even for a business trip. But where would we live? We could go almost anywhere.

我下定决心，再次同她在一起时，我永远不离开她了，即使为了生意，也不分离。我们到何处定居？任何地方，我们都可以去。

that引导宾语从句。

读书笔记

091 Love You Forever 永远爱你

今日关键语导读 Today's Key Points

《永远爱你》是一本经典的图画书，书中集合了爱与成长的主题，让人开怀的同时也发人深省。幽默、夸张、潇洒又带动感的画风，创造出形形色色神情及肢体语言夸大的人物，令读者边读边笑地享受《永远爱你》带来的乐趣。开放性的结局也让读者可以继续编故事。这是一本适合亲子共读或孩子自己“悦”读的图画书。

障碍词先听为快 Words and Expressions

rock [rɔk] vt. 摇动；使摇晃

pull [pul] vt. 拉；拔；拖

shelf [ʃelf] n. 架子；搁板；搁板状物

refrigerator [ri'fridʒəreitə] n. 冰箱，冷藏库

flush [flʌʃ] vt. 使齐平；发红，使发亮；用水冲洗

crawl [krɔːl] vt. 爬行；缓慢地行进

forth [fɔːθ] adv. 向前，向外；自……以后

rock [rɔk] n. 岩石，石头，摇滚乐 v. 摇晃，摇动，震动

好英文娓娓动听 Beautiful stories

A mother held her new baby and very slowly rocked him back

and forth, back and forth, back and forth. And while she held him, she sang: I'll love you forever, I'll like you always. As long as I'm living my baby you'll be. The baby grew. He grew and he grew and he grew. He grew until he was two years old, and he ran all around the house. He pulled all the books off the shelves. He pulled all the food out of the refrigerator and he took his mother's watch and flushed it down the toilet. Sometimes his mother would say, "This kid is driving me crazy!" But at night time, when that two-year-old was quiet, she opened the door to his room, crawled across the floor, looked up over the side of his bed; and if he was really asleep she picked him up and rocked him back and forth, back and forth, back and forth. While she rocked him she sang: I'll love you forever, I'll like you always. As long as I'm living, my baby you'll be.

The little boy grew. He grew and he grew and he grew. He grew until he was nine years old. And he never wanted to come in for dinner, he never wanted to take a bath, and when grandma visited he always said bad words. Sometimes his mother wanted to sell him to the zoo!

But at night time, when he was asleep, the mother quietly opened the door to his room, crawled across the floor and looked up over the side of the bed. If he was really asleep, she picked up that nine-year-old boy and rocked him back and forth, back and forth, back and forth. And while she rocked him she sang:

I'll love you forever, I'll like you for always. As long as I'm living my baby you'll be.

The boy grew. He grew and he grew and he grew. He grew until he was a teenager. He had strange friends and he wore strange clothes and he listened to strange music. Sometimes the mother felt like she was in a zoo!

But at night time, when that teenager was asleep, the mother opened the door to his room, crawled across the floor and looked up over the side of the bed. If he was really asleep she picked up that great big boy and rocked him back and forth, back and forth, back and forth. While she rocked him she sang:

I'll love you forever, I'll like you for always. As long as I'm living my baby you'll be.

That teenager grew. He grew and he grew and he grew. He grew until he was a grown-up man. He left home and got a house across town. But sometimes on dark nights the mother got into her car and drove across town. If all the lights in her son's house were out, she opened his bedroom window, crawled across the floor, and looked up over the side of his bed. If that great big man was really asleep she picked him up and rocked him back and forth, back and forth, back and forth. And while she rocked him she sang:

I'll love you forever, I'll like you for always. As long as I'm living my baby you'll be.

长难句解析

A mother held her new baby and very slowly rocked him back and forth, back and forth, back and forth.

一个妈妈抱着刚出生的小宝宝，非常轻柔地摇晃着他，来来回回，来来回回，来来回回。

back and forth反复地，来回地。

Sometimes his mother would say, "This kid is driving me crazy!"

有时候他的妈妈会说："这个小孩把我给逼疯了！"

drive sb. crazy 让某人疯狂。

While she rocked him she sang: I'll love you forever, I'll like you always. As long as I'm living, my baby you'll be.

她摇晃他的时候，会唱到：我将永远爱你，我将一直都喜欢你，只要我在人世间，你都是我的宝贝儿。

as long as只要，还可表示"和…一样长"的意思。

But at night time, when that teenager was asleep, the mother opened the door to his room, crawled across the floor and looked up over the side of the bed.

但是一到了晚上，当这个少年安安静静地躺在床上时，妈妈会推开房门，安安静静地走到他的床边，看他是不是睡着了。

at night 在晚上、夜晚，when引导时间状语从句；be asleep 睡觉；crawl across爬过；look up向上看；the side of 在……的一边。

092 Ulysses 尤利西斯

今日关键语导读 Today's Key Points

《尤利西斯》是爱尔兰现代主义作家詹姆斯·乔伊斯于1922年出版的长篇小说。是意识流小说的代表作，并被誉为20世纪百大英文小说之首。小说以时间为顺序，描述了主人公，苦闷彷徨的都柏林小市民，广告推销员利奥波德·布卢姆在1904年6月16日一昼夜之内在都柏林的种种日常经历。

障碍词先听为快 Words and Expressions

lore [lɔː,lɔə] n. 知识；学问；全部传说

chide [tʃaid] vt. 责骂；斥责

truant ['truːənt] adj. 旷课的；偷懒的

malign [mə'lain] vt. 诽谤，污蔑；中伤，说坏话

stud [stʌd] vt. 散布；用许多饰钮等装饰

bridle ['braidl] n. 缰绳；马勒；系带；约束物

pilgrim ['pilgrim] n. 朝圣者；漫游者；（美）最初的移民

withal [wi'ðɔːl] adv. 而且，加之；同样

comether [kəu'meðə] n. 友谊；事情；引诱（等于come-hither）

tumble ['tʌmbl] n. 跌倒；翻斤斗；跌跤

—Dialectic, Stephen answered: and from his mother how to bring thoughts into the world. What he learnt from his other wife Myrto (absit nomen!) Socratididion's Epipsychidion, no man, not a woman, will ever know. But neither the midwife's lore nor the caudlectures saved him from the archons of Sinn Fein and their noggin of hemlock.

—But Ann Hathaway? Mr Best's quiet voice said forgetfully. Yes, we seem to be forgetting her as Shakespeare himself forgot her.

His look went from brooder's beard to carper's skull, to remind, to chide them not unkindly, then to the bald pink Lollard costard, guiltless though maligned.

—He had a good Groatsworth of Wit, Stephen said, and no truant memory. He carried a memory in his wallet as he trudged to Romeville whistling The Girl I Left Behind Me. If the earthquake did not time it we should know where to place poor Wat, sitting in his form, the cry of hounds, the studded bridle and her blue windows. That memory, Venus and Adonis, lay in the bedchamber of every light-of-love in London. Is Katharine the shrew illfavoured? Hortensio calls her young and beautiful. Do you think the writer of Antony and Cleopatra, a passionate pilgrim, had his eyes in the back of his head that he chose the ugliest doxy in all Warwickshire to lie withal? Good: he left her and gained the world of men. But his boywomen are the women of a boy. Their life, thought, speech are lent them by males. He chose badly? He was chosen, it seems to me. If others have their will Ann hath a way. By cock, she was to blame. She put the comether on him, sweet and twenty-six. The grey-eyed goddess who bends over the boy Adonis, stooping to conquer, as prologue to the swelling act, is a boldfaced Stratford wench who tumbles in a cornfield a lover younger than herself.

And my turn? When?

Come!

—Ryefield, Mr Best said brightly, gladly, raising his new book, gladly brightly.

长难句解析

What he learnt from his other wife Myrto (absit nomen!) Socratididion's Epipsychidion, no man, not a woman, will ever know.

他从另一个老婆默尔托（名字是无所谓的！），苏格拉底的灵魂的分身那儿学到了什么，任何男人或女人都永远不得而知。

His look went from brooder's beard to carper's skull, to remind, to chide them not unkindly, then to the bald pink lollard costard, guiltless though maligned.

他的视线从冥思着的那个人的胡子扫到吹毛求疵者的脑壳，宛若在提醒他们，和颜悦色地责备他们，然后又转向那尽管无辜却受到迫害的罗拉德派那粉红色的秃脑袋。

go from...to...，从……到……;bald“秃头的，无毛的”，注意与plain区分。

He carried a memory in his wallet as he trudged to Romeville whistling. The Girl I Left Behind Me.

当他用口哨吹着《我撇下的姑娘》，朝罗马维尔吃力地走着的时候，他的行囊里就装有记忆

as 引导时间状语从句，表示当……的时候。

If the earthquake did not time it we should know where to place poor Wat, sitting in his form, the cry of hounds, the studded bridle and her blue windows.

即便那场地震不曾记载下来，我们也应知道，该把蹲在窝里的可怜的小兔，猎犬的吠声，镂饰的缰绳，她那蓝色的窗户，放在他一生的哪个时期。

句中的place，sitting 都应该理解为名词的放置的意思，翻译是首先直译再将文字联系上下文进行整理。

The grey-eyed goddess who bends over the boy Adonis, stooping to conquer, as prologue to the swelling act, is a boldfaced Stratford wench who tumbles in a cornfield a lover younger than herself.

灰眼睛的女神伏在少年阿都尼身上，屈就取胜。这就是厚脸皮的斯特拉特福荡妇，她曾把比自己年轻的情人压翻在麦田里。

who引导定语从句；stoop的v.-ing形式为现在分词作状语，表伴随；这个长句，is前面部分做整个句子的主语。

读书笔记

093 Kidnapped 诱拐

今日关键语导读 Today's Key Points

罗伯特·路易斯·史蒂文森于1850年生于苏格兰的爱丁堡。他受训成为一名律师，但21岁时他下决心要当一名作家。他最著名的作品有：《诱拐》《金银岛》和《化身博士》。本书讲述了在1745年苏格兰的艰难岁月。苏格兰高地人向英格兰乔治国王发动了战争，但失败了。乔治国王的部队把很多苏格兰高地人赶出了他们的家园。

来自苏格兰低地的戴维·鲍尔弗并不为英格兰部队而烦恼。当他离家去开始新生活时，他并没有预料到任何麻烦或危险。但是，麻烦很快接踵而至。他见到了他那很有钱的叔叔，但他叔叔获悉自己有这样一个穷侄子时一点儿也不高兴。危险一个接一个。戴维来到苏格兰高地，在那儿他遇见了艾伦·布雷克，一个骄傲的斯图尔特人。斯图尔特人既恨英格兰人，又恨效忠乔治国王的坎贝尔人，所以艾伦对于戴维来说是一个危险的朋友。

接着，他们身边发生了一宗谋杀案。戴维和艾伦开始了在荒山野岭上的逃亡……

障碍词先听为快 Words and Expressions

cabin ['kæbin] n. 小屋；客舱；船舱

sailor ['seilə] n. 水手，海员；乘船者

slave [sleiv] n. 奴隶；从动装置

violent ['vaiələnt] adj. 暴力的；猛烈的

sheet [ʃiːt] n. 薄片，纸张；薄板；床单

cupboard ['kʌbəd] n. 碗柜；食橱

whisky ['(h)wiski] n. 威士忌酒

fixedly ['fiksidli] adv. 固定地，不屈地，坚定不移地

好英文娓娓动听 Beautiful stories

So I was carried up into the sunlight a few minutes later, and put in a cabin where some of the sailors were sleeping. It was a wonderful feeling to see the daylight and to be able to talk to people again. I lay in the cabin for several days, and after a while began to feel better. The sailors were kind to me in their way. They brought me food and drink, and told me about their families at home. I discovered from them that the ship was sailing to the Carolinas, in North America. There the captain was planning to sell me as a slave, to work in a rich man's house or on a farm.

I also learnt that both the ship's officers, Mr Riach and Mr Shuan, enjoyed drinking far too much. The sailors liked Mr Shuan, but said that he was sometimes violent when he had drunk a lot. One of the sailors was a young boy, called Ransome. His job was to bring meals to the captain and officers in the round-house, a big cabin on the top of the ship, where the officers slept and ate. When Ransome dropped something or did something wrong, Mr Shuan used to hit him, and I often saw the poor boy crying.

One night, about nine o'clock, I heard one of the sailors in the cabin saying quietly to the others, 'Shuan's killed him at last!'We all knew who he meant. Just then the captain came in. I was surprised to see him walk towards me and say kindly, "My man, We Want ye to help us in the round-house. From now on, ye'll sleep there instead of Ransome." As he spoke, two sailors carried Ransome into the cabin. His face was as white as a sheet, and he did not move. My blood ran cold when I saw him.

I obeyed the captain, and ran to the round-house. It was a large room, with a table, a bench and locked cupboards. All the best food and drink was kept there, under the captain's eyes, as well as the guns. When I entered, I saw Mr Shuan sitting at the table, with a bottle of whisky in front of him. He did not seem to notice what was happening around him, and was looking fixedly at the table.

长难句解析

His job was to bring meals to the captain and officers in the round-house, a big cabin on the top of the ship, where the officers slept and ate.

他的工作是给后甲板室（即船顶上的一个大机舱）里的船长和高级船员送饭。高级船员吃住都在后甲板室里。

on the top of 在……顶端；where引导的是地点状语从句。

I was surprised to see him walk towards me and say kindly, "My man, We Want ye to help us in the round-house. From now on, ye'll sleep there instead of Ransome."

我很吃惊地看见他走向我，和蔼地对我说："小伙子，我们需要你到后甲板室给我们帮忙。从现在起，你就代替兰塞姆睡在那儿。"

be surprised to 对……感到惊讶；from now on从现在开始；句中的"ye"是方言，指"you"；instead of 而不是，代替。

All the best food and drink was kept there, under the captain's eyes, as well as the guns.

最好的食品和饮料都放在那儿，就在船长的眼皮底下，也在枪口保护之下。

under one's eyes 在……眼皮下；as well as也、又、和……一样。

读书笔记

094 A Streetcar Named Desire 欲望号街车

今日关键语导读 Today's Key Points

《欲望号街车》是美国剧作家田纳西·威廉斯诸多作品中的扛鼎之作，女主人公布兰奇是典型的南方淑女，从小娇生惯养，受过旧式的南方教育。家庭败落以后，不肯放弃旧日的生活方式，逐渐堕落腐化，后来不得不投靠妹妹斯黛拉。但又与妹夫斯坦利粗暴的生活方式格格不入，继而遭妹夫强奸，最后被送进疯人院。威廉斯笔下的这部悲剧不是简单的生活，而是一个在社会文明还较为落后、男权独唱大戏的时代社会背景下，一个试图与这样一个社会反抗的女性的故事。该剧展现了现代社会中野蛮残忍的势力是如何无情地蹂躏生活中无力的弱者。

障碍词先听为快 Words and Expressions

telegram ['teligræm] n. 电报

millionaire [ˌmiljə'nεə] n. 百万富翁；大富豪

goddam ['gɒddæm] adj. 诅咒的；讨厌的

deceit [di'siːt] n. 欺骗；谎言；欺诈手段

ragpicker ['rægipikə(r)] n. 拾破烂的人

sprinkle ['spriŋkl] v. 洒，撒；下稀疏小雨；喷撒

liquor ['likə] n. 酒，含酒精饮料；溶液；液体；烈酒

incredible [in'kredəbl] adj. 难以置信的，惊人的

scalding ['skɔːldiŋ] adj. 滚烫的；尖刻的

Stanley: Was this before or after you got the telegram?

Blanche: Telegram? Telegram...Oh, as a matter of fact, my wire...

Stanley: As a matter of fact, there wasn't no wire at all.

(Stanley pushes Blanche, she falls down at the bed.)

Blanche: Oh!

Stanley: And there isn't no millionaire. And Mitch didn't come in here with roses' cause I know where he is. There isn't a goddam thing but imagination and lies and deceit and tricks. And look at yourself! Take a look at yourself in that worn-out Mardi Gras outfit, rented for fifty cents from some ragpicker, and with the crazy crown on, what kind of a queen do you think you are? You know that I've been on to you from the start, and not once did you pull the wool over this boy's eyes. You come in here and you sprinkle the place with powder and you spray perfume. And you stick a paper lantern over the light bulb and lo and behold, the place has turned into Egypt, and you are the Queen of the Nile, sitting on your throne swilling down my liquor. And you know what I say? Ha! Ha! Do you hear me? Ha! Ha! Ha!

Blance: Stella? I weight now what I weighed the summer you left Bella Reve, the summer Dad died and you left us...It's just incredible.

Stella: Blanche, how well you look. Are you sure you don't want another?

Blanche: Well, well, maybe just one little tiny nip more, sort of to put the stopper on, so to speak...Now don't get worried, you sister hasn't turned into a drunkard, She's just all shaken up and hot and dirty and tired. Waiter! Waiter!

Stella: You want it hot?

Blanche: Scalding. Stella!

Stella: What is it, hon?

Blanche: there's only two rooms, I don't see where you're going to put me?

Stella: We're going to put you right in here.

Blanche: Well, what kind of bed's this-one of those collapsible things? Does it feel all right?

Stella: Oh, wonderful, honey, I don't like a bed that gives much.

Blanche: But Stella! There's no door between the two rooms, and Stanley-will it be decent?

Stella: Stanley is Polish, you know.

Blanche: Oh, yes. Something like Irish, isn't it? Well- I brought some nice clothes to meet all your lovely friends in Well, I'm afraid you won't think they are lovely. Well-anyhow-I brought nice clothes and I'll ware them. I guess you're hoping I'll say I'll put up at a hotel, but I'm not going to put up at a hotel. I've got to be near you, Stella. I've got to be with you, Stella. I can't be alone! Because - as you must have noticed I'm - not very well...

Stella: You do seem a little...

Blanche: Will Stanley like me, or will I just be a visiting in-law? I couldn't stand that, Stella.

Stella: You'll get along fine together, - if you'll just try not to compare him with an officer.

Blanche: He was an officer?

Stella:He was a Master Sergeant in the Engineer's Corps. Decorated four times!

Blanche: He had those on when you met him?

Stella: I assure you I wasn't just blinded by all the brass. That's not what I.... But of course there were things to adjust myself to later on. Such as his civilian background!

Blanche: How did he take it when you said I was coming? Oh, he's on the road a good deal... and...

Blanche: Oh, travels? Good!

Stella: I mean- isn't it...... I can hardly stand it when he is away for a night......

Blanche: Why? Stella!

Stella: when he's away for a week I nearly go wild! Gracious! And when he comes back I cry on his lap like a baby...I guess that is what is meant by being in love...

长难句解析

You know that I've been on to you from the start, and not once did you pull the wool over this boy's eyes. You come in here and you sprinkle the place with powder and you spray perfume. And you stick a paper lantern over the light bulb and lo and behold, the place has turned into Egypt, and you are the Queen of the Nile, sitting on your throne swilling down my liquor.

知道吗，从一开始我就对你一清二楚，你一次都没能蒙骗过我的眼睛。你一来到这儿就在这地方洒上香粉，洒满香水。还把一个纸灯笼罩在灯泡上，你瞧，这地方变成埃及王国了，而你就是尼罗河女王。坐上你的王座，喝着我的酒。

that引导宾语从句；句中的and为连词，连接多个分句。

There's only two rooms, I don't see where you're going to put me?

这只有两个房间你安排我住哪里?

where 引导的句子放在see后作宾语成分；put一词为安排、安置的意思，为及物动词。

I assure you I wasn't just blinded by all the brass. That's not what I.... But of course there were things to adjust myself to later on. Such as his civilian background!

我可不是被那些迷住的，我不是那样的……但是的确有些事情我原来不知道。比如他的平民身份！

assure sb. sth. 向某人保证某事；adjust...to 调整；later on 一会儿；Such as 例如，句中用到了there be 句型。

When he's away for a week I nearly go wild! Gracious! And when he comes back I cry on his lap like a baby...I guess that is what is meant by being in love.

他要是离开我一周，我就要疯了！天啊！当他回来的时候，我抱着他哭得像个小孩……嗯，这就是爱的感觉吧。

when 引导时间状语从句；go wild 解释为疯狂；come back 回来；that引导宾语从句；what引导表语从句。

读书笔记

095 Great Expectations 远大前程

今日关键语导读 Today's Key Points

《远大前程》是英国作家查尔斯·狄更斯晚年写成的教育小说。故事背景为1812年圣诞节前夕至1840年冬天，主角孤儿皮普以自叙式口吻，叙述从7岁开始的三个人生阶段。此小说贯彻了狄更斯文以载道的风格，透过剧中孤儿命运的跌宕起落，表达了他对生命和人性的看法。

障碍词先听为快 Words and Expressions

dramatic [drə'mætik] adj. 戏剧的；引人注目的；激动人心的

witness ['witnis] n. 证人；目击者；证据 v. 目击；证明

feeble ['fiːbl] adj. 微弱的，无力的；虚弱的；薄弱的

hesitate ['heziteit] v. 踌躇，犹豫；不愿 vt. 踌躇，犹豫；有疑虑，不愿意

gasp [gɑːsp] n. 喘气

inherit [in'herit] vt. 继承；遗传而得 vi. 成为继承人

forbid [fə'bid] vt. 禁止；妨碍，阻止

whisper ['(h)wispə] n. 私语；谣传；飒飒的声音 v. 耳语；密谈；飒飒地响

forge [fɔːdʒ] n. 熔炉，锻铁炉；铁工厂 v. 伪造；做锻工；前进

miserable ['mizərəbl] adj. 悲惨的；痛苦的；卑鄙的

convict ['kɔnvikt] vt. 证明……有罪；宣告……有罪 n. 罪犯

One Saturday evening, when I had been apprenticed to Joe for four years, he and I were sitting in the pub, with some of the villagers, listening to Mr. Wopsle. He was giving a dramatic reading of a newspaper report of a murder trial, and we all enjoyed watching him act the main characters. His witnesses were old and feeble, his lawyers were clever and sharp-eyed, and his accused was a violent, wicked murderer. Suddenly we became aware of a strange gentleman who had also been listening, and was now looking coldly at us. Well! he said to us, biting the side of his finger. So you've decided the accused was the murderer, have you? 'Sir, 'answered Mr. Wopsle firmly, yes, I do think he is guilty. We all nodded our heads in agreement. But, said the stranger, do you or do you not know that the law of England supposes every man to be innocent until he is proved to be guilty? Sir, began Mr. Wopsle, as an Englishman myself, I-Come! said the stranger, don't avoid the question. Either you know it, or you don't know it. Which is it? Of course I know it, answered poor Mr. Wopsle. Then why didn't you say so at first? Another question. Do you know that this trial isn't finished yet?

Mr. Wopsle hesitated, and we all began to have a rather bad opinion of him. And you were going to say that the accused was guilty, before the end of the trial, before he has been proved guilty! We realized that the unfortunate Wopsle had no understanding of the law, or indeed anything at all. Now the stranger stood in front of our little group. I'm looking for the blacksmith, Joe Gargery, he said, and his apprentice, Pip. He did not recognize me but I knew he was the gentleman I had met on the stairs when visiting Miss Havisham. There was even the same smell of per—fumed soap on his large hands. I want to speak to you two in private, he said, and so Joe and I left the pub and walked home with him. My name is Jaggers, and I'm a lawyer, he said, when he reached the forge. Joe Gargery, I am sent by someone who suggests canceling this boy's apprenticeship to you. Would you want any money, if you lost your apprentice? 'I'd never stand in Pip's way, never, 'said Joe, staring. The answer is no. Don't try to change that answer later, said Mr. Jaggers .Now, what I have to say, and remember, I'm only an agent, I don't speak for myself, is that this young man has great expectations. Joe and I gasped, and looked at each other. I have been told to say that he will be very rich when he is older. In addition, the person who sent me wants the young man to be removed from his home and educated as a gentleman who expects to inherit a fortune.'

My dream had come true. Miss Havisham was making me rich! Now, Mr. Pip, continued the lawyer, there are two conditions. The first is that you always use the name of Pip. The second is that the name of the person who has been so generous to you must remain a secret, until that person chooses to tell you. You are forbidden to ask any questions or try to discover who the person is. Do you accept these conditions? My heart was beating fast as I whispered, Yes'. Now, to details. I have been given enough money for you to live the life of a gentleman in London while you are studying. You will come to me to ask for whatever you need. I suggest Mr

Matthew Pocket as a teacher. I remembered that was the name of one of Miss Havisham 's relations, the one who did not visit her often. You must buy some new clothes. Shall I leave you twenty pounds? He counted twenty coins out of his large purse onto the table. And when can you come to London? Next Saturday? I agreed, feeling very confused. He looked at Joe, who seemed even more confused. Well, Joe Gargery? Perhaps, I only say perhaps, I promise nothing, he said, throwing his purse carelessly from one hand to another, perhaps I have been told to give you a present when you lose your apprentice. 'Joe put his great strong hand on my shoulder in the gentlest possible way.

Pip can go freely to fortune and happiness, he knows that. But if you think that money can ever pay me back for losing the little child who came to the forge and always the best of friends! He could not continue. Dear good Joe! I was so ready to leave you, and so ungrateful to you! I can see you now, with your strong blacksmith's arm in front of your eyes, and your shoulders shaking, and tears on your cheeks. But at the time I was so excited by my good luck that I forgot what I owed to Joe. Mr Jaggers clearly thought Joe was a fool for refusing money, and left the house, reminding me to go straight to his office in London in a week's time. Joe told Biddy what had happened, and both congratulated me. They were very quiet and sad at first, because I would be leaving them, but I promised I would never forget them and would often return to visit them. Biddy tried to explain the good news to my sister, but the poor woman could not understand. As Joe and Biddy became a little more cheerful, discussing my possible plans for the future, I became more miserable. Now that I could be a gentleman, as I had always wished, I was not sure if I wanted to leave my home, which was full of happy memories. That week passed slowly. I took a last walk through the churchyard to the marshes. At least I need never think about my convict again. No doubt he was dead by now.

长难句解析

Suddenly we became aware of a strange gentleman who had also been listening，and was now looking coldly at us. "Well!" he said to us，biting the side of his finger.

突然，我们注意到一位陌生人也在听。现在正冷眼看着我们。喂！他边咬着手指边对我们说。

“become aware of”等同于“be aware of”意为发觉、意识到、who引导定语从句；“biting the side of his finger”动名词作状语。

I do think he is guilty. We all nodded our heads in agreement. "But," said the stranger, "do you or do you not know that the law of England supposes every man to be innocent until he is proved to be guilty?"

我想他是有罪的。我们都点点头表示同意。“但是，”陌生人说，“你们知不知道英国的法律，推测每个人是无罪的，直到他被证实是无罪的？”

这一段文字中do均有强调意味，而“I do think he is guilty.”这句中的do强调意思最强烈；be proved to意为“被证明是”。

“Now，Mr. Pip,” continued the lawyer, “there are two conditions. The first is that you always use the name of Pip. The second is that the name of the person who has been so generous to you must remain a secret, until that person chooses to tell you.”

“喂，匹普先生，”这位律师接着说，“有两个条件：首先，你永远使用匹普这个名字。第二，对你如此慷慨的那个人的名字必须保秘，直到时机成熟了，那个人会告诉你的。”

The first...The second...构成排列句式，两个“that”均引导表语从句；“be generous to”意为“对……慷慨的”。

“Well, Joe Gargery? Perhaps, I only say perhaps, I promise nothing,” he said, throwing his purse carelessly from one hand to another, “perhaps I have been told to give you a present when you lose your apprentice.”

“喂，乔·葛吉瑞，或许，我只讲或许，我没有什么许诺，”他漫不经心地从一只手到另一只手扔着他的钱袋说，“也许我已经讲过，当你失去你的徒弟时给你一份礼物。”

“Perhaps, I only say perhaps,”此处重复使用perhaps，表示强调语气；“throwing his purse carelessly from one hand to another”动名词作状语。

I can see you now, with your strong blacksmith's arm in front of your eyes, and your shoulders shaking, and tears on your cheeks. But at the time I was so excited by my good luck that I forgot what I owed to Joe.

现在，我能看到在你眼前用那强壮的铁匠手臂捂着双眼，你的肩膀颤抖着，脸颊挂着泪水。但是，我的好运使我如此兴奋，我忘记要感谢乔。

“with your strong blacksmith's arm in front of your eyes”为独立主格结构；shaking动名词作状语；that引导定语从句；what引导定语从句中的宾语从句。

读书笔记

096 The Magic Faraway Tree 远方的魔法树

今日关键语导读 Today's Key Points

《远方的魔法树》，作者伊妮德·布莱顿，这是一部童话故事，曾被评为一百部英国人最喜爱的小说之一。讲述了魔法森林中的一棵魔法树上，居住着许多奇奇怪怪的精灵、仙子和小动物。一天，三个小孩误入魔法森林，由此展开了一段奇幻历险。

障碍词先听为快 Words and Expressions

peculiar [pi'kjuːljə] adj. 奇怪的，古怪的；异常的 n. 专有特权，专有财产

peep [piːp] v. 窥视，偷看；（小鸟等）唧唧地叫 n. 窥视；唧唧声；隐现；慢慢露出

Faraway ['fɑːrəwei] adj. 遥远的；恍惚的

stream [striːm] n. 河流，小河，川，溪 vt. & vi. 流，流动

biscuit ['biskit] n. <英>饼干；<美>软烤饼

butter ['bʌtə] n. 黄油；黄油状的食品；奉承话；焊膏 vt. 抹黄油于……上；用黄油煎食物；讨好

worry ['wʌri] n. 担心；烦恼 v. 担心；担心；烦恼；撕咬

promise ['prɔmis] 许诺，允诺；希望 v. 允诺，许诺；有指望，有前途

Mother saw their disappointed faces and smiled. "I suppose you want to take Dick to see those peculiar friends of yours," she said. "Well now, listen-if you are good children today, and do the jobs you have to do, I'll give you a whole day's holiday tomorrow! Then you may take your dinner and your tea and go to visit any friends you like. How would you like that?" "Oh, Mother, thank you!" cried the children in delight, "A whole day!" said Bessie. "Why, Dick, we can show you everything!" "And maybe let you peep into whatever land is at the top of the Faraway Tree," whispered Fanny. "Oh, what fun!" So they did their work well after tea and looked forward to the next day. Dick dug hard, and Jo was pleased with him. It was going to be fun to have a cousin with them, able to work and play and enjoy everything, too! When they went to bed that night they left the doors of their rooms open so that they might call to one another.

"Sleep well, Dick!" called Bessie. "I hope it's fine tomorrow! What fun we shall have!" "Good night, Bessie!" called back Dick. "I can't tell you how I'm longing for tomorrow. I know I shan't be able to sleep tonight!" But he did -and so did all the others. When Mother came up at ten o'clock she peeped in at the children, and not one was awake.

Jo woke first next day. He sat up and looked out of the window. The sun streamed in, warm and bright. Jo's heart jumped for joy. He leaned over to Dick's bed and shook him.

"Wake up!" he said. "It's tomorrow now and we're going to the Enchanted Wood!" Off to the Enchanted Wood.

The children ate their breakfast quickly. Mother told Bessie and Fanny to cut sandwiches for themselves and to take a small chocolate cake from the larder.

"You can take a packet of biscuits, too," she said, "and there are apples in that dish over there. If you are hungry when you come home tonight I will bake you some potatoes in the oven, and you can eat them in their skins with salt and butter." "Oooh, Mother-we shall be hungry!" said Jo at once. "Hurry up with those sandwiches, Bessie and Fanny. We want to start off as soon as possible." "Now don't be too late home, or I shall worry," said Mother. "Look after your cousin, Jo." "Yes, I will," promised Jo.

长难句解析

Mother saw their disappointed faces and smiled. "I suppose you want to take Dick to see those peculiar friends of yours," she said.

母亲看到他们失望的脸，笑了。“我觉得你想带迪克去见你那些奇特的朋友，”她说。

take sb. to sth.“带某人看某物”

"Oh, Mother, thank you!" cried the children in delight, "A whole day!" said Bessie.

“哦，妈妈，谢谢你！”孩子们喜悦地叫喊着，“一整天！”贝茜说。

in delight 在喜悦中

When they went to bed that night they left the doors of their rooms open so that they might call to one another.

那天晚上他们上床睡觉时，将自己的房门敞开，以便他们可以互相交谈。

when引导时间状语从句，so...that“如此……以至于……”。

If you are hungry when you come home tonight I will bake you some potatoes in the oven, and you can eat them in their skins with salt and butter.

如果你今晚回到家中饿了的话，我将为你在炉子上烤一些土豆片，你可以连皮就着盐和黄油一起吃。

if引导条件状语从句，when引导时间状语从句。

读书笔记

097 In the Moon Below 在月亮下面

今日关键语导读 Today's Key Points

《在月亮下面》是由英国作家罗维纳·阿金耶米所写的一部科幻题材的小说，小说讲述了由于人类对环境的破坏，用来阻挡太阳光的臭氧层裂开了一个洞，虽然人类制造了人工臭氧层，但是在2522年这个人工臭氧层也失去了保护作用，人类将面临怎样的选择呢？

障碍词先听为快 Words and Expressions

across [ə'krɔs] prep. 穿过 adv. 横过

shout [ʃaut] vt.& vi. 呼喊 n. 大叫

jump [dʒʌmp] vt. 跳 vi. 暴涨 n. 猛长

ship [ʃip] n. 船 vt. 把……装上船

fast [fa:st] adj. 快的 vi. 禁食

commander [kə'ma:ndə] n. 指挥官

march [ma:tʃ] v. 进军，进展

guard [ga:d] n. 警卫 vt. 保卫

gate [geit] n. 门；闸门 vt. 给……装大门

aeroplane ['ɛərəplein] n. 飞机

"No, thank you," Kith answered. "I'd like you to look at these numbers." Kith gave Captain Seru his book.

Captain Seru looked at the numbers. Suddenly, her face changed. "No, no," she said. "I don't want to talk. It's late and I'm tired. Sit down and have a drink."

Kith and Rilla sat down. There was a big window in Captain Seru's room. Kith looked out of the window at the dark sky. He saw the Moon. It was cold and white in the dark sky.

"Captain Seru," he began. "It's important. Look at those numbers carefully. The AOL is beginning to—"

"Stop!" captain Seru stood up and put her hands in her pockets. She went to the window and looked at the sky.

On Friday, after three weeks in space, Kith and Rilla finished work and left Ship OM-45 on a space plane to Kisangani. Kiahphoned Adai and Rilla phoned Commander Zadak in Australia. The next morning they took an aeroplane to Sydney. A taxi took them from the airport to Commander Zadak's office, some kilometres north of Sydney.

"Wait for us here," Kith said to the taxi driver.

Kith and Rilla walked to the gate. About ten guards stood in front of the gate. Across the road, a train waited.

"RillaOM-45," Rilla said. "To see Commander Zadak at four-thirty."

"Let me call the Commander' soffice," the guard said.

Kith and Rilla waited. It was hot and Kith began to feel thirsty.

The guard came back. "I'm sorry," he said. "The Commander can't see you."

"But I talked to the Commander yesterday," Rilla said.

"He wanted to see us at four-thirty." "The Commander is leaving on the train in three minutes," the guard said.

"Can we wait and see him here?" Kith asked.

"No!" the guard shouted. "Get out of here!"

Kith and Rilla walked back to the taxi.

"Where's the driver?" Kith asked.

"Look! He's sitting under that tree," Rilla said.

Just then, Commander Zadak came out of the gate. He was a very tall, big man with blue eyes and a lot of white hair. Two guards marched in front of him, and two guards marched behind him. They all carried guns.

"There he is!" Rilla cried. "Commander!" And she began to run along the road to him.

"Commander Zadak did not stop. A guard opened the door of the train and the Commander got in. Slowly, the train began to move."

Kith ran to the taxi and jumped in. Then he drove the taxi fast down the road. The taxi driver saw him and ran after him. The train began to move faster. Suddenly, Kith drove the taxi off the road. He drove in front of the train and stopped.

The train came nearer. And then the train stopped, very near the taxi and some guards jumped off. Kith opened the door an got out of the taxi.

"Put up your hands!" the guards shouted.

Two of the guards began to hit Kith. "Stop that!" someone shouted. "Bring him over here!" It was Commander Zadak. Kith stood in front of the Commander. Just then, Rilla arrived.

"Oh, it's you!" Commander Zadak said. He did not smile. "Rilla, your father's going to be angry." "We want to talk to you, Commander," Rilla said. "It's very important."

"Very well. I'm listening."

长难句解析

A taxi took them from the airport to Commander Zadak's office, some kilometers north of Sydney.

一辆出租车把他们从机场带到了悉尼以北几公里以外的扎达克司令的办公室。

take sb. from“从……带到……”。

Just then, Commander Zadak came out of the gate. He was a very tall, big man with blue eyes and a lot of white hair.

正说着，扎达克司令出现在大门口。他高大魁梧，蓝眼睛，长着一头浓密的白发。

came out of“从……出来”，a lot of=lots of“大量的”。

"There he is!" Rilla cried. "Commander!" And she began to run along the road to him.

"他在那儿！"瑞拉喊了起来，"扎达克司令！"她随即顺着马路朝他跑去。

there 等表地点的副词放句首句子用倒装，begin to do sth."开始做某事"。

读书笔记

098 Silas Marner 织工马南

今日关键语导读 Today's Key Points

19世纪早期的英国僻静的乡村，生活一成不变，四季交替，对于住在大房子里的乡绅及其全家和对于住在小草屋里的村民来说都是一样的。任何新鲜和古怪的事情在像福洛这样的村庄里都会遭到猜疑。

织工西拉斯·马南就很古怪。他独自居住，没人知道他的家庭情况？他脸色苍白，眼神怪异，并且总是瞪着眼睛，因为他每天都要在织机上干很长时间的活，甚至星期天也干，而星期天他应该去教堂。他一定是魔鬼的朋友，村民们相互这么说。

可怜的西拉斯！他是一个忧伤、孤独的人，他唯一的朋友就是那些闪光的金币，那是他织布挣来的，被他藏在地板下面。但是变故总会发生，即便在瑞福洛这样安静的村庄里。乡绅的两个儿子之间有一个秘密，这导致争吵、抢夺，以及死亡。那是在一个下雪的夜晚，在离西拉斯的草屋不远的地方……

障碍词先听为快 Words and Expressions

unloved [ʌn'lʌvd] adj. 未被爱的，未被喜爱的

weaver ['wiːvə] n. 织工，编织者；[鸟]织巢鸟，[虫]豉豆，织网蜘蛛

pretend [pri'tend] v. 假装；伪装；（尤指儿童）（在游戏中）装扮；自诩

firmly ['fəːmli] adv. 坚固地；稳固地；坚定地；坚决地

confess [kən'fes] vt. & vi. 承认；聆听（某人的）忏悔（或告罪、告解）；（尤指罗马天主教会）忏悔；悔过 vt. 听……忏悔

cottage ['kɔtidʒ] n. 小屋，村舍；（农舍式的）小别墅；（郊外的）新式住宅，（大院内的）单幢住宅；乡下房子，小房子

orphan ['ɔːfən] n. 孤儿 vt. 使成为孤儿 adj. 孤儿的；无双亲的

jealously ['dʒeləsi] adv. 妒忌地，猜疑地

好英文娓娓动听 Beautiful stories

There on the bed was his unloved wife. He only looked at her for a moment, but for the rest of his life he never forgot her sad, tired face.

The weaver had come back with the doctor, and was sitting by the fire, with the children on his knees. The little one was awake, but her wide open blue eyes looked up into Godfrey's face without recognizing him at all. The father was glad of this, but also a little sad, especially when he saw the small hand pull lovingly at the weaver's grey hair.

"So, who's going to take care of the child?" Godfrey asked, pretending not to show much interest.

"I am," replied Silas firmly. "The mother's dead, and I suppose the child hasn't got a father. She's alone in the world, and so am I. My money's gone, I don't know where, and she's come, I don't know where from. I don't understand it at all, but I'm going to keep her."

"Poor little thing!" said Godfrey. "Let me give you something for her clothes." He put his hand in his pocket and gave Silas some coins.

As he walked back to the Red House, he felt very relieved. Nobody would recognize his dead wife, and soon his secret would be buried with her. Now he could talk of love to Nancy. He could promise to be a good husband to her. Only Dunstan knew about the secret marriage, and perhaps Dunstan would never come home. "What a good thing I didn't confess everything to the Squire!" he thought. "Now I can make Nancy and myself happy And the child? Well, it won't matter to her whether I'm her father or not."

That week the dead woman was buried in Raveloe, and the child stayed at the weaver's cottage. The villagers were very surprised that Silas had decided to keep her, but they liked him for wanting to help an orphan. The women, especially, were very ready to give him useful advice on taking care of children.

Dolly Winthrop came every day to help Silas. "It's no trouble," she said. "I get up early, so I've got plenty of time. And I can bring you some of Aaron's old baby clothes, so you won't need to spend a lot of money on the child. I can wash her, and give her food, and—"

"Ye—es," said silas, hesitating. He was looking a little jealously at the baby in Dolly's arms. "That's very kind of you. But—but I want to do everything for her myself! I want her to be fond of me! She's my child!"

"Don't worry," said Dolly gently, giving him the child. "Look, she loves you the best. See, she's smiling at you!" And so Silas learnt how to take care of the little girl. He called her Eppie, which had been his little sister's name. His life was quite different now.

When he was working and living only for his gold, he had not been interested in the world outside his cottage, or the people he sometimes met. But now that he had another reason for living, he had to look outward. He spent hours in the fields with Eppie, happily rediscovering the plants he used to know so well. Together they visited his neighbors, who were always delighted to see him and his adopted child. His days and evenings were full, taking care of a trusting, loving child.

长难句解析

There on the bed was his unloved wife. He only looked at her for a moment, but for the rest of his life he never forgot her sad, tired face.

床上躺着他已经不再爱的妻子。他只看了她一会儿，但终生都没有忘记她那张忧伤疲惫的脸。

look at“注视”，for a moment，是指片刻、一会儿。

The weaver had come back with the doctor, and was sitting by the fire, with the children on his knees. The little one was awake, but her wide open blue eyes looked up into Godfrey's face without recognizing him at all.

织布匠（马南）是和大夫一起回来的，他坐在火炉旁，抱着孩子。小家伙醒着，她睁大了蓝眼睛盯着戈弗雷的脸看，可是根本没认出他来。

come back 回来，with the children on his knees 是with的复合结构（with+宾语+介词短语）look up into，朝……看去；not at all，一点也不。

"I am," replied Silas firmly. "The mother's dead, and I suppose the child hasn't got a father. She's alone in the world, and so am I. My money's gone, I don't know where, and she's come, I don't know where from."

"我，"西拉斯坚决地说，"她妈妈死了，我想孩子也没有爸爸，她像我一样在这个世上孤苦零丁。我的钱不知到哪儿去了，而她不知从哪儿来。这一切我都不明白，可我一定要抚养她。"

mother's = mother has；so am I 译为"我也一样"（若为so I am 意思则变为肯定对方说的话）Eg：So do I，表示"我也是"，—I like watching TV. —So do I. So I do，表示强调，赞同别人对自己的说法，比如说，—You like watching TV. --So I do.

As he walked back to the Red House, he felt very relieved.

回红屋的路上，戈弗雷异常轻松。

as,"作为"，此处译为"当……的时候"。

Well, it won't matter to her whether I'm her father or not.

嗨，我是不是她父亲对她也并不重要。

whether or not 固定搭配“无论、是否、不管”

When he was working and living only for his gold, he had not been interested in the world outside his cottage, or the people he sometimes met. But now that he had another reason for living, he had to look outward. He spent hours in the fields with Eppie, happily rediscovering the plants he used to know so well.

当他为金子而工作而生活的时候，他对屋外的世界，对那些偶然见到的人们毫无兴趣。现在生活的目的变了，他不得不开始看看外面的世界。他花几个小时陪埃比在地里玩，又愉快地重新发现了那些他曾经熟悉过的植物。

when 引导时间状语从句；now that固定搭配，译为“既然”；spend time with sb. on/in sth/v-ing 花费时间陪某人做某事。

读书笔记

099 The Paper Bag Princess 纸袋公主

今日关键语导读 Today's Key Points

故事中公主和王子一开始就要“幸福地生活在一起”了，可是火龙却把王子掠走了，还把城堡烧得一干二净。公主只好穿上一个纸袋，然后勇敢地追赶火龙，要救出王子。公主用自己的机智打败了火龙。谁知王子却嫌公主衣衫褴褛，公主气坏了，骂王子是一个没用的家伙，然后扬长而去。

这个故事颠覆了以往童话故事中的王子和公主形象。首先，公主表现得更加有智慧和力量，传统童话中都是公主等着王子的拯救，而这个童话却把两个角色彻底做了调换。其次，公主表现得更有主见，当王子责怪公主时，公主马上还以颜色，毫不犹豫地弃他而去。

障碍词先听为快 Words and Expressions

smash [smæʃ] vt. 粉碎；使破产；溃裂

clothesline ['kləuzlain] n. 晒衣绳

grab [græb] v.敲；攫取

stick [stik] vt. 刺，戳；伸出

fantastic [fæn'tæstik] adj. 奇异的；空想的；极好的；不可思议的

meatball ['miːtbɔːl] n. 肉丸子

whisper ['(h)wispə] vi. 耳语；密谈；飒飒地响

tangled ['tæŋgld] adj. 紊乱的；纠缠的

bum [bʌm] n. 流浪汉

fiercest [fiəsist] adj. 最凶猛的；最猛烈的

好英文娓娓动听 Beautiful stories

Elizabeth was a beautiful princess. She lived in a castle and had expensive princess clothes. She was going to marry a prince named Ronald.

Unfortunately, a dragon smashed her castle, burned all her clothesline with his fiery breath, and carried off Prince Ronald.

Elizabeth decided to chase the dragon and get Ronald back.

She looked everywhere for something to wear, but the only thing she could find that was not burnt was a paper bag. So she put on the paper bag and followed the dragon.

He was easy to follow, because he left a trail of burnt forests and horses' bones.

Finally, Elizabeth came to a cave with a large door that had a huge knocker on it. She took hold of the knocker and banged on the door.

The dragon stuck his nose out of the door and said, "well, a princess! I love to eat Princesses, but I have already eaten a whole castle today. I am very busy dragon. Come back tomorrow."

He slammed the door so fast that Elizabeth almost got he nose caught.

Elizabeth grabbed the knocker and banged on the door again.

The dragon stuck his nose out of the door and said, "Go away. I love to eat Princess, but I have already eaten a whole castle today. I am a very busy dragon. Come back tomorrow."

"Wait," shouted Elizabeth. "Is it true that you are the smartest and fiercest dragon in the whole world?"

"Yes," said the dragon.

"Is it true," said Elizabeth, "that you can burn up ten forests with your fiery breath?"

"Oh, yes," said the dragon, and he took a huge, deep breath and breathed out so much fire that he burnt up fifty forests.

"Fantastic," said Elizabeth, and the dragon took another huge breath and breathed out so much fire that he hunt up one hundred forests.

"Magnificent," said Elizabeth, and the dragon took another huge breath, but this time nothing came out. The dragon didn't even have enough fire left to cook a meatball.

Elizabeth said, "Dragon, is it true that you can fly around the world in just seconds?"

"Yes." said the dragon, and jumped up and flew all the way around the world in just ten seconds.

He was very tired when he got back, but Elizabeth shouted, "Fantastic, do it again!"

So the dragon jumped up and flew around the whole world in just twenty seconds.

When he got back he was too tired to talk, and he lay down and went straight to sleep.

Elizabeth whispered, very softly, "Hey, dragon." The dragon didn't move at all.

She lifted up the dragon's ear and put her head right inside. She shouted as loud as she could, "Hey, dragon!"

The dragon was so tired he didn't even move.

Elizabeth walked right over the dragon and opened the door to the cave.

There was Prince Ronald. He looked at her and said, "Elizabeth, you are a mess! you smell like ashes, your hair is all tangled and you are wearing a dirty old paper bag. Come back when you are dressed like a real princess."

"Ronald," said Elizabeth, "your clothes are really pretty and your hair is very neat. You look like a real prince, but you a bum."

They didn't married after all.

长难句解析

She looked everywhere for something to wear, but the only thing she could find that was not burnt was a paper bag. So she put on the paper bag and followed the dragon.

她东找找、西找找，想找些东西穿在身上；可是唯一没被烧掉的东西，就剩下一个纸袋了。她只好穿上纸袋，追着火龙而去。

look for "寻找"；she could find作后置定语，that也引导一个定语从句，修饰the only thing；put on "穿上"。

Finally, Elizabeth came to a cave with a large door that had a huge knocker on it. She took hold of the knocker and banged on the door.

最后，依莉莎來到了一座山洞前，山洞巨大的门上头有一个门环。于是，她握起门环，用力地敲下去。

that引导定语从句，指代词是large door。

The dragon stuck his nose out of the door and said, “well, a princess! I love to eat Princesses, but I have already eaten a whole castle today. I am very busy dragon. Come back tomorrow.”

火龙把它的鼻子探出门外，说：“好啊！，是个公主呢！我最爱吃公主了，不过我今天已经吃了一整座城堡。现在累昏了，你还是明天再来吧。”

love to do sth. 表示爱做某事，have done是现在完成时，表示事情已完成并有一定影响。

There was Prince Ronald. He looked at her and said, “Elizabeth, you are a mess! you smell like ashes, your hair is all tangled and you are wearing a dirty old paper bag. Come back when you are dressed like a real princess.”

雷诺王子就在里面。他一看到依莉莎，就不停地数落依莉莎：“你简直一团糟，闻起来就有灰尘味。你的头发乱糟糟的，还有你竟然穿着一件脏兮兮的旧纸袋。还是等你打扮得像个真正的公主再来找我吧。”

look at“注视”，come back“回来”；when引导时间状语从句。

读书笔记

读书笔记

读书笔记